St Kildan Heritage

St Kildan Heritage

Calum Ferguson

acair

Text copyright © Calum Ferguson

First published in 2006 by Acair, Limited
7 James Street, Stornoway, Scotland HS1 2QN
www.acairbooks.com
info@acairbooks.com

The right of Calum Ferguson to be identified as the author of the work has
been asserted by him in accordance with the Copyright, Designs and Patents
Act 1988.

A CIP catalogue record for this title is available from the British Library.

Text and cover designed by Margaret Anne Macleod.

Printed by Gomer Press, Llandysul, Wales.

ISBN 0 86152 684 8
EAN 9 7808615 26840

Note:
Hiort Far na laigh a' ghrian, by the same author, was published by Acair in 1995.
This new, much requested English version seeks to share the original
with a wider readership.

Contents

Contents

Contents

TOWARDS THE CLIFF EDGE (1852 onwards)

Contents

Foreword

Throughout the islands of the Outer Hebrides, the harvest of 1928 was so poor that, by the following February, the crofters' meal chests and potato-stores were nearly empty. In Lewis, many families in rural communities were forced to eke out what little food they had left. The island's winters are usually very wet and windy, but seldom are they excessively cold. The first three months of 1929 were different. The cold was so intense that not only the lochs and streams froze but also some of the wells from which families drew their drinking-water. Snowdrifts closed the single-lane gravel track linking the outlying communities of the Eye Peninsula to Stornoway, the island's only town. Known as *Rathad an Rìgh* (The King's Highway), the track remained impassable for weeks on end.

In the communities of Port Mholair and Port nan Giùran at the outmost end of the Eye Peninsula, families were suffering serious food shortages. As the weeks passed, news of the growing crisis was conveyed to the authorities at Stornoway by telegraph, and a herring-drifter carrying oatmeal, flour, sugar and margarine was despatched to relieve the situation.

As I was only a year old at the time of that crisis, I cannot remember the arrival of the herring-drifter at Port nan Giùran, nor the sense of euphoria as men laden with sacks of groceries appeared at Ceann an Loch, the hamlet of black-houses where we lived. Yet, living in one of those black-houses and, later, in a well appointed 'white-house', I well remember how remote the town seemed to be during my formative years of the 1930s. For crofters urgently needing to buy supplies in the town, transport was by a rickety, ill-sprung 'omnibus' or, more commonly, by horse and cart travelling over the rutted *Rathad an Rìgh*. In summer, most people visiting the town chose to travel the eleven miles by Shanks's pony!

Our little hamlet was only eleven miles from Stornoway, yet I was not able to savour the sights and sounds of that busy little fishing port until I was aged eight. I remember being awestruck by so many strange smells and sounds and, not least, by my encountering so many unfamiliar faces. How wonderful was the sight of so many shops lining the streets: ships' chandlers, cobblers, ironmongers, drapers, bakers, tobacconists and, most memorable of all, the Italian cafè with its unforgettable aroma of coffee mixed with the alluring fragrance of ice-cream cones and wafers.

Reading through some of the numerous books written about St Kilda between 1697 and 1930, I was struck by the many similarities between conditions on that little archipelago, lying forty miles off the coast of North Uist, and those of my native community of the 1930s. Food was cooked in pots hung over the peat fire in the living-room. In common with eight other families in our village, we lived in *taighean-dubha* (black-houses), with the cattle and poultry sharing our accommodation under the one thatched roof. In that respect we were unlike the St Kildans, who had graduated to gabled 'white-houses' sixty years earlier.

Fowling was central to St Kilda's economy as fishing was to that of Lewis. Animal husbandry and the growing of oats and potatoes were important on both islands, and implements such as the spade, fork, sickle, hoe and *tairsgear* (peat-cutter) were essential to both lifestyles. Like the St Kildan schoolchildren, children from the crofting villages of Lewis began their primary education knowing only the Gaelic language; yet they were taught in a foreign tongue - English.

On Hiort, consanguineous marriages through the generations made everybody in the community related to everybody else. This gave the community a sense of cohesion – it was, in a very real sense, a clan. In both communities, the families relied on each other in times of need, and not least in coping with tragedies, when, all too frequently, boats foundered or when the young died of disease or through accidents. When a young islander decided to leave, whether to gain experience of the outside world or because of some less happy circumstance,

Foreword

the departure was keenly felt by the whole community. I well remember the kindness of our neighbours before I set off on my first outing to a college in Glasgow. There was a sense of occasion as I visited the eight houses at our end of the village and, with their fondly expressed blessings, received a precious half-crown, a carefully ironed handkerchief, a half-dozen eggs or, perhaps, a well-used fountain-pen. The scene before I boarded the bus to take me to 'the steamer' was so like Alice MacLachlan's diary entry, written on Hiort on 31st August 1906:

> *They went off in great glee — Norman McQuien, Neil Gillies and Ewen Gillies. There was lamenting at the pier and kissing any amount.*

In Lewis, dancing, singing, recitation of *bàrdachd* (poetry) and the playing of the melodeon, bagpipes and jew's harp were as much part of the culture as psalm-singing and church attendance. As I was growing up, I learned not only psalms, hymns and catechisms, but also countless traditional Gaelic songs and pieces of *bàrdachd*. Dances in village halls and, depending on the weather, at the crossroads, were regular occurrences. The talents of the singers, musicians and bards who provided the community with entertainment were universally admired. There was a time when St Kildans shared with the rest of the Highlands and Islands the love of instrumental and vocal music and *bàrdachd*. Alas, in the last three or four generations on Hiort, the oppressive brand of Calvinism introduced by the Rev MacDonald of Ferintosh (the Apostle of the North) in the 1820s, '30s and '40s killed off the desire to compose songs or poetry. Indeed, the singing or recitation of any composition except the Psalms of David came to be regarded as 'foolish and profane'. By 1930, the population had dwindled and the living conditions had deteriorated to such an extent that the islanders petitioned the government for assistance to evacuate the island.

My fascination with Hiort began when two families of Glasgow-born cousins were evacuated to our community at the beginning of the Second World War. Three of the children of one family, two boys and a girl, were the offspring of Bessie MacQueen of St Kilda and Norman MacKenzie, a relation of my mother. Bessie's brother, Finlay, was married to Marion MacKenzie of Aird, another relation of my mother. Bessie and Finlay were the children of Finlay MacQueen, famous in his day for his climbing skills.

In 1944, Hiort became a dominant subject of conversation in our family for a different reason. My father was Second Skipper of the *Walwyn's Castle,* a minesweeper sent to retrieve the remains of the air-crew of the Sunderland Flying-boat ML858 which crashed on Hiort in 1944. I well remember, when he came home on leave, the high emotion of the *Hiortaich* who called to see him to quiz him about the condition of the houses which they had vacated fourteen years earlier. Though he was unable to report on individual dwellings, it seemed enough comfort for them to be told that the roofs appeared to be intact. Though they had made a new life for themselves in places far from St Kilda, their homeland continued to haunt their minds.

For those of us who have been privileged to witness the stupendous sea cliffs of the archipelago, and then to step ashore to the sights and sounds of Hiort, the experience was awe-inspiring and unforgettable. Is it any wonder that the natives who were evacuated in 1930 chose to forget the wretchedness and deprivation that drove them from their island fortress and yearned to return to its unique environment?

Calum Ferguson

THE ISOLATION ISLE
(before 1730)

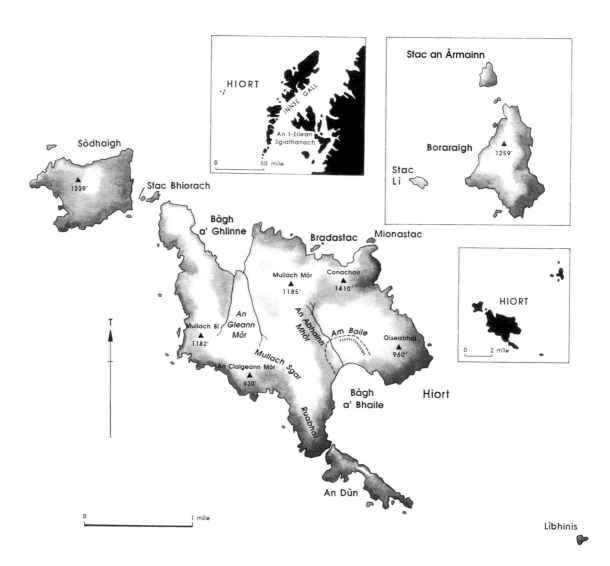

1. St Kildan Roots

Early modern humans had reached Britain by around 30,000 years ago, but within 3,000 years they were driven out by the advance of the last Ice Age. Until comparatively recently, archaeologists believed that the repopulation of Britain after the Ice Age took the form of sporadic forays from mainland Europe. Studies by a team of European scientists recently published in the *Journal of Quaternary Science* suggest that a wave of migration coincided with a sudden rise in temperature and the northwards spread of herd animals such as wild horse and deer. The archaeologists looked for evidence of their return in ancient caves in western and northern England. The team discovered that repopulation began as far back as 16,000 years ago. The oldest bones studied in Britain were a group of neck vertebrae from wild horses discovered in a cave at Cheddar Gorge, Somerset. Cut marks on the bones showed that the animals had been butchered by humans.

Carbon-dating of the bones from butchered animals found in Belgium and Germany were found to be only slightly earlier. This suggests a rapid advance of people from mainland Europe. Their progress was helped by the fact that Britain at that time was not an island but a peninsula joined to the northern tip of Denmark. An area in the south of the North Sea and much of the present English Channel was dry land, thus forming a wide corridor between mainland Britain and the rest of Europe. The scientists suggest that the movement of animals across this same land connection triggered the wave of human migration. There is much evidence that the hunters brought with them spears and knives, used to kill and then dismember their prey. Analysis of flint tools specific to the late glacial period shows that these early settlers were highly mobile and covered large distances. At that time much of the land was covered by dense forest, and settlements were located in clearings along the coast.

About 4,000 BC, a new wave of people from the Continent began to colonise the south of Britain. No-one can be certain of the kind of vessel they used to continue their exploration along the west coast of Britain and to colonise offshore islands as far north as Shetland. Around this time huge circular earthworks called 'henges', built in places throughout the southern half of Britain, are thought to have been 'cathedrals' to the Neolithic gods. The new colonists had knowledge of agriculture and fishing, so that their lifestyle was somewhat different from that of the original settlers. Over the next thousand years or so, the two peoples gradually merged to become one expanding population occupying the coastal plains and fertile valleys. Islands made particularly attractive sites for settlements, not least because they offered natural protection from invasion.

One island that offered near total protection from invaders was Hiort, the largest of the four islands of the St Kildan archipelago, lying about sixty miles west of Harris in the Outer Hebrides. Hiort is about two miles long east-west and about the same north-south. It has five peaks over 900 feet high. The highest is Conachair, which rises to 1,397 feet – a third of the height of Ben Nevis. Its summit is close to an awesome cliff more than 1,000 feet high, the tallest sea cliff in the British Isles. Sitting near the summit to watch fulmar riding the up-draughts that surge up the cliff face, one finds it difficult to imagine how anybody would willingly venture down that wild and dangerous precipice to ensnare sea fowl or, occasionally, to retrieve an errant ewe. Such hazardous activities were but mere chores to the St Kildans, whose livelihood to a large extent centred on fowling and animal husbandry.

Of the other three islands in the group, the *Dùn* lies nearest to Hiort and is separated from it by a channel which is only fifty yards wide. It consists of a narrow finger of land which gives Village Bay some protection from southerly storms. Soay, the second biggest island of the archipelago, lies north-west of Hiort, from which it is separated by a quarter of a mile of open sea. It is a land area of about 240 acres, being 1,200 feet at its highest point. Boreray, about four miles to the north of Hiort, has an area of 187 acres and, like Soay, is surrounded by a wall of sheer rock, hundreds of feet high.

If we consider the miles of treacherous sea they had to cross from the main islands of the Outer Hebrides, it is astonishing that, thousands of years ago, families managed to reach and colonise St Kilda. From shards found on Hiort in recent years, archaeologists have established that there were people living there some 6,000 years ago. From that time until about one thousand years ago, little is known of the islanders. All that can be said with any degree of certainty is that they relied on the flesh and eggs of seabirds as an important food source.

Until the middle of the ninth century, the Outer Hebrides was regarded as part of Pictland, which occupied the northern half of the country we now know as Scotland. By that time permanent Norse settlements were being established throughout the Hebrides, Galloway, Man and Ireland. A new race of people, of mixed Norse and Celtic ancestry, the *Gall-Gàidheil*, had come into existence, and they proved to be every bit as ruthless as the Norsemen.

From about 900 AD, Norway ruled the northern and western seas and islands of Scotland. Until the Battle of Largs in 1263, the islands off the western and northern coasts of Britain, from the Isle of Man to Shetland, were under the control of the Norsemen. During that period the Norse language was predominant in those areas. On the Scottish mainland, including much of the Lowlands, the people spoke Gaelic and referred to the Outer Hebrides as *Innse Gall*, 'the Foreigners' Isles'. It is safe to assume that for a long time St Kilda was occupied by a people who spoke Norse. A number of St Kildan place-names are of Norse origin: for example, Oiseabhal (East hill), Ruabhal (Red Hill), Soay (Sheep Isle), Cambair (Ridge) and Bradastac (Steep Stack).

According to one of the Norse sagas, a ship carrying an Icelandic bishop was on a voyage to Norway in 1202 when a storm drove it as far as

the islands that are called Hirter.

If 'Hirter' was Hiort, then it would make this the earliest literary reference to St Kilda. It would also make the ship at least 300 miles off course!

In 1263, the Battle of Largs brought Norse rule in the British Isles to an end. Afterwards, King Alexander III of Scotland purchased the kingdom of Man and the Isles from Norway, and the islands north of Kintyre were given to the progeny of Somerled. St Kilda was included in that treaty.

In the fourteenth century, the Inner and Outer Hebrides were governed by John MacDonald, Lord of the Isles, whose stronghold was on Loch Finlaggan in Islay. In due course of time, John MacDonald granted St Kilda and other territories to his son Reginald; that inheritance was sanctioned by King Robert II. After a couple of generations, the power of the Lord of the Isles was broken and, in 1493, the Lordship of the Isles was forfeit to the Scottish Crown. Ownership of St Kilda passed to MacDonald of Sleat in Skye.

Early references to Hiort are in two documents written in the sixteenth century. In 1527, Hector Boece, the first Principal of the University of Aberdeen, wrote:

> *The last and outmaist Ile is namit Hirtha ... in this Ile is gret nowmer of scheip ... This Ile is circulit on every syd with roche craggis; and na baitis may land at it but allanerly at ane place ...*

About twenty years later, Donald Munro, Dean of Argyll and the Isles, wrote an account of his exploratory journey through his diocese, which included remote communities such as that of St Kilda. He described Hiort as having numerous fields well fertilised with manure, and producing an abundance of grass and corn for sheep which were

> *bigger and more handsome with longer tails than on any neighbouring islands.*

The islanders he thought of as

> *ignorant creatures who were without much education or religion.*

At the time of Dean Munro, St Kilda was owned by MacLeod of Harris, yet he was not the man directly involved with the islanders' welfare or their problems. MacLeod, the proprietor, received an annual payment from his lessee (known as the Steward), who travelled to St Kilda in summer to collect rent from each householder. The Steward was usually accompanied by a minister whose function was to baptise children born in the previous twelve months. The rent was in the form of money, smoked mutton, smoked wild fowl and smoked seal.

When Martin Martin visited St Kilda in 1697, there were three churches on Hiort:

> *The first of these is called Christ Chappel, near the village; there is a brazen cross lies upon the altar, not exceeding a foot in length; the body is completely done, distended and has a crown on; all in the crucified posture. ... The second of these chappels bears the name of St Columba, the third of St Brianan; both being built after the manner of Christ's Chappel; having church-yards belonging to them.*

The foundation for some of those chapels may have been laid centuries earlier. From the seventh century, Irish monks founded monasteries in Scotland, notably on the isles of Iona, Eigg and Lismore in the Inner Hebrides. They also established churches in the Outer

Hebrides, Orkney, Shetland, The Faeroes and Iceland. Some holy men from those centres travelled to even more remote places and established hermitages where they were able to worship alone or in small groups.

Martin described the people of Hiort as being energetic and fond of sports. In summer they played shinty with great enthusiasm on the *Gaineamh*, the expanse of sand at the head of Village Bay. Stripped to their shirts, the teams competed for 'eggs, fowl, hooks or tobacco'.

Some thirty years after Martin's visit, a smallpox epidemic reduced the population of twenty-one families to three adults and twenty-six children. Until that happened, generations of the same people had lived on St Kilda from time immemorial. After the epidemic, new people were brought in from other islands of the Outer Hebrides and from Skye.

In the eighteenth century, the Steward collected the rent in the form of tweeds, feathers, meat, fowl, oil, cattle, horses, sheep or barley. At the end of his stay he took with him all that he and his retinue had collected in addition to produce that was surplus to the community's own needs. Back in Skye he sold the St Kildan produce to the tenants living in other parts of the Chief's estates. What remained was sent south to the commercial markets.

Not all of the proprietor's representatives were honest in their dealings with the islanders. At the end of the seventeenth century, a steward tried to extort one additional sheep from every family on the island. When the islanders refused to pay, he was forced to withdraw his claim. The Rev John Lane, who was Church of Scotland minister to the Isles from 1782 to 1790, described the tacksman of St Kilda as

> *a charity-schoolmaster in that place who, having forgot his former insignificance, has assumed all the turbulent pride of a purse-proud pedagogue, to keep the inhabitants under.*

In 1799 Harris and St Kilda were sold to Captain Alexander MacLeod for £15,000. Fifty years later, the property was again sold to another member of the Clan MacLeod. In 1871, Norman MacLeod, the twenty-second chieftain of the clan, paid £300 for St Kilda. It remained in the possession of that clan for the next sixty years, i.e. until after the population was evacuated.

Apart from the devastation caused by the smallpox epidemic of 1729, the event that in recent centuries had the most damaging effect on the St Kildan community was the mass emigration of the youngest and ablest of its people to Australia in 1852. Of the thirty-six emigrants who sailed from Liverpool, only eighteen reached Melbourne, the others having succumbed to diseases contracted on board the ship.

Markets for St Kilda produce changed over time, and by the end of the nineteenth century the demand for salted gannet flesh and fulmar oil had petered out. As yachts and ships carrying tourists to the island became commonplace, the St Kildans quickly learned to communicate in English. They produced more tweed and knitted socks to sell to the tourists. Their own diet was changing too, as they took fewer birds from the cliffs, and instead imported tea, sugar, flour and fruit such as apples, oranges and pears. They also began to devote less time to agriculture. Describing crofting on Hiort in 1878, John MacDiarmid wrote:

> *The return it gives is miserable. From a barrel of potatoes (about 2 cwt) scarcely three barrels will be lifted … with oats the return is never above two and a half times the quantity of the seed sown.*

MacDiarmid's assessment contrasts with those given by writers in earlier centuries. For example, in 1549 Donald Monro, Dean of Argyll and the Isles, wrote as follows:

> *… mane laich* [valley] *sa far as it is manurit of it, is abundant in corn and grising* [grazing], *namelie for scheip …*

About forty years later, an anonymous writer appears to have been impressed by St Kilda's productivity:

> *Irt* … is maist fertile in scheip and foullis, quhairof it payis ane great matter yeirlie to … McCloyd and his factors. Albeit they use na pleuchis* [ploughs], *but delvis their corn land with spaddis, yet they pay yierlie 60 bollis victual.*

The presence of toxic chemicals, unwittingly introduced by the islanders in recent centuries, may have reduced the fertility of their arable land. In a recent analysis of soil samples taken from crofts and midden pits on Hiort, scientists from the University of Aberdeen discovered high concentrations of pollutants such as lead, zinc, cadmium and arsenic. The source for those pollutants was the thousands of seabird carcasses and offal discarded in the middens. Seabirds tend to have elevated levels of potentially toxic metals in their organs – resulting, perhaps, from the ever increasing volume of pollutants which have been entering marine eco-systems since the beginning of the Industrial Revolution. Before sowing their oats and barley in the spring, the islanders spread the manure from the middens across the fields.

In the nineteenth and twentieth centuries, the population continued to decline, mainly as a result of emigration and infant mortality. Eventually, it became clear that the community was so reduced that it could not be sustained. The islanders were evacuated at their own request in August 1930.

---

* The Gaelic spelling of the name of the main island is Hiort (pronounced *hirst*). Gaels apply the same name to the archipelago of St Kilda. Books and maps published over the centuries employ different spellings of the name: Irt, Hirt, Hirta, Hirte and Hirtha. An inhabitant of Hiort is called a Hiortach. Some inhabitants of Harris and the Uists refer to St Kilda as Tirt or Tiort (pronounced *tirst*), and a St Kildan as a Tirteach or Tiortach.

2. Cleite Gàdaig

It is inferred that the composer of this lively St Kildan song was a young woman who pokes fun at Dòmhnall, an admirer. Because of his advanced years, or perhaps some disability such as vertigo, Dòmhnall is unable or unwilling to scale high cliffs.
The composer invents a little stack called the *Gàdag* on to which he and she venture together. A *gàdag* was a small corn-stack, equivalent to twelve sheaves of oats, the contribution from each crofter to the feeding of the communal bull. Thus, *Cleit a' Ghàdaig* (the Cliff of *Gàdag*) would not present too great a challenge!

The Chorus, which consists of series of vocables, imitates the lively skirl of seabirds such as kittiwakes.

Tha fleasgach anns a' bhaile seo
Ris an can iad Dòmhnall,
'S ged gheibheadh e an saoghal,
Gu saothraicheadh e mòine.

Sèist

Inn ala oro i, o inn al ala;
Inn ala oro i, uru ru-i uru ru-i;
Inn ala oro i, o inn al ala.

Ged bhiodh tu a' bruidhinn rium
'S a' briodas rium an-còmhnaidh,
Cha tugadh tu na h-uighean dhomh
Nuair shuidheadh tu Didòmhnaich.

Sèist

'S truagh nach eil mo leannan s'
Ann an ìochdar Leac na Gàdaig,
Acfhainn air a smioradh air,
Is mise bhith gu h-àrd oirr'.

Sèist

There's a bachelor in this village
By the name of Donald,
And though he'd have the world's riches,
He'd continue to work peats.*

Chorus

Inn ala oro i, o inn al ala;
Inn ala oro i, uru ru-i uru ru-i;
Inn ala oro i, o inn al ala

Even though you talk with me
And chat me up continually,
You'd even refuse to get eggs for me
When you relax on Sunday.

Chorus

I wish that my sweetheart
Were at the foot of the *Gàdag* Flagstone,
Secure in his (climbing) gear,
And I at the top.

Chorus

* Fuel used for cooking and heating

3. The Staller's House

The short rocky beach at Village Bay was the only place on Hiort from which boats could operate. Launching and landing were possible only during spells when both weather and tidal conditions were favourable. But for all its shortcomings, the island community could scarcely have existed without it.

Unlike Hiort, Boreray, which is entirely girt by huge forbidding cliffs, does not afford any form of safe haven. Only the most agile, intrepid visitor dare attempt access to this mysterious isle. At only two locations, each situated at opposite sides of Boreray, can the visitor land, and that by jumping from a boat which is never motionless. After climbing clear of the rushing current, the visitor may look up to see the precipitous cliff above, rising hundreds of feet towards the fertile pastures crowning this fortress-like outpost of the British Isles.

The name, (in the Gaelic of the St Kildans it was pronounced Boighearaigh or '*boy-err-aye*') is probably derived from two Norse words: 'northarri' – farther north; and 'ey' – an island. Alternatively, the root may be 'borgar-ey' – a fortified island or an island on which a fort has been built. Most commentators prefer 'borgar-ey' as the derivation.

To the south of the summit, i.e. on the side visible from Hiort, there is a broad slope of peaty soil enriched each year by tons of guana, the droppings from the island's huge population of gannets and puffins. It is not surprising that, many generations ago, crops were grown there. Small ribbon-fields, long since overgrown with grass, are clearly visible, looking as if a huge comb had been drawn down the slope. Whether Boreray at one time supported a population separate from that of Hiort is an intriguing question. What we do know for certain is that, in recorded history, no-one lived on Boreray except for the short periods when groups from Hiort visited it during the months of summer and autumn to kill gannets and puffins, or to look after their sheep. According to the Rev MacAulay, there was a circle of prayer-stones on Boreray as well as a temple and chapel. There are numerous cleits on the island, just as there are on Hiort.

Taigh an Stallair (The Staller's House), near the highest point on the island, was designed to provide protection from invaders and from severe weather. Though all trace of it has long since disappeared, early writers' descriptions of it suggest that it was skilfully built and would have required the participation of many hands in its construction. Earth houses of similar design have been discovered at *Tàbost* in Lewis and Loch Portain in North Uist. However, the Staller's House differed in one important respect: it was built into a hillock, so that one walked straight into it rather than having to descend into it as if into a coal pit.

Duncan Kennedy of Ardchattan was missionary to St Kilda from 1857 till 1862. During that period he was visited by his niece, Ann Kennedy, a young woman who was fascinated by the antiquities of St Kilda. She befriended Euphemia MacCrimmon, a tradition-bearer, who was able to give her a wealth of information. In a letter to a friend, Ann described the Staller's House:

The building was underground except for a small facade which allowed for the entrance. It was raised on tall pillars of stones, said to have been hewn at the Castle Dùn in Village Bay.* It was quite round within with stone wedges protruding on which one might hang one's clothes. There were six closets within, each with a name of its own. The Rastalla was big enough as to provide accommodation for twenty men, sleeping head to foot. The Ralighe again was not quite as commodious. In front of the Bàir-ruighe was a long midden of ashes the purpose of which was to give the house some shelter from the force of the wind.

Ann Kennedy states that, at one time, the men and women from Hiort who visited Boreray for the purpose of harvesting fowl and tending sheep used to sleep in the Staller's House, but that 'the roof collapsed twenty years ago' (i.e. around 1840). Euphemia MacCrimmon had told her that, when she was young, she had been inside the Staller's House and could remember seeing writing on some of the stones in the interior. She could also remember seeing an altar stone on Boreray and another on Soay.

It is astonishing that men were capable of building such a commodious building on such a small and remote island. Who were the men who performed such a feat of design and construction? Of whom were they so afraid that they felt compelled to travel to the farthest limits of Europe to build such a refuge? Whoever they were, we can infer that they were practised builders, physically strong and of determined and independent spirit. Unfortunately, not a trace of the Staller's House is to be seen on Boreray. In the latter half of the nineteenth century fowlers from Hiort removed all trace of the building. They plundered the stones to build cleits, the little pyramid-like, drystone stores in which the carcasses of birds were preserved by the action of the wind.

It used to be said on Hiort that the Staller was himself an islander who, in the distant past, became so incensed by a steward's excessive demands for rent that he chose a group of fellow islanders and went with them into voluntary exile on Boreray, where they would be free from tyranny and able to repulse all attempts at invasion. There was another tradition that may have been closer to the truth: that the forebears of the original people of Hiort had crossed the sea from Uist, bringing with them the know-how and, possibly, the tools necessary to build earth-houses such as that at Loch Portain and Tàbost.

In her letter, Ann Kennedy provides an Anglicised version of the Gaelic names of the different parts of the Staller's House:

* This claim has long since been discounted on the grounds that there were plenty of suitable rocks on Boreray. By what means could the rocks be transported the four miles from the Dùn? That task accomplished, how could they be lifted to the top of Boreray?

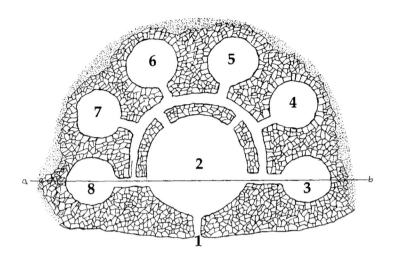

1. Bàir na Ruighe – The Shieling Roadway or Entrance
2. An Teallach – The Hearth
3. Ràth an Stallair – The Staller's Stronghold
4. Ràth an Lighiche – The Doctor's Stronghold
5. Ràth nam Bearan – The Young Men's Stronghold
6. Na Simidearan – The Tools or Weapons?
7. Leabaidh nan Con – The Dogs' Bed
8. Leabaidh an Teallaich – The Hearth Bed (which like 3 was the only compartment within sight of the fire)

Archaic Gaelic words

bàir – a path

bearan – a young man

ruighe – a shieling

ràth – a stronghold

simid – a mallet; cf. scimitar

stallair from *stalla* – an overhanging cliff

4. Thulgag bhòidheach

(verses 2 and 3 by CF)

In verse 1 (the only one to survive), the composer sees the boat as a little dimple or dent in the surface of the ocean. To the spectator looking down from the clifftops of Hiort, small boats might well appear as 'dimples' in the great expanse of the ocean. Another St Kildan boat celebrated in song (p.48) was named the *Faiche*, a word which means 'a nook or niche in a rock, serving as shelter for a lobster or edible crab'.

1 Thulgag bhòidheach, thulgag bhòidheach;
Thulgag bhòidheach null gu Sòdhaigh:
Thulgag eile seo; thulgag eile seo;

Thulgag eile seo; null chon nan eileanan.

Beautiful Dimple, beautiful Dimple;
Beautiful Dimple heading for Soay:
Another Dimple here; another Dimple here;

Another Dimple here, bound for the islands.

2 Ruiteag air sàl i; ruiteag air sàl i;

Ruiteag air sàl i, aotrom àlainn;

Cuinneag fo ràmh i; cuinneag fo ràmh i;

Cuinneag air snàmh i, aonrag aighearach.

Kittiwake afloat is she; kittiwake afloat is she;

Kittiwake afloat is she, buoyant and graceful;

A rowing-boat is she; A rowing-boat is she;

A vessel afloat is she, spirited and festive.

3 Cuideachd an eunlaith; cuideachd an eunlaith;
Cuideachd an eunlaith, aoibhneach sgiamhach;
Greadhnachas beadarach, greadhnachas beadarach,
Greadhnachas ciatach eun a' ceilearadh.

Birds for company; birds for company;
Birds for company, cheerful and graceful;
A pleasure so lively;a pleasure so lively;
A pleasure so lovely, the chiming of birds.

5. Attire

When Martin visited St Kilda in 1697, there were islanders still living who at one time were clad in sheepskins. The skins were sewn together by use of the bones or beaks of seabirds such as the oystercatcher. This had been the mode of dress of the islanders from ancient times. At the end of the seventeenth century, it was usual for men to wear *breacan an fhèilidh** (the belted plaid), which, at that time, was commonly worn throughout the Gàidhealtachd. It consisted of a heavy tartan plaid which reached to their knees and was secured at the waist by means of a leather belt.

Over the plaid they wore a short doublet that reached to the waist. On weekdays they wore short hoods, whereas on Sundays they wore bonnets. Trousers which were wide and open at the knees were favoured by a few men. Except in summer, when they went barefoot, they wore stockings and shoes. Their stockings were made of woven cloth and their shoes of leather which they tanned using the roots of tormentil, a plant growing locally.

The women also went barefoot in summer, but for the rest of the year they wore *cuaranan iteach* (feathered slippers) made from the heads and necks of mature gannets. They cut the gannet's head above the eyes and removed the skull. The crown of the head served as the back of the heel. With the lower end of the head sewn, the foot entered into the skin, as into a slipper. A pair of those *cuaranan iteach* lasted no more than five days. If the feathered side was next to the ground, it lasted for only three or four. However, that was not of great concern to the islanders, as they were able to catch hundreds of gannets during the month of March.

The women's headgear was a linen cloth drawn horizontally across the brow and at the back falling a foot and a half in length to a point below the shoulders. A long lock of hair hung down each cheek to the breasts, its lower end tied with a knot. Their upper garment, a plaid, was fastened on their breasts with a large circular buckle made of brass. Traditionally, when the Steward** brought his wife to the island, she wore a similar buckle, but one made of silver. However, the Steward's wife of Martin's generation had broken with tradition by visiting the island wearing a different style of dress which did not require a buckle of any kind.

Two centuries ago, both male and female St Kildans wore flannel shirts which they doffed before going to bed. Whether they wore nightgowns or similar is not known.

Wedding rings were not worn on Hiort. A married woman was distinguished by a white frill worn in front of the headscarf. In the first half of the nineteenth century married women in other parts of the Outer Hebrides wore a white fillet in their hair.

* the kilt in its present form had not been invented

** In effect, he was the tenant who was the interface between the islanders and the proprietor. Also known as the 'factor', he visited St Kilda each summer to collect rent from all the householders. He paid an annual sum to the landowner.

In the middle of the eighteen century, the St Kildans wore clothes made from coarse tweed woven on the island. The tweed was warm to wear and was produced in a variety of colours: mainly black, white, grey and brown, the natural colours of the island sheep. Yellow was the only artificial colour used. Though the people in the rest of the Hebrides were practised in the art of dying wool, using lichens and plants such as rue, water-lily and nettles, the St Kildans were ignorant of those skills. Nor were the weavers of the island as skilful as weavers elsewhere.

Little linen was manufactured on the island, and such as there was was very coarse.

Even the most image-conscious islander owned only one shirt. They normally wore woollen underwear.

In 1848, the men wore trousers and vests of coarse blue cloth, with blanket shirts. On Sundays they wore jackets. Their clothes were made at home from wool plucked (not shorn) from their own sheep, and spun by the women using a spinning wheel. Some women preferred to spin by means of a *dealgan* (spindle), a method used since ancient times. The dyeing and spinning of the thread was women's work. The men were responsible for weaving cloth and tailoring garments for both sexes. They were also the shoemakers. However, the quality of the leather shoes they produced was poor and was described by a visitor as being

> *as hard as box-irons, and not unlike them in shape.*

On her head the St Kildan woman wore a cotton handkerchief which was tied under her chin; all cotton goods were, of course, imported or given by visitors as gifts. She had a gown of coarse cloth which was dyed blue, or blue with a thin purple stripe, fastened at the breast with an iron skewer. Tied at the waist with a worsted cord of dull colours, the skirt reached down to just above the knees. As in previous centuries, the women were barefoot in summer even when they went to church. However, in church they covered their heads with plaids, fastened at the breast with a copper brooch made from old pennies hammered into thin discs.

In the nineteenth century, the ever-increasing number of yachts and passenger steamers visiting Hiort was having an effect on the way of life of the islanders. James Wilson (1842) says that the prevailing dress of the males was

> *very like that of the fishermen of the Long Island: small flat blue bonnets, coarse yellowish-white woollen jerkins and trousers also of coarse woollen stuff of mixed colours similar to that of heather stalks.*

T.S. Muir (1858) informs us that he found the males and females very decently and comfortably dressed and, in that respect at least, presenting a very favourable contrast to their equivalents in the Western Isles generally.

6. A St Kildan Waulking Song

They work hard at this employment, first making use of their hands and then of their feet. When they are at this work, they sing the whole time, one of their number acting the part of a prime chantress whom all the rest follow.

(Martin, 1697)

The following words in the *Òran Luaidh* are archaic or have a specialised St Kildan application:

ball-sinnsir – an heirloom

coimheach – awesome

cuaran iteach – a feathered slipper; a shoe rather like a moccasin made from the skin of a gannet

hiùra – This word may be a variant of *iùbhrach* – a ship under sail; a stately woman

iorrach – the member of the crew who sang the *iorram*

iorram – a work-song which has a regular rhythm; on a row-boat, the beat of the

iorram established the rhythm of the oars. The word can also mean 'an elegy'

linne – a deep pool; the four miles of open sea separating Hiort from Boreray was known as *An Linne*

liosdadh – meaning uncertain; perhaps, 'select' or 'special'; compare the army 'listed for bravery'

mogais – an anchor consisting of a bag made from tough stalks of heather or from perforated seal-skin and filled with heavy stones

Sèist	Chorus
Agus Ò, iorrach a' chuain;	And O, the ocean chant-man;
Agus Ò, 's na hiùra bhòaich;	And O, the beautiful;
Agus Ò, iorrach a' chuain.	And O, the ocean chant-man.
Dhèanainn an clò bàn dhut,	I'd make white tweed for you,
Snàth mar an sìoman reamhar;	Woollen thread as thick as a rope;
Sèist	Chorus
Dhèanainn dhut an cuaran iteach,	I'd make for you feathered slippers,
A luaidh 's a liosdaidh nam fearaibh;	My love, my special one of all men;
Sèist	Chorus
Bheirinn dhut a' mhogais phrìseil,	I'd give you the precious mogais,
'S am ball-sinnsir bh' aig mo sheanair;	And the heirloom given by my grandpa;
Sèist	Chorus
Mo ghaol sealgair a' bhigein	My love the hunter of the birds,
'S moiche thig thar linne choimhich;	Earliest home across the wild channel;
Sèist	Chorus
Mo ghaol maraiche nan tonn –	My love the mariner of the deep,
'S mòr am fonn bhiodh air a mhalaidh.	Wonderful the cheer on his brow.
Sèist	Chorus

© Alasdair Alpin MacGregor Collection (N.M.S.)

Annie, widow of John Gillies, shortly before leaving Hiort

7. Native Animals

Hiort boasted species of domestic animal – horses, cattle, sheep, dogs and cats. Until the Hebridean blackface was introduced in the nineteenth century, the breed of sheep reared on Hiort was closely akin to that now known as the Soay sheep. 'An Account Given to Sir Robert Sibbald'* by Sir George MacKenzie, Lord Registrar, includes the following description:

> *their sheep upon the island of Hirta are far different from all others, having long legs, long horns and instead of wool, a blewish hair upon them, for the figure and description it seems to approach in resemblance the Ovis Chilensis (Chilean sheep).*

According to present-day zoologists, Soay sheep are

> *a remarkable survivor of the type of domestic sheep that people kept in the Bronze Age.*

There were around 300 sheep on Hiort in the middle of the nineteenth century and an unknown number on Soay and Boreray. Those on Soay belonged to the proprietor and ran wild. They were caught only when their wool was to be plucked in summer. More than a dozen *buailtean cròthaidh* (folds) may still be seen in the Gleann Mòr. Those were used mainly for holding the ewes at milking-time. Each *buaile,* with walls of turf and stone, consists of a main pen for the ewes and between two and five smaller compartments for the lambs.

Dogs were numerous on Hiort. They were small, lean animals described by one observer as 'mongrel collies' and by another as 'a mixture of terrier, spaniel and water dog'. They were trained to round up sheep and hunt puffins. At an early age, their canine teeth were filed down or broken so that there was less chance of their tearing the flesh of sheep during the *ruagadh* (periodic round-up). In spite of that radical dental treatment, the lean collies of Hiort were sometimes able to injure other domestic animals and were generally distrusted by visitors to the island. See Alice MacLachlan's diary, p.207. Contrariwise, MacAulay was impressed by their 'wonderful sagacity' and by their being capable of bringing to their masters five or six puffins at a time having been trained to hunt on their own. Before St Kilda was evacuated in 1930, the islanders drowned** their dogs by tying heavy rocks round their necks and throwing them off the end of the pier.

* Sir Robert Sibbald (1641-1722) was a physician, geographer and natural historian. Although he was born in Edinburgh, his parents fled with their young family to Linlithgow in 1645 to avoid the plague. Sibbald witnessed the sacking of Dundee by General Monk in 1651. Professor of Medicine at the University of Edinburgh, he founded the Royal College of Physicians in Edinburgh (1681) and was physician to King James VII. He was also Cartographer Royal for Scotland.

** Prior to the inception of veterinarian services and the RSPCA, drowning was a common method of disposing of surplus dogs and cats throughout rural Scotland.

In Martin's time there were no more than eighteen horses on the island. They were

> *of a red colour, very low and smooth skinned, being employed in carrying turf and corn.*

By 1759, the number had dwindled to ten. A century later, Sands reported that

> *There are no horses on the island now, the work they did is now done by women.*

After visiting Stornoway a year or two before the Evacuation, a young St Kildan girl reported that the most memorable part of her visit was, for the first time, seeing a horse!

Martin reported that there were about ninety head of cattle on Hiort.

> *... small and great, have their foreheads white and black, which is discernible at a great distance, are of low stature, but fat and sweet beef.*

Eighty years later, when John MacDiarmid visited Hiort, he found that the island's herd consisted of twenty-one cows, twenty-seven heifers, twelve calves and a bull that was eight or nine years old. Gàrradh a' Ghlinne is a semi-circular dyke, nearly a mile long, running from a point high on Mullach Bì to the Mullach Mòr and was built to control the movement of cattle and sheep. Cheese made from the milk of the cattle mixed with that of the ewes found a ready market on the Scottish mainland.

The only wild animal was (and is) the mouse, which, since cats were evacuated along with the human population in 1930, has become exceedingly numerous, particularly in and around the Village.

Martin left an intriguing account of a discovery which might suggest that, at one time, there was a deer population on Hiort:

> *Some years ago, a pair of large deer antlers were found in the top of Oterveaul-hill* [Oiseabhal] *almost a foot under ground, and a wooden dish full of deer's grease.*

While it is feasible that deer were introduced at some time in the island's long history, it seems more likely that the antlers and deer grease were imported in ancient times and used by islanders in some form of pagan ceremony.

8. Cas na Caora Hiortaich, Ò!

This humorous ditty celebrates the temperamental nature of a particular St Kildan ewe. St Kildan sheep were known to rush headlong down precipitous cliffs at the sight of a human being. Many descendants of sheep left on Hiort after the Evacuation live in the vicinity of the Village and are quite docile – not so the sheep on Soay and Boreray!

Cas na caora Hiortaich, ò!	*A leg of the St Kildan ewe, o!*
Hiortaich, Hiortaich, Hiortaich, ò!	*St Kildan, St Kildan, St Kildan, o!*
Cas na caora Hiortaich, ò!	*A leg of the St Kildan ewe, o!*
B' e siud a' chas bha sgiobalta.	*What a speedy leg it was.*
Siud a' chaora bha grinn,	*What a wonderful ewe she was,*
Dh'fhàsadh an dath air a druim.	*Colour growing naturally on her back.*
Chan iarradh i crotal no sùith	*No need for lichen-dye nor for soot –*
Ach snìomh na clòimh gu briogaisean.	*Just spin the wool into trousers.*
Siud a' chaora bha luath	*What a speedy ewe was she*
Nuair a thigeadh i mun cuairt;	*When dodging about;*
Cha robh h-aon anns an taobh tuath	*There was nobody on the north side*
An uair sin chuireadh it' aiste.	*Who could pull a tuft out of her.*
Chaidh an t-uan leis fhèin	*Her lamb wandered off by itself*
Null ann an siud leis an sprèidh;	*Over yonder with the flock;*
Sin nuair a chaidh ise na bèist,	*That was when she went crazy*
Nuair a theann a seinn gu gliogadaich!	*And her bleating became a bellowing!*
Siud a' chaor' anns an robh sgeun;	*What a wild-eyed ewe she was,*
Cha do chleachd i bhith air sliabh;	*Unaccustomed to being on the hill;*
'S ann aig baile bha i riamh;	*Ever around the village she'd been,*
Is grinn am feur a dh'itheadh i.	*Eating her favourite greenery.*

9. Tha Giullan Agam Fhìn

(Unfortunately, the original words to this lively tune have not been discovered; the following words are by the author)

Dannsaidh mi le Fionnlagh –
M' ulaidh air, cho sunndach;
Is seach gu bheil mo ghiullan mear,
Miridh e ri cunntais.
Dìridh e na creagan cas
Chunntadh nan uighean dhomh;
Streapaidh e an Stiodhaigh Ghlas
Cùl Bhoraraigh –
Streapaidh e an Stiodhaigh Ghlas
Chunntadh uighean dhomh.

I'll dance with Finlay –
My darling is so light-hearted;
And since he is so lively,
He'll begin counting.
Steep rocks he will climb
To count eggs for me;
He'll scale the Grey Cliff-path
Behind Boreray –
He'll scale the Grey Cliff-path
To count eggs for me.

Pòsaidh giullan Màiri
Caileag laghach àlainn,
Is seach gu bheil an dithis cleas,
Nach danns iad dhuinn an-dràsta.
Dìridh e na creagan cas –
'S e gheibh uighean di;
Streapaidh e a' Bhearraidh Gheal
'N taobh Oiseabhal;
Streapaidh e a' Bhearraidh Gheal –
'S e gheibh uighean di.

The lad will marry Màiri,
A nice lovely girl,
And since the two are so light-footed,
They will now dance for us.
He will climb the steep rocks –
He's the one who'll get eggs for her;
He'll climb the White Pass
At the back of Oiseabhal;
He'll climb the White Pass –
He's the one who'll get eggs for her.

Gleusaidh sinn na fidhlean
'S cluinnear sinn an Ìle,
Is seach gu bheil an comann deas
Air stapadaich na ruidhle,
Dìreamaid na creagan cas
Chunntadh ghugachan;
Dìreamaid an Staca Bhreac –
Stùc Bhradastac:
Dìreamaid an Staca Bhreac
Chunntadh ghugachan.

We'll tune the fiddles,
We'll be heard all the way to Islay,
And as the company is so good
At step-dancing in the reel,
We'll climb the steep rocks
To count nestling gannets;
We'll climb the Mottled Stack –
Stack of Bradastac:
We'll climb the Mottled Stack
To count nestling gannets.

Dèanamaid an ruidhle
Do dh'Fhionnlagh beag na fidhle –
Fionnlagh lurach beag cho mear,
'S e 'n giullan agam fhìn e.
Cluichidh e mun Staca Lì,
'S eòinridh a' magadh air;
Cluichidh e air Mullach Bì,
'S raon Chonachair;
Cluichich e air Mullach Bì
'S eòinridh a' magadh air.

Fulmair is làmhaidh
'S buthaigir an àigh dhomh
Gheibh mo ghiullan measg nan creag
Na annlann do na càirdean.
Cuiridh e gu danns' sinn,
Fionnlagh a' feadalaich;
Gìbean ris a' ghanntar,
'S ceòl aighearach;
Gìbean ris a' ghanntar
'S Fionnlagh a' feadalaich.

Let's do the reel
To little Finlay's fiddle tune –
Little Finlay so attractive and lively,
He is my very own laddie.
He'll play around the Stac Lì,
With the seabirds a-mocking him;
He will play on Mullach Bì
And on the plain of Conachar;
He will play on Mullach Bì
With the seabirds a-mocking him.

A fulmar, a razorbill
And the delightful puffin
My lad will find among the rocks
As food for our friends.
He'll put us all a-dancing,
Finlay a-whistling;
Gìbean* against food shortage
And lively music;
Gìbean against hunger
And Finlay a-whistling.

* *gìbean* – fowl fat (not to be confused with *giaban* – a gizzard)

10. For Lack of a *Bramach-Innilt*

In the middle of the nineteenth century, when Alexander Carmichael* was in Uist collecting material for his *Carmina Gadelica*, he visited Balranald (Baile Raghnaill), one of the most productive farms in the Outer Hebrides. There he heard a moving account of how eighteen St Kildans 'in a frail coracle' had arrived one year in the late spring, hoping to purchase oats and barley seed. As soon as they landed, the local people quickly gathered on the shore to help them and convey them to the farmhouse. Each of the eighteen was given dry clothes and a substantial meal, and while their order of oats and barley seed was being prepared, they sat by a blazing fire chatting to their hostess, the wife of MacDonald, the farm tenant. The St Kildans explained that they had undertaken their voyage out of desperation, their own harvest having been destroyed by storms the previous autumn. The conversation between Mrs MacDonald and the St Kildans was long remembered.

'Am bi pòsadh agus baisteadh agaibh ann an Tiort?'

'O ghà'ag [ghràdhag] ghaolach, cha bhi pòsadh no baisteadh againn – is ann a tha sinn chun a dhol a dhìth. Ciamar a phòsadh no a bhaisteadh sinn – nach d' eug a' bhramach-innilt? Agus chan urrainn dhuinne clann a bhith againn, agus is ann a tha sinn, a ghà'ag, an annar a dhol a dhìth.'

'Ciod e an rud a tha anns a' bhramach-innilt?'

'Tha, a ghà'ag, am boireannach a tha am bun na bratha [mnatha] a tha cur na cloinne chun an t-saoghail.'

'Do you have marriages and baptisms on Hiort?'

'O darling beloved, we have neither marriages nor baptisms. In fact, we are going to ruin, for we can neither marry nor baptise, now that our *bramach-innilt* is dead. We cannot now have children and, indeed, darling beloved, we are on the verge of ruin.'

'What manner of creature is a *bramach-innilt?*'

'The *bramach-innilt*, dear, is the female who helps wives put children into the world.'

* Author of *Carmina Gadelica* (Ortha nan Gaidheal), Hymns and Incantations with Notes on Words, Rites and Customs, etc.

It is said that the eighteen St Kildans delivered the recital of their misfortunes loudly and in unison. Their performance caused much amusement at the time: the artless simplicity, the peculiar words and the lisping accent.

The farmhands helped the travellers to launch their craft, and watched as the vessel, heavily laden with the sacks of seed-corn, set off to fight against the waves rolling in from the open ocean.

According to those who told Carmichael of the encounter, the St Kildans' vessel foundered with the loss of everybody on board. If such a tragedy ever occurred, it must have been a devastating blow to a community which, reportedly, was already 'on the verge of ruin'.

The story has a number of inconsistencies. Carmichael says that the St Kildans arrived in 'a frail coracle', carrying eighteen persons. He surely meant to use the word 'currach' rather than 'coracle' as the latter is, indeed, a frail craft built to accommodate one person and is used for fishing on gentle-flowing rivers. By contrast, the currach is a much more robust vessel* built to sail on the open sea. Even then, it is difficult to believe that even a currach, capable of carrying a crew of eighteen together with a considerable weight of cargo, was ever used by the St Kildans. Why was it necessary for eighteen men to leave the community in the spring when the harvesting of mature gannets was in full swing?

In spite of these questions, the story rings true in some respects. Balranald supplied grain to many communities in the southern isles of the Outer Hebrides. The term *bramach-innilt* (midwife) was used only on St Kilda. It was said that, in their dealings with strangers, the St Kildans of yore were inclined to whinge and plead poverty. If that were the case, it would seem likely that they would list their misfortunes in the hope that they might move the listener to pity, and thus get favourable terms for their business dealings.

* The *Navigatio Sancti Brendani Abbatis*, a manuscript of the tenth century, contains a detailed description of the construction of the vessel in which St Brendan, an Irish abbot of the sixth century, claimed to have sailed north from Ireland and reached lands far to the north-west of Newfoundland. The vessel was quite like the currachs still made in County Kerry. Sceptics could not accept that such a fragile vessel would survive a voyage in the open sea. Tim Severin, a British navigation scholar, constructed a currach, following the details given in the tenth century manuscript. He and his helpers built a wooden frame; tanned ox-hides with oak bark; stretched them across the frame; sewed them with leather thread; and smeared the hides with animal fat which made them resistant to salt water. Determined to prove that a voyage across the Atlantic in a such a craft was possible, he and his crew embarked from the south of Ireland in 1976. They followed a route that took them close to Iceland and Greenland, and finally landed in Newfoundland. This was similar to the route that Leif Erickson would have taken in the tenth century.

11. A St Kildan in Glasgow

One of the inhabitants of St Kilda some time ago being wind-bound in the Isle of Harries, was prevailed on by some of them that traded with Glascow to go thither with them. He was astonished at the length of the Voyage, and of the great Kingdoms, as he thought 'em, that is Isles, by which they sail'd; the largest in his way did not exceed twenty four Miles in length, but he consider'd how much they exceeded his own little Native Country.

"Upon his arrival at Glascow, he was like one who had dropp'd from the Clouds into a new World, whose Language, Habits, etc. were in all respects new to him: he never imagin'd such big Houses of Stone were made with hands; and for the Pavements of the Streets; he thought it must be altogether Natural; for he could not believe that Men would be at pains to beat it into the ground to walk upon. He stood dumb at the door of his Lodging with the greatest admiration; and when he saw a Coach and two Horses, he thought it a little House they were drawing at their Tail with Men in it: but he condemn'd the Coach-man for a Fool to sit so uneasy, for he thought it safer to sit on the horses back. The Mechanism of the Coach-Wheel, and its running about, was the greatest of all Wonders.

"When he went through the Streets, he desired to have one lead him by the hand. Thomas Ross, a Merchant, and others, that took the diversion to carry him through the Town, ask'd his Opinion of the high Church? He answer'd that it was a large Rock, yet there were some in St Kilda much higher, but that these were the best Caves he ever saw; for that was the Idea which he conceiv'd of the Pillars and Arches upon which the Church stands. When they carried him into the Church, he was yet more surpriz'd, and held up his hands with admiration, wondering how it was possible for Men to build such a prodigious Fabrick, which he supposed to be the largest in the Universe. He could not imagine what the Pews were design'd for and he fancied that the People who wore Masks (not knowing whether they were Men or Women) had been guilty of some ill thing for which they dar'd not shew their Faces. He was amaz'd to see Women wearing Patches, and fancied them to have been Blisters. Pendants seem'd to him the most ridiculous of all things; he condemned Perriwigs mightily, and much more the Powder us'd i them: in fine, he condemned all things as superfluous, he saw not in his own Country. When he heard the Church-Bells ring, he was under a mighty Consternation, as if the Fabrick of the World had been in great Disorder. He did not think there had been so many People in the World, as in the City of Glasgow..."

(excerpt from Martin Martin's *A Voyage to Saint Kilda*, 1697)

12. Ciod e Bhiodh tu 'g Iarraidh?

Words unknown

13. Òran na h-Inghinn

Words unknown

© Donald MacCormick (N.M.S.)

Mrs Mackinnon of No 1

14. Fearchar and the Dougan

There were good reasons why remote coastal communities should have been fearful of the sight of foreign ships approaching their shores. Between 1530 and 1780, North African pirates known as Barbary Corsairs abducted and enslaved more than one million Europeans. They not only attacked ships at sea but also landed on unguarded beaches, often at night, to snatch the unwary. In 1631, almost all the inhabitants of the village of Baltimore, in Ireland, were taken. Some of those captured were ransomed, but most were forced to work as galley slaves, labourers and concubines for Muslim overlords in small North African states which became Morocco, Tunisia, Algeria and Libya.

Though there is no mention of St Kildans being taken by slavers, it is likely that news of the activities of North African pirates would have reached the islanders and made them fearful of strangers. In its long history Hiort was sometimes visited by men who brought misery to the islanders by attempting to steal property and to abuse the women. On one occasion, a group of armed men intent on robbery set sail from Harris. They landed and began to round up the sheep. The islanders attacked them with knives and their fishing rods and sent them packing.

Among the most disastrous episodes recalled in the folklore of the island was that perpetrated by Fearchar and the Dougan, two villains who claimed to be natives of the Isle of Lewis. Talkative and amiable, the visitors were ever ready to entertain the *bodaich* (old men) with stories and songs. Little did the islanders suspect that they were wolves in sheep's clothing.

One day Fearchar and the Dougan said that they were going to climb to the top of Oiseabhal to gather heather for rope-making. Having been on the hill for only a short time, they came running back down to the Village and breathlessly stuttered out the dreadful news that a fleet of pirate ships was approaching Gob na h-Àirde from the east and that, within the hour, a horde of bloodthirsty foreigners would disembark and come swarming into the Village.

The news quickly spread and the panic-stricken women began to gather the children and prepared to secrete them in *Taigh an t-Sìthiche*. However, the two conspirators managed to dissuade them from retreating underground, saying that the pirates would soon discover their hideaway and treat them mercilessly. Some of the men began to sharpen their scythes and flensing-knives, preparing to resist the invaders. Others argued that their only way to save the community was to rush away from the Village and hide the women and children in cleits on the cliffs at the back of Conachair where no foreigner would ever find them.

> *"There's no time for you to do any such thing," cried The Dougan. "The pirates will soon be rounding Rubha Cholla and before you can say 'Sgian', they will be within sight of the houses and the air will fill with their drumbeats and warcries!"*

"Salvation for us there is none!" wailed the bodaich. "Our little community is going to be at the mercy of those godless pirates. Let us all retreat into God's house and pray."

Fearchar and the Dougan agreed that that was an excellent plan for, they said, however barbarous the foreigners, they would never desecrate a holy place.

"Greas ort! Greas Ort! Hurry inside now and cling to the horns of the altar," shouted Fearchar.

Very soon every man, woman and child was packed within the walls of the chapel. Shaking with fear, they awaited the terrifying noise of the rampaging foreigners. For a time all was quiet. When the warcries and the drumbeat of the advancing pirates were not heard, one St Kildan overcame his fear and tried to open the chapel door to investigate. There was panic when he discovered that the door was locked from without with boulders stacked up to prevent the occupants from escaping. Fearchar and The Dougan had set the thatch alight and were dancing round the burning building like wild savages. After a time, they became tired of their celebration and sat together on a knoll, watching the smoke and the flames while they discussed how they could transport the St Kildans' cattle and sheep to the Scottish mainland.

"It amazes me," declared Fearchar, "that the entire population was so gullible as to allow themselves to be herded into the chapel like sheep!"

"Strange feeling," said the Dougan, "that we are the only two people living in the whole of St Kilda."

But one person survived the holocaust – a *cailleach* (old woman) who had spent several weeks tending cattle on the grazings of the Gleann Mòr, on the far side of the island. It so happened that her return to the Village coincided with the very time of the inferno at the chapel. On her homeward journey, she rested at the Blàr* – the high saddle separating the two glens of Hiort. There she observed the pall of smoke rising from the chapel and heard the cries of the victims trapped within. Tearfully she hurried down the brae in the vain hope that somehow she could help her family and friends. As she progressed, the cries of those trapped faded and, after only a few minutes, they were replaced by absolute silence. She paused at Clach na Gruagaich. Not a soul could she see moving about the Village – that is, until Fearchar and the Dougan appeared from a house shouting and laughing and throwing sacks of feathers on to the burning church.

* Shown as Blaid on Matheson's detailed map of 1927, this is the peat-moor which, for many centuries, provided the islanders with their fuel. In my native village in Lewis, our *sliabh-mònach* (peat-moor) was also known as Am Blàr and pronounced by some as Am Blàid.

Hidden by smoke from the burning building, the *cailleach* slunk fearfully to her right until she reached Tobar na Cille – a well at the foot of Mullach Sgàr. As she sat by the well she remembered that close by there was a cave* to which islanders in olden times sometimes retreated if they felt their lives to be in danger. Cold, hungry and frightened, she clambered into the cave. Indeed, she lived in the cave for many days and nights.

Occasionally, hunger forced her to sally forth to look for food. She did so only at night, when she thought Fearchar and The Dougan might be asleep. She took eggs stored in cleits and, from her own house, a small quantity of grain which she reduced to meal by pounding it between two stones.

Towards the end of the summer the Factor's galley anchored in the bay. As the skiff bringing the Factor and members of his retinue was approaching the shore, Fearchar and the Dougan walked down to meet them. The villains wrung their hands as they recited their account of how they arrived on the island to find the charred remains of the islanders in the church. Needless to say, the Factor and his men were shocked by the news that the island's entire population had perished. Approaching the ruins of the chapel, they became aware of a human voice whimpering among the rocks nearby.

> *"Come out!" demanded the Factor. "Approach us, for you needn't fear us! We're here to protect you!"*

Slowly, the *cailleach* emerged and cautiously made her way down from her hiding-place. Fearchar and the Dougan were gripped by panic as the old woman told of her ordeal: how she had seen the two strangers celebrating at the scene of the disaster and how, half-starved and ill with the cold, she had determined to live long enough to tell the Factor the true story.

Fearchar and The Dougan were overpowered and, after binding them hand and foot, the Factor decided that their trial should take place there and then. Though the villains pled their innocence, it didn't take the Factor and his men long to decide that they and only they were guilty of a mass murder. Their punishment was that they were to be banished for life to Stac an Àrmainn, a stack close to Boreray, four miles north-east of Hiort. With their limbs still bound with ropes, Fearchar and the Dougan were placed sitting on a thwart in the boat ready to be ferried out to the galley. No longer protesting their innocence, the two began to worry about the problems of surviving on the cold austere stump of Stac an Àrmainn. Above the creaking of the oars in the rowlocks, the Factor heard Fearchar say to his fellow prisoner,

> *"They couldn't have chosen a colder more desolate prison for us. I hope you've remembered to bring the steel and tinder-box with you so that we can at least try to make a fire."*

---

* Uamh Cailleach Bheag Ruabhail (The Cave of the Little Old Woman of Ruabhal), supposed to have been the hiding-place of the *cailleach*, is by the shore of Village Bay, to the south-east of Mullach Sgar and about half a mile from the Village.

© A. M. Cockburn (S.S.S.)

Dùgan's 'botha' on Soay

When the Factor heard mention of the arsonists' fire-making tools, he was enraged and, with clenched fist, advanced on the two men. Seeing the fury on the Factor's face, Fearchar Mòr leapt overboard and was immediately swallowed in the sea. The Factor then directed that the boat be rowed past the galley and along the south shore of the Dùn on a course that would take them to Soay.

Within a few yards of the cliffs of Soay, the Dougan, quivering with fright, was released from his bonds and forced to jump ashore. Abandoned on that wild, inhospitable isle, the prisoner began to look for a place of shelter. In due course, he found a shallow cave at the entrance of which he built a wall of boulders to protect himself from the fury of the Atlantic gales. The cave was known to the St Kildans as Botha an Dùgain (The Dougan's Bothy).

After visiting Soay in 1876, John Sands described Botha an Dùgain in such a way as to lend some credence to the folk-tale.

> He found shelter under an over-hanging rock. He deepened the floor area by the use of his dirk and fortified the entrance by building a wall of boulders, so that a doorway of only two feet square was left. Years later, the man's skeleton and dirk were found within. The Botha is a very rudimentary home, yet six girls stay there each summer while they hunt the puffin which they prize for the feathers.

In his autobiography, Calum MacQueen,* who as a twenty-four year old emigrated to Australia, gives a slightly different version of the story of 'The Burning of the Temple':

> There were two men in the 13th or 14th century, probably not of St Kilda themselves, were one day on the east side of the island near Mount Orachival where there was a lot of heather and dry ferns. They made two large bundles and cried out, "The ships are coming. Run under the protection of the Trinity." There was a Temple in the cemetery built of birch. My father said it was as high as himself. They all went to the temple. The two brought the bundles to the door and set fire in hope of destroying all the people. All the people of the island, except one woman, were burnt there; the woman hid until a boat came. She was more than a mile from the houses in one of the stone huts, some of which were scattered about in my time. She got food out of the houses. One day, two men were paddling where she was in hiding and one said he smelt fire; the other said it was only their own. When the proprietor came to meet the people of the island, he saw only two men. Presently however, one woman was seen coming.

* See 'Calum MacQueen', p.164

The two men told the proprietor the story of the ship that visited the island and the people went to the Temple for protection but the place took fire. The proprietor then asked the woman who said, "Don't believe it. It was they." They took them away but decided not to kill the men. They put Big Farquhar on Stac an Armainn without fire or anything but he went to follow the boat and was drowned. The other they put on Soay. He made a hut against a big rock (I have slept there). They later found the bones of Dougan in the hut.

In olden times the Hiortaich were suspicious of any unrecognised ship approaching the island and sometimes became so fearful that they retreated to distant caves or cleits.

The Factor (left) representing the owner of the island visited Hiort once a year to claim the rent!

15. Cha b' e Sgiobadh na *Faiche*

The woman who composed this song has seen the safe return of one of two boats which had sailed from Hiort. She anxiously awaits the return of the *Faiche*, the second boat, crewed by her husband, son, nephew and three brothers.

Cha b' e sgiobadh na *Faiche*	The crew of the *Faiche* did not make
Ghabh Diciadain an t-aiseag;	The (return) voyage on Wednesday;
Gur e sgeula nan creach mura beò sibh.	How tragic my tale if you haven't survived.
Gur e chùm sibh cho fad' uam	Perhaps you have been delayed
Am muir àrd 's a' ghaoth chas oirbh,	By the high seas and the wild wind,
Chòir nach faod sibh an ceartuair thoirt seòl dhi.	Unable to raise your sails.
Gur e turas gun bhuannachd	Some inauspicious business
Thug air falbh an duin'-uasal	Prompted the gentleman to leave,
Gus an t-aon mhac thoirt uamsa seo, Dòmhnall.	Taking from me Donald, my only son.
Dh'fhalbh mo mhac 's mo thriùir bhràithrean,	My son is away, as are my three brothers
Aona mhac piuthar mo mhàthar;	And my sister's only boy;
Sgeul as cruaidh' thig no thàinig, m' fhear pòsta.	But the hardest of all to bear is the fate of my husband.
'S e chur mi tharraing na luatha	What caused me to draw the ashes
'S a thoirt leis air an ruamhar,	And to scatter them on the field
Na fir a bhith bhuam 's gun brath beò orr';	Is that the men are absent with no news of them;
Mi gun shùgradh gun mhire	I am bereft of joy and of pleasure
Am shuidh' air ùrlar a' ghlinne –	Sitting on the floor of the glen,
Tha mo shùilean a' sileadh, 's tric deòir orr'.	My eyes often shedding tears.

6. Red Ruairi, the Impostor

The story of Fearchar and the Dougan may have been a fiction, a cautionary tale told and retold to generations of St Kildans to warn the young of the danger of putting their trust in glib Lewismen and other personable strangers. By contrast, the villainous Red Ruairi (Ruairidh Ruadh) was an historic figure, authenticated by none other than the notable Martin Martin, tutor to the family of the Chief of MacLeod of Skye.

Of all the preachers who ever held sway on Hiort, the most imperious was Ruairi. In his *Voyage to St Kilda*, Martin describes Ruari as

> *a comely, well-proportioned fellow, red-haired, and exceeding all the inhabitants of St Kilda in strength, climbing, etc.*

Ruairi was illiterate and had never been beyond the bounds of St Kilda – not even to visit the other islands of the Outer Hebrides. Apart from chatting with members of the crew of the Steward's galley who were as illiterate as he was himself, he had never had an opportunity of conversing with anybody except his fellow-islanders. He was rebellious by nature and his father, reputedly an honest man, often told him that if he continued to be so disobedient and strong-willed, he would come to a sticky end. When he was aged eighteen, he went fishing on a Sunday – something that had been taboo on Hiort long before a minister had become resident on the island. Those who had witnessed Ruairi striding cockily towards Rubha Cholla with his fishing-rod on his shoulder were aghast. Had they really seen what they had seen?

A few hours later, Ruairi reappeared and entered the Village, carrying his rod and several bream suspended from a string. People stood in the doorways of their houses, quietly murmuring their disapproval.

"I have great news for all the folk at this moment looking at me," exclaimed Ruairi. "As I was coming home by the Lag bho Thuath, I met a stranger dressed in Lowland garb. You'll never guess who he was! He was John the Baptist."

"Be quiet, you foolish, blasphemous boy," declared one old woman who laughed nervously and retreated indoors. Over her shoulder she shouted, "Stop your lies or God will bring down a judgement on you."

"No! No! Don't leave me!" cried Ruairi. "Listen to me now. Listen to what happened to me up in the Lag bho Thuath. It's the most wonderful news. The *Gall* I met really was John the Baptist, and when he told me who he was, my mind went into such a great disorder and I fell flat on the ground. But that saintly figure told me not to fear him, for he had been sent straight to me to instruct me in the laws of Heaven."

On hearing the commotion, the islander appointed by the Steward to be the 'Officer of Hiort' appeared on the scene. "*A Ruairidh Ruaidh na mallachd!*" he cried scornfully, "you are the only Hiortach since the beginning of time to go fishing on the Sabbath Day.

Are you telling us that you, the breaker of the Sabbath, are the one chosen to instruct us in the laws of Heaven?"

"That indeed I am," replied Ruairi, "though the fact of it surprises no-one more than it surprises myself!"

Leaving his audience gobsmacked, the red-haired, freckle-faced fisherman turned away and stride off to his home, where he took to his bed. News of Ruairi's claim to fame spread quickly. By nightfall everybody was on tenterhooks waiting to see what would happen when the self-proclaimed visionary emerged from his parents' home.

Ruairi stayed in his *crùb* for the rest of the day, but on the following morning his mother appeared from the gloom of their home to report that her son had spoken in a foreign language during the night. With bated breath, the villagers waited for Ruairi to appear. However, he didn't do so that day; nor on the following day; but at the open doorway of his home, curious neighbours could hear him, recumbent in his *crùb*, reciting strange mantras and, occasionally, declaiming single words that the audience had never heard before. On the third morning, his mother came out of the house to confide that there was a further development during the night. After a time, the dishevelled figure of Ruairi emerged to tell of his latest experience. "The Blessed Baptist came to me for a second time – the very man who baptised our Lord Jesus Christ. He came to me straight from the pages of the New Testament and the words he spake were 'Guranodugo, Buranbuhasi'. Those, my friends, were his very words, which come from the language of the Holy Land!"

Not surprisingly, there was no-one on Hiort who had knowledge of the ancient language of the Holy Land, nor, indeed, of any land furth of St Kilda! What did all the mumbo-jumbo mean? It didn't take Ruairi long to enlighten them.

"I am to be your shepherd, chosen from among you to lead you in the new laws of Saint John. 'Guranodugo' is a holy commandment directing us to fast all day Friday. Nobody must taste food of any kind, nor take even as much as a sniff of tobacco-snuff on that day. Obey that commandment, for, if we obey it, Heaven will be shown which souls are the wheat and which the chaff; who are to be saved and who lost for all eternity."

There were sceptics among the people of the island, and none more so than Ruairi's own father, who denounced his son as one who would cause the community untold grief. In spite of that admonition, more and more of the islanders began to obey Ruairi's edicts, and, as the years passed, the impostor became bolder and imposed increasingly punitive penalties on his neighbours. He asserted that some of their deceased relatives were 'nominated saints in Heaven' and that, in the hereafter, the function of those nominated saints was to propose a similar status for members of their families still living. Each of the nominated saints was to be commemorated with a feast at which the entire community would partake of boiled beef or mutton and fowl. On those feast days, the family of each saint-in-waiting was required to provide all the food. Ruairi himself was always to be the chief guest and a share of the food had to be sent separately to his wife and family.

There were more laws in the pipeline! Ruairi commanded the head of each household to take a sheep from his flock and kill it on the threshold of his home; a sizeable portion of the meat from the animal was to be presented to Ruairi. Instead of a knife, the instrument used to dispatch the animal had to be the *cas-chrom,* an appallingly blunt instrument which, as Martin Martin observed, had a cutting-edge almost half an inch thick.

Their self-appointed priest then introduced further humiliating penances. He forced individuals to stand in cold water, even in the depths of winter, and stay there for as long as it pleased him. He forbade the use of the Lord's Prayer, the Psalms and the Ten Commandments. Instead of those, he substituted gibberish of his own. All the women in his congregation were required to visit him in order to learn new hymns. During those sessions, he succeeded in 'debauching some of the simple women'.

Red Ruairi consecrated the little hillock on which, according to himself, he had had his first meeting with Heaven's emissary. He named it *Preas Eòin Baistich* (John the Baptist's Bush) and forbade anybody to walk on it or for any cattle or sheep to graze on it. Any animal found on the hillock was to be slaughtered immediately and its meat divided equally between the owner and Ruairi. Anybody refusing to obey that edict was liable to be excluded from the congregation – a fate which, according to Ruairi, would be reckoned against them in the hereafter.

For much of the second half of the seventeenth century, the people of Hiort were dominated by the physically powerful figure who reigned over them with tyrannical laws and prohibitions. The first challenge to his authority came from one of his own cousins: Lewis (alias Muldonich), who flatly refused to kill one of his best-loved ewes after she had given birth to triplets. The animal had been found grazing on the supposedly sacred 'bush'. In spite of Red Ruairi's fury, Lewis refused to budge. When Heaven failed to strike the rebel down, some of the neighbours began to lose faith in the preacher's celestial influence. The rot had set in! Others refused to slaughter their animals for so-called 'religious festivals'.

It was a busy time of the year and the fowlers were out on the stacks. Ruairi, who rarely participated in those secular pursuits, met the Factor's wife and told her it was time for him to come to her home to instruct her in the new theology. The woman told her husband. When Ruairi arrived to conduct his tutorial, he assumed that only he and the woman were on the premises. After a brief discussion on matters theological, he proceeded to embrace the woman and to kiss her. He broke off in great alarm when he discovered the Factor at his elbow.

"Is this the way John the Baptist has told you to instruct the women of Hiort?" demanded the Factor.

Ruairi begged the Factor to forgive him and promised never to repeat such disgraceful behaviour. His show of remorse was such that the Factor forgave him but allowed an account of the incident to be made public. The friendship between the two men was patched up, and in due course, Ruairi asked the Factor to become his 'sponsor' at the baptism of one of his children. In his *Voyage to St Kilda*, Martin describes what the ceremony of sponsorship entailed:

> *When there is an opportunity of being sponsor to each other and it is thought necessary to enter into bonds of friendship at baptism, the inhabitants of the Western Isles supply this ceremony by tasting a drop of each other's blood.**

* Reminiscent of the ceremony by which men of the Blackfoot tribe of North America became 'blood brothers'.

In spite of his promise to behave with due decorum, Red Ruairi allowed himself to fall into his former lecherous ways. It so happened that a carpenter from the Isle of Harris travelled to Hiort to mend a boat damaged in a storm. He took with him his son, who, one evening, decided to eavesdrop on one of Ruairi's night-time instructional services for women. The boy saw and heard more than he had bargained for! As soon as the service ended, he ran to his father and reported all. The Steward happened to arrive on the island soon afterwards and was given a full account of what the boy had seen.

Though resident in Harris, the Rev John Campbell was responsible for the spiritual welfare of the St Kildans. He visited Hiort with Martin and called the people together. The minister preached a sermon in which he told them that there was a false prophet in their midst. He rounded on Red Ruairi and denounced him as an impostor.

There was so much evidence against Ruairi that the St Kildans who had previously been afraid of him spoke out against him. The minister directed the people to go to the so-called 'Bush of St John the Baptist', the patch of ground round on which the impostor had instructed his congregation to built a dry-stone wall. With Ruairi a reluctant volunteer, they demolished the wall and scattered the stones far and wide so that future generations would not look on them as 'monuments to the folly and ignorance' of their ancestors.

The village graveyard

Though Martin gives quite a full account of the rise and fall of Red Ruairi, he does not mention how, in the end, he was persuaded to leave Hiort. Tradition has it that the Steward delivered a bogus message from the Chief of the MacLeods inviting the self-declared Prophet of Hiort to visit him in Dunvegan. Had such an invitation been issued by the Chief, Ruairi would have had to regard it more as a command than as a request.

In any case, at the last moment, Ruairi embarked on the vessel that was to take Martin and the Rev John Campbell to Harris. He was held for a time on the isle of Pabbay off the coast of Harris and afterwards was transported to Skye, where he was tried before the Presbytery of that island.

Before the Presbytery, Ruairi confessed to his wrongdoings. As a punishment, he was committed to life as a *diol-dèirce* – a beggar – never allowed to leave the island but forced to travel from one community to another, confessing all that he had done, not least by jeopardizing the souls of the poor people who had followed him.

Of course Ruairi never again returned to St Kilda, and within a generation almost everybody had forgotten him and his tyranny. They remembered him only through ceilidh-house imitations of his night-time sermons to women.

17. D' Dhà Shùil Bheag Bhiolach

The composer of this lullaby had a mischievous sense of humour! One can imagine her rocking the cradle in which a baby lies trying to focus on the crooner as it drifts off to sleep. The composer draws on her experience of hunting for puffin on Boreray or Soay. Looking into a burrow, she can see the beady little eyes of the occupant looking out and awaiting its inescapable fate: oblivion! The piece, recorded by James Ross for the School of Scottish Studies, is made all the more strange because of the so-called 'St Kildan lisp' by which the word *ruig* (reach) is transmuted to leig.

D' dhà shùil bheag bhiolach	Your two sharp little eyes
Gham choimhead tron toll,	Watching me from within the burrow,
'S cha leig mi ort; cha leig mi ort.	And I can't reach you; I can't reach you.
Tha càch aig am beinn, 's tha mis' aig a' chloinn,	The others are out on the ben, and I'm left with the kids,
'S cha leig mi ort; cha leig mi ort.	And I can't reach you; I can't reach you.
D' dhà shùil bheag bhiolach	Your two sharp little eyes
Gham choimhead tron toll,	Watching me from within the burrow,
'S cha leig mi ort; cha leig mi ort.	And I can't reach you; I can't reach you.
Ma thig Ailean gu baile 's gun ruig e dh'alam,	If Alan comes back home and reaches me,
Bidh sinn aoibhneach, Ò;	We'll be happy, O;
Bidh sinn aoibhneach, Ò.	We'll be happy, O.
D' dhà shùil bheag bhiolach	Your two sharp little eyes
Gam choimhead tron toll,	Watching me from within the burrow,
'S cha leig mi ort; cha leig mi ort.	And I can't reach you; I can't reach you.

Manx shearwater

18. Music and Merriment

Until about 1820, when the spirit of the people slowly crumbled, the earliest reports describe them as being light-hearted and fond of partying, singing and dancing. Both men and women liked to compose *bàrdachd* and enjoyed listening to both vocal and instrumental music. According to Martin, the only musical instrument on the island was a trump (jew's harp) which 'disposes them to dance mightily'. The Rev Kenneth MacAulay, who visited Hiort in 1764, was impressed by the St Kildans' love of music and entertainment:

The power of music is felt everywhere: that divine art has charms enough to conquer the most savage heart. The St Kildans are enthusiastically fond of it, whether in the vocal or the instrumental way. The lowest tinklings of the latter throws them into ecstasy of joy. I have seen them dancing to a bad violin – much to my satisfaction. Even the old women in the isle act their part in the great assemblies, and the most agile dancers are here, as well as everywhere else, great favourites. They delight much in singing and their voices are abundantly tuneful. The women, while cutting down the barley in a field, or grinding their grain on their hand-mills in the house, are almost constantly employed in that way; and the men, if pulling the oar, exert all their strength of their skill in animating the party, by chanting away some spirited songs, adapted to the business in hand.

The minister advising the youth! (John Sands)

At Michelmas (29th September), pony races were held on a racecourse stretching from the Gaineamh* to the cluster of houses that was Am Baile (The Village). There was great excitement on such occasions as the young men took turns to ride their mounts without saddles or bridles, using only halters to control the ponies. On that day, each housewife baked a *srùdhan* – a large five-cornered bannock which, as tradition demanded, had to be consumed on that same day. According to Carmichael's *Carmina Gadelica*, feasting, dancing and the celebration of the *srùdhan* were prevalent throughout the Outer Hebrides.

By 1758, the tradition of baking the *srùdhan* had been discontinued on Hiort. Indeed, by the end of the eighteenth century, all evidence of the islanders' former *joie de vivre* had largely disappeared. In his book *Account of the Island of St Kilda and the Neighbouring Islands*, 1799, Robert Campbell records that Christmas, Good Friday and Michelmas continued to be observed – but by fasting rather than by feasting and merrymaking. Yet one festival of the age of *horo-gheallaidh* (merrymaking) survived. Like Gaels elsewhere in Scotland, the St Kildans continued to enjoy the *Callainn* (Hogmanay) on 12th January, the date of the New Year by the obsolete Julian Calendar. In his diary notes for 1887, George Murray says that he accompanied men from Hiort 'to catch sheep for a New Year Feast'.

* the stretch of sand appearing along the head of the Bay in summer but disappearing during late autumn storms

19. Smallpox

Of the many tragic events in the history of St Kilda, none was more devastating than that which occurred in 1729. In the autumn of that year the community was in fair fettle. There were sufficient fit young men and women to reap the oats and barley and to engage in the more challenging work of fowling.

On his rent-collecting visit to Hiort in summer, the Steward usually met the islanders' requirements of salt, storage barrels, gutting-knives, wooden boards etc. Even so, there was a time when the St Kildans were prepared to travel the sixty sea miles to Harris, to barter goods at the busy little fishing village at the head of the sheltered sea-loch called the Òb.*

They did so only if they owned a boat which they considered seaworthy. A voyage to the Òb was not undertaken lightly, for the seas between Hiort and the south of Harris were often treacherous, even during the Yellow Months.

As the September weather was fair, seven men set off in the *sgoth* which at that time happened to be the St Kildans' only boat. Taking account of the north-flowing tide, the *sgoth* sailed into the south-easterly breeze. Rising high above the other Harris hills, the bulky blue dome of the Clisham sat beckoning on the eastern horizon.

When the St Kildans were about five miles west of the island of Taransay, they steered south-eastwards, allowing the ebbing tide to carry them towards their destination. As they journeyed along the coast, they debated why, at each hamlet they passed, bonfires were burning, sending columns of whitish-grey smoke high into the sky. Even a mile from the coast, the travellers could smell burning *fiteach* (straw).** It was inconceivable, they agreed, that the Hearaich (Harris folk) were burning precious sooty thatch off their black-houses that should be used as fertiliser on their fields. Not until they beached their boat at the Òb did they discover the awful truth. The smoke they had seen was, indeed, from burning *fiteach* – the straw bedding on which individuals or, in many cases, whole families had died of *a' bhreac* (smallpox).

It is likely that the visitors, who were naturally fearful of infectious diseases, were aware that smallpox was highly infectious and deadly. Generations of the St Kildans had known the Òb as a busy little fishing village, but on this occasion only one person was to be seen – an emaciated woman who was down on the shore gathering limpets.

"*Dhachaigh leibh! Dhachaigh leibh!*" (Go home! Go home!") she shouted.

---

* It was the custom for St Kildans coming to the Òb to trade, to sleep overnight in bothies at a small headland called Ceann Tùlabhaig. The grass-covered ruins of the bothies are still visible.

** According to the Rev Neil MacKenzie, who was resident on St Kilda 1829-43, one summer was so wet that the islanders failed to dry their peats. Consequently, they were forced to burn *fiteach* for cooking – 'a very inefficient fuel'.

The woman warned the visitors against setting foot ashore. She told them of a disaster that had struck Harris and urged them to return home. Grateful for her advice, the St Kildans threw on to the beach fish which they had caught off Taransay. Cold and hungry after their long voyage, they debated whether they should risk going ashore. In the end they decided to retreat to the bothies on the headland of Ceann Tùlabhaig, and there to have a meal. After eating they slept for a few hours, then prepared to set off on the voyage westwards.

Just as they were about to shove their boat off the shingle, one of their number, Donald MacDonald left the boat, saying to his friends, "Providence has directed me to this place. God willing, I will be able to help the people here and will return to see my mother next summer."

The *sgoth* sailed away, and after a voyage that took many hours, arrived back in Loch a' Bhaile (Village Bay) just as the weather was turning sour. Strong winds and sleety rain engulfed the island and the inhabitants sat round their peat fires waiting for the weather to clear.

On the day after the *Callainn*, the first gannets were seen in the northern sky. They were the scouts leading a multitude of around 100,000 which, in the following weeks, responded to the instinct to return from the ocean. Day after day hundreds became thousands, and then tens of thousands, which all converged on increasingly congested nesting-sites on Boreray, Stac Lì and Stac an Àrmainn. By mid-February, the skies and seas saw the return of the *làmhaidh* (razorbill), which laid eggs so palatable that the best climbers on St Kilda were prepared to risk their lives by climbing to the top of a pinnacle called the Stac Bhiorach to get a few dozen.

At the beginning of March, excited children ran home to report that they had seen the first *buthaigir* (puffin) fishing at Geò na h-Eige, at the back of the Village. Within a week, everybody turned out to see hundreds of newly-arrived puffins fishing for cuddies all over Village Bay. March was one of the best times of the year when flocks of different species of bird were seen arriving back from the ocean, filling the skies and occupying every available niche in the crags. Already the first fowling-parties were out collecting eggs on the cliffs and inshore stacks . The weather improved steadily throughout the spring and summer, and the fowlers brought home ever increasing numbers of carcasses of adult gannets and young fulmar. Some of those were preserved in peat-ash or in ash from burnt seaweed. Others were stored in cleits where the salt wind off the ocean would dry them quickly as it rushed through the gaps in the drystone walls.

August was the month for 'stealing' gugas (fledgling gannets). Only the best behaved boys and girls were allowed to go on fowling expeditions. All through the Black Months, children were encouraged to be self-disciplined and focused in everything they did. Any individual who was *sgeòtalach* (undisciplined) was excluded from expeditions to Boreray and the stacks, where any misconduct on their part could result in tragic consequences for themselves and for others. In mid-August, 1729, the *sgoth* transported to Boreray a fowling-party consisting of four men and eight children. The group had sufficient provisions to last for a fortnight. It was expected that in about ten days the *sgoth* would return to collect the fowling-party and its catch of birds. On Boreray spirits were high. Apart from the scores of gugas taken by the old hands during the first two days, the tally despatched by the youngsters was high.

The group had been working on Boreray for only three days when one of the men noticed, far to the east, a boat tacking towards Hiort from the direction of Harris. It was unusual for the islanders to have visitors late in August. As ever, the Steward with his retinue had paid his rent-collecting visit in June and had departed a month later. The men on Boreray debated the reason for the strangers' visit as they watched the boat approach Hiort and finally disappear behind Rubha an Uisge, at the foot of Oiseabhal.

When the boat entered Village Bay, as many St Kildans as saw the boat ran down to the shore to help drag her ashore. However, when she came within shouting distance of the Dìollaid – the shelving rock on which boats were hauled out of the sea – the stranger stood off. A member of her crew called to the islanders that they had sailed all the way from the Òb to deliver the sad news that, while in Harris, Donald MacDonald had succumbed to smallpox. The visitors refused to accept hospitality ashore, saying that the disease which had killed Donald was so contagious that, if they were to land, their breath might defile the pure air of the island. They rowed the boat close enough to the Dìollaid, to enable one of their number to land a small sea-chest containing Donald MacDonald's possessions.

That evening, a wake was held in the former home of the dead man. Apart from the members of the fowling-party, who at that very time were settling themselves down for the night in the Staller's House on Boreray, the entire community attended the wake. The prayers over, Donald's mother opened her son's sea-chest and began to distribute its contents among her neighbours.

Unbeknown to her, she also distributed a virus so terrible that, within a fortnight, almost everyone present was either dead or dying.

Towards the end of the third week on Boreray, the men and boys were looking forward to the arrival of the *sgoth* and their own return to the embrace of their families. On what they assumed was to be their last night of dossing down in the Staller's House, a northerly storm blew up, so that the *Linne* became a maelstrom of roaring, windswept breakers. It took the storm three days to subside, but, as often happened, within a few hours of the storm passing and the waves subsiding, the sun shone and the sea became flat-calm. The conditions were perfect for the boat to set off from Village Bay and cross the four miles to Boreray. Hours passed and yet no boat appeared. As night fell, the castaways on Boreray began to realise that some calamitous event had taken place on Hiort.

Day after day passed and still the *sgoth* failed to appear. Although the castaways had shelter and food, they were deeply concerned about their families at home. One morning they got a hint of what was happening when the children detected a smell of burning *fiteach* on the south-westerly breeze.

Autumn passed and the dark howling gales of winter followed. The castaways' store of oatmeal and cheese had been consumed long before winter set in. Fortunately, there were about four hundred sheep on the island and the men occasionally slaughtered one, not only for its mutton but also for its precious skin. As their clothing was inadequate for the harsh weather of the Black Months, they had to don sheepskins sewn together with the bones of seabirds.

The gannets and the razorbills returning in the spring must have been a welcome sight. Their eggs would have broken the monotony of their diet.

It was summer before the castaways were rescued after the Steward's galley called at Hiort to collect the annual rent.

One can only imagine the joy felt by the castaways as they were helped aboard the Steward's galley at Boreray. But their joy was soon replaced by grief when they learned the fate of their families and friends. Smallpox* had killed seventeen of the heads of Hiort's twenty-one families. For the first year thereafter, responsibility for looking after the twenty-six orphans must have fallen to the four adults who survived. However, MacLeod, the proprietor who owned the archipelago, made certain that Hiort would not become a desert island. Some families may have volunteered to take the place of those wiped out by the epidemic. Others who were trouble-makers in Skye and the islands of the Outer Hebrides may have been conveniently removed from their usual habitat and given free passage to St Kilda! The following, an excerpt from the Minutes of the Directors of the SSPCK for 1731, mentions

> *Hirta, which Island by the yearly transporting of people to it, will soon be populous again.*

Nach tu bh' ann a Hiort! (I wish that you were resident in Hiort!) is a saying with which all Gaels are familiar. It is tinged with irony and recalls a time when mischief-makers were unceremoniously removed to St Kilda.

---

* Smallpox, which originated in India or Egypt over 3,000 years ago, was one of the most devastating diseases known. No effective treatment for it was developed, so that it killed 30% of those infected. In 1798, Edward Jenner demonstrated that inoculation with cowpox could protect against the disease, but in spite of Jenner's discovery, progress with its application worldwide was extremely slow. In the early 1950s some fifty million cases of smallpox occurred in the world each year. In 1967, the World Health Organisation launched an international campaign aimed at eradicating man's 'ancient scourge'. So successful was that campaign that smallpox was finally pushed back to the Horn of Africa, and then to one single victim in Somalia in 1977. The successful eradication of smallpox worldwide was certified by the World Health Assembly in 1980.

© James Smith

Approaching the west side of Harris

20. Crucifix and Dirk

In 1705, the Rev Alexander Buchan became a resident of St Kilda, the first minister to do so since the Reformation. He had been sent by the Presbytery of Edinburgh

> *to root out the pagan and Popish superstitious customs*

of the inhabitants. During his twenty-five years on Hiort he and his wife worked hard to teach the children the Protestant beliefs of the Established Church and to improve the living conditions of the whole congregation by using gifts of money sent by fellow Christians in Edinburgh and elsewhere. His wife is credited with having taught the women how to knit.

In 1752, *A Description of St Kilda*, a book by the Rev Alexander Buchan, was published by Jean, his daughter. In the introduction to the book, Jean Buchan says that her father died of 'a dreadful disease' in 1730. It is probable that the cause of death was smallpox. Jean Buchan writes that she was sent to the Scottish mainland to improve her education. The ship on which she travelled was wrecked at Kintyre in Argyll, but she was rescued and continued her journey to Glasgow, where she received her schooling. While in Edinburgh, she was knocked down and suffered a broken jaw when a horse bolted. As a result of the accident, she earned her living as a seamstress.

The book appeared six years after the Jacobites' defeat at the Battle of Culloden, and at a time when efforts were being made to smother the Gaelic language and to erase all things associated with the culture of the Highland clans: their weapons, tartans and bagpipes. It is not surprising that the book doesn't mention the language of the St Kildans!

The wording of the dedication is a reminder of how submissive the once proud people of the Highlands and Islands had become after Culloden. On account of the cruelty and ferocity with which he treated his defeated enemies, the Duke of Cumberland was known to the Gaels as 'The Butcher'. Whether Jean Buchan's dedication ensured that the book reached the Duke is not known.

Remote though Hiort was in the eighteenth century, it is interesting to read that it was by no means isolated from the other islands of the Outer Hebrides. Indeed, it shows that there was even some intercourse between St Kilda and the Scottish mainland. It reiterates Martin's impression that the people of Hiort were energetic and happy – this in spite of the fact that the population had been devastated by smallpox in 1729. Significantly, it describes the ancient ritual of the St Kildan marriage service – a ritual which, in due course, the Rev Buchan abolished.

When a couple decided to marry, the entire community gathered at Eaglais Chrìosda (the Church of Christ), which was located close to the Village. The *maor* (presiding officer) or other person nominated to conduct the service stood before the congregation and demanded to know if any person present wished to object to the marriage's taking place. If nobody objected, the *maor* proceeded with the ritual. After promising to be faithful to one another through good times and through bad, the bride and groom watched as the *maor* drew a dirk from its sheath. With the dirk in view of everybody present, the bride and groom swore yet again that they would be faithful to one another. To consecrate the marriage, the *maor* then led the couple to the altar, on which lay a brass cross a foot long and bearing an effigy of the crucified Christ with the crown of thorns on his head. With their right hands on the cross, the couple repeated the vows, signifying that their spoken words were binding in the eyes of God and man.

After the marriage service the community celebrated the occasion by dancing to the music of bagpipes. Taking their marriage vows in the way described, fifteen St Kildan couples were married by the Rev John Campbell on 17th June 1697 – seven years before the arrival of the Rev Alexander Buchan. It may have been the last occasion on which the cross and dirk were used.

Because of its association with Roman Catholicism, the cross, so prominent at one time in the life of the people, was spirited away from St Kilda and may have been destroyed. However, long after the crucifix was withdrawn from religious services, it continued in the minds of the people to be regarded as the symbol of marital honesty, truthfulness and constancy. Whenever a St Kildan was asked to swear to tell the truth, he did so by swearing on the crucifix: *"Air crois an Tì Bheannaichte!"* ("Upon the cross of the Blessed One!").

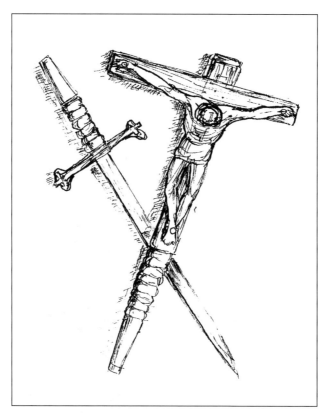

Crucifix and dirk

21. Gur Ann Thall ann an Sòdhaigh

In the Rev Neil MacKenzie's collection, two versions of this song are given. The second version was published in *An Gàidheal* No. 5 and has been published many times since then.

A' Chiad Tionndadh

'S gur ann san t-samhradh a shiubhail
Rinn na h-uighean mo lèir-chreach,
Nuair a thugadh uam Ìomhar –
Fàth mo mhisneachd gu lèir e.

'S gur ann thall ann an Sòdhaigh
Dh'fhàg mi 'n t-òg nach robh leumach –
Is tu nach fhalbhadh le
    m' fhacal
'S nach innseadh na breugan.

Thu bhith muigh sa
    Gheodh' Chumhainn,
Gur cianail dubhach ad dhèidh mi;
'S thu bhith muigh feadh nan stuaghan
'S am muir gad fhuasgladh o chèile.

Ach seachd beannachd do mhàthar
Gad chumail sàmhach ri chèile –
Gun robh d' fhuil air a' chloich ud
Is do lotan air leum oirr'.

'S gur diombach den eug mi,
Cha chaomhail leam fhèin e,
Nach leig thu gu d' mhàthair
Gu i càradh do lèine.

Bidh mo chuid de na h-eunaibh
Anns na neulaibh ag èigheach,
Is mo chuid de na h-uighean
Aig a' bhuidhinn as trèine.

Bliadhn' an t-samhraidh sa 'n-uiridh
Rinn na h-uighean mo lèireadh;
Gur ann thall ann an Sòdhaigh
Dh'fhàg mi 'n t-òg nach robh leumach.

The First Version

Last summer, the egg-gathering
Gave me reason to be grief-stricken
When Ivor was taken from me –
He who was my mainstay.

Over yonder in Soay
I left the virtuous youth
Who would not repeat (to others)
    anything I said
And who would not tell lies.

The thought of you alone out in the
    Narrow Gully
Pains and depresses me;
And that you are out in the breakers
With the sea tearing you apart.

May your mother's sevenfold blessings
Keep you gently intact –
Your blood was on yon rock
Where your wounds bled.

I resent death;
I dislike it,
That prevents your return to your mother
That I may prepare your shroud.

My share of the birds will be
Calling free from the sky;
And my share of the eggs
Will belong to the fittest (gatherers).

A year last summer
The eggs brought me grief;
It was over yonder in Soay
That I left my virtuous youth.

Nuair a thàinig do phiuthar,	When your sister arrived,
Cha robh sinn subhach le chèile;	We were both upset;
Cha tig thu gu d' mhàthair	You won't come to (me) your mother
Gus càradh do lèine.	That I may prepare a shroud for you.

The following version of the same elegy was collected from Margaret MacDonald, a servant at the farm of Baile Raghnaill in North Uist in 1815.

Gur ann thall ann an Sòdhaigh	It was over yonder in Soay
Dh'fhàg mi 'n t-òganach gleusta,	That I left the fine lad,
Urradh dhèanadh mo thacar	The paragon who was my support,
'S thabhairt dhachaigh na sprèidhe.	Ever ready to bring home the flock.
'S ged a chaidh thu sa chreig ud,	Although you ventured into that cliff,
Cha b' e 'n t-eagal a lèir thu –	It was not fear which destroyed you –
'S ann a rinn do chas sraonadh,	Your foot slipped,
'S cha do dh'fhaod thu riamh èirigh.	And you lay prostrate.
Bha d' fhuil air a' chloich ud,	Your blood stained that rock,
Bha do lot an dèidh leumaidh;	For your wound bled;
Bha thu muigh air bhàrr stuaighe,	You were out on the wave-tops,
'S muir gad fhuasgladh o chèile.	With the sea tearing you asunder.
Nuair a thàinig do bhràthair,	When your brother arrived,
Cha do chaomhainn e 'n èigheadh;	He was not restrained in his grief;
Bha sinn dubhach is cràiteach	We were disconsolate in our grief
Gad amharc an cèin uainn.	Seeing you receding from us.
A sheachd beannachd nan càirdean	The seven blessings of your relations
'S a lon làidir na feuma,	And the strong useful climbing-rope,
Tha mo chuid-s' de na h-eunaibh	My share of the birds
Anns na neulaibh ag èigheach.	Are calling from the skies.
Tha mo chuid-s' de na h-uighibh	My share of the eggs
Aig a' bhuidhinn as treubhaich';	Will belong to the strongest gatherers;
'S ann thall ann an Sòdhaigh	It was in Soay yonder
Dh'fhàg mi 'n t-òganach gleusta.	That I left the fine lad.

OLDEN TIMES
(1730-1852)

MacCrimmon's Lament

Tha osag nam beann gu fann ag imeachd,
Gach sruthan is allt gu mall le bruthach;
Tha ealtainn nan speur feadh gheugan dubhach;
A' caoidh gun d' dh'fhalbh 's nach till e tuilleadh.

Tha 'n fhairge fa-dheòidh làn bròin is mulaid,
Tha 'm bàta fo sheòl ach dhiùlt i siubhal;
Tha gàirich nan tonn le fuaim neo-shubhach
Ag ràdh gun d' dh'fhalbh, 's nach till e tuilleadh.

(Lament by Donald MacCrimmon, 1745)

The breeze of the bens is gently blowing,
The brooks in the glens are softly flowing;
On darkened boughs the birds are silent;
They mourn for him who's gone forever.

Its dirge of woe, the sea is sighing,
The boat under sail unmoved is lying;
The voice of the waves in sadness saying,
The last is gone; we'll see him never.

(Tr. Lachlan McBean 1888)

This was the age in which the influences of the outside world began to impinge so heavily, that the fabric of the old community crumbled. After the smallpox epidemic it became necessary to boost the population by introducing new blood from other islands. In the decades that followed, a strong self-confident Hiort was re-established. In the minds of the islanders religion began to dominate as never before. Attending prayer-meetings and sermons took precedence over all other activities. In 1852, the most youthful and energetic members of the community abandoned the island and went in search of a better lifestyle in Australia. That exodus was the beginning of the end of the once self-sufficient community of Hiort.

22. Lady Grange

Rachel Chiesley (1682-1746) was married to James Erskine, who as the Scottish Lord Advocate, took the title Lord Grange. Before entering into that high office, James Erskine had to swear loyalty to the Hanoverian King George, the Protestant king who had replaced the Catholic King James. For the sake of his career it was convenient for Erskine to take the oath of allegiance, but in his heart, he remained a Jacobite – a loyal subject of King James. His brother was the Earl of Mar, leader of the Jacobite Uprising of 1715 which had petered out after the indecisive Battle of Sheriffmuir. In spite of that upset on the battlefield, a number of Scots nobles continued to conspire against the Hanoverian King and to look for support for yet another Jacobite uprising.

Rachel and James Erskine quarrelled constantly and, in spite of the efforts of their eight children, they finally separated in 1730. One of the reasons for the tension between the husband and wife was their allegiance to two different royal dynasties. It is said that their quarrel came to a head after Lady Grange overheard a conversation between her husband and a number of Scottish nobles who favoured the overthrow of King George. Alarming news was brought to Lord Grange that his wife was spreading rumours regarding his political leanings. Fearing that even the suspicion of his disloyalty might result in his being charged with high treason, he decided to remove the cause of the problem.

Counter-rumours began to spread in Edinburgh suggesting that Lady Grange had become insane. Shortly afterwards she was declared officially dead. While her funeral was being staged at Greyfriars Church in Edinburgh, a group of Highlanders hired by someone close to her husband, abducted Lady Grange and held her in a 'safe house' until they were able to spirit her out of the city. The kidnappers, with their prisoner, journeyed from the Lowlands into the Highlands.

On the Isle of Skye, both MacDonald of Sleat and MacLeod of Dunvegan were sympathetic to Lord Grange's political leanings and agreed to hide Lady Grange in one of the most remote corners of their island possessions. First the prisoner was ferried to Heisgeir, a tiny island situated west of North Uist. In spite of the charade at Greyfriars Church, rumours began to circulate that Lady Grange had been kidnapped and was being held against her will in some remote place in the north of Scotland. Her relatives, including her eight children, searched for her but failed to find her.

Having spent two years on Heisgeir, Lady Grange was transported to St Kilda, where a house was specially prepared for her – one which was better appointed than that of the native people. According to Donald MacLeod of Berneray (Harris), it was

> *A house or cottage of two apartments, tolerably well furnished ... forty feet long, with an inner room and a chimney in it, a curtained bed, armchair, table and other articles.*

Having examined the ruins of the house which had been demolished some years earlier, Lachlan MacLean in 1838 stated that

> *it measured only about twenty feet by ten … it is divided in the centre by a partition of rude loose stones. In one of these compartments sat Finlay MacDonald every night for seven years, and Lady Grange in the other … thus making the entire of her ladyship's accommodation ten feet semi-lunar!*

Finlay MacDonald, an islander, had been given responsibility for the prisoner's welfare, but was also charged with preventing her from contacting the outside world.

The St Kildans felt sorry for Rachel and they often brought her gifts of birds, eggs or flowers that they had picked from the glens. Despite all their kindnesses, the only thing she wanted was to be allowed to tell her family that she was still alive. Finlay presented her with a wicker chair which, it is said, he had made, and which she treasured for the rest of her life.

Lady Grange regularly wrote letters which she carefully tied to pieces of wood and set afloat on the outgoing tide. None of them brought her release from her exile. But after eight years on Hiort she finally did manage to contact the outside world. A servant girl who was going to Glenelg managed to smuggle out one of Rachel's letters sewn into her petticoat. From Glenelg, sympathizers conveyed the letter to Edinburgh, where Rachel's relatives and friends immediately mounted an expedition to rescue her. Weeks later, a boat arrived in Village Bay and Finlay MacDonald was unable to prevent her crew from rescuing his prisoner. It is said that Finlay had become very attached to Rachel and was glad her ordeal was finally over. Before leaving Hiort, she gave Finlay twelve shillings in recognition of his kindness to her. During her years on Hiort, she failed to learn the Gaelic language. The following poem, expressing admiration of the St Kildans, is said to have been composed by Lady Grange.

> When gathering clouds the blackening sky deform,
> And sweeping whirlwinds swell the heaving storm,
> While far at sea their solitary skiff,
> The faithful matrons climb the shelving cliff;
> With tears of love and anguish heaven implore
> To guide the labouring bark to Kilda's shore.
> Each marks her shroudless husband, pale, aghast,
> Rise from the deep and ride the driving blast.
> The storm is hushed, the prospering breezes play,
> They mark the whitening canvas far away;
> With faithful hearts – the only wealth they boast –
> They hail the storm-tossed nation to the coast.
> Up springs the jovial dance, the festive lay,
> And night repays the labours of the day.

Lady Grange was taken to the Isle of Skye.

As it was not yet safe for her to return to Edinburgh, she settled down on that island and, in fact, died there in 1746, the year of the Jacobites' crushing defeat at the Battle of Culloden.

Letter said to have been written by Lady Grange while on St Kilda, 1738

23. The Well of Virtues

There were seven wells on Hiort.

Tobar nam Buadh – The Well of Virtues (Gael. *buadh* – a virtue)

Tobar Chiolda – The Spring Well (Norse *kelda* – a spring)

Tobar a' Chlèirich – The Clergyman's Well (Gael. *clèireach* – a clergyman or clerk)

Tobar na Cille – The Church Well (Gael. *cill* – a church)

Tobar Ghil a' Chille – The Well in the Ravine by the Church (Norse *gil* – a ravine).

Tobar a' Mhinisteir – The Minister's Well (Gael. *ministear* – a minister)

Tobar a' Chonastain – The Constable's Well? The origin of the word *conastan* is uncertain. The word may have been the St Kildan variant of *conastapal* (constable), a ground-officer appointed by the Steward to look after his interests.

Of those seven wells, Tobar nam Buadh is the best known. It is located in the Gleann Mòr in the north-west of the island, more than a mile from Village Bay. The water of this well was believed to have healing properties, and invalids travelled, even from other islands of the Outer Hebrides, in the hope of being cured of their maladies. The pagan belief that spirits resided in wells, rocks, lochs etc. continued well into the nineteenth century. To propitiate the spirit guarding Tobar nam Buadh, it was necessary for those who drank of its water to leave a small gift such as shells, pebbles or buttons on the lintel of the well.

Even if a drink of its cold clear water did not immediately ease the invalid's condition, the experience of sitting by the burbling waters of Tobar nam Buadh, in the solitude of the Gleann Mòr, would in itself have been recompense for travelling afar to that strangely peaceful and unforgettable place.

The Well of Virtues

In the Great Glen, looking from the ruins of Airigh Mhòr (The Big Shieling) to the island of Soay in the middle distance

24. Laoidh na Tobrach

In this hymn, the Rev Neil MacKenzie uses the supposed properties of the Well of Virtues as a metaphor for the healing powers of the Gospel and of God's love.

Tobar nam buadh tha shuas sa ghleannan,	O Well of Virtues up in the glen,
Neo-thruaillidh, fallainn do stòr;	Pure and health-giving is your store;
Chuala mi 'm fuaim mus d' fhuair mi faisg ort –	I heard your murmur ere I drew near –
Gur fuaran gast' thu tha beò.	Most generous fountain in existence.

A' sruthadh bho chàrn tha àirde chreagach	Flowing from a hill tall and rocky
Do làn co-fhreagradh gach uair;	With water abundant and inexhaustible;
Mur tig ort crith-thalmhainn a spealgas creagan,	Even in a rock-splitting earthquake*
Chan fhalbh thu 'm feast gu Là Luain.	You will not fail, never to the world's end.

An tobar tha fìorghlan, aotrom, soilleir,	The well that is pure, light and bright,
Gun aon nì doilleir fo d' ghruaidh,	Unblemished, under your canopy,
Tha sìor shruthadh sìos a-riamh bhon chruinnicheadh	Since the Creation flowing down
Riamh air fearann 's air cuan.	Continuously over land and sea.

* alluding to the earthquake (reported by Martin to have taken place in 1698) during which some of the gannet rocks at Boreray split and fell into the sea

25. The Fowler's Gear

The *lomhainn* or *lon* was the St Kildan's climbing-rope and was, for many generations, his most prized possession. When the fowling season was over, the *lon* was carefully stored away in a dry loft. At the beginning of the following season, every inch of it was carefully examined to ensure that it was in perfect condition. Writing in 1764, MacAulay stated that the *lon* was

> *made out of a strong, raw cowhide, salted for that purpose and cut circularly into three thongs of equal length.*

Cutting a rawhide into a continuous narrow strip took skill and patience and was traditionally left to one man who had learned the art from his forebears. First, he had to be certain that the hide was properly cured. With the hairy side of the hide on the ground, the cutting was done *deiseal* (clockwise), spiralling inwards until it came to the very middle. No fowler worth his salt would use a strip cut *tuathal* (anti-clockwise), as moving 'against the sun' was regarded as unnatural and was associated with the black arts. The rawhide thongs were wound together and covered with *peilid* (sheepskin) to protect them from jagged rocks while under tension. The most precious *ball-sinnsir* (heirloom) a father could leave to his eldest son was his *lon*, considered to be worth at least two of St Kilda's best cattle. It was expected to last for two generations, and if there were no sons, it was bequeathed to a daughter.

Later climbing-ropes were made of horse-hair and, again, covered with *peilid*. When Richard Kearton visited Hiort in 1896, he bought what he thought was the last *lon ghaoisde* (horse-hair climbing-rope) on the island. It was fifty-two feet long and weighed three pounds. By that time, many of the islanders were making their climbing-ropes from manila rope imported from Glasgow.

Invariably, the anchorman was stronger and heavier than the one suspended against the cliff-face; the latter more nimble and skilled at 'stealing' eggs or birds. The two had to agree where the anchorman should position himself, for if the rock on which he stood were to give way, they would both die. In the eighteenth and nineteenth centuries, many of the bardic compositions on Hiort were in memory of men and women who died in accidents on fowling expeditions (see Section 28).

Human existence was regarded as inescapably perilous, as if, throughout his life on earth, man was living on the edge of a precipice. When a St Kildan died, whether in a fowling accident or even through old age, he or she was said to have 'gone over',* as if the person had plunged off a cliff and into eternity.

John MacLeod, the factor, witnessed a dramatic rescue while he was visiting Hiort around 1750. He had ventured near the rim of a precipice and spotted two fowlers at work. The anchorman, the elder of the two, was feeding out the *lon,* which was coiled at his feet.

---

* "Chaidh e leatha"

Below him, his companion was collecting eggs. Only half of the rope had been fed out when the rock supporting the man below gave way. Shouting at the top of his voice, he plunged towards what seemed like certain death, taking with him all the slack rope until only a few fathoms of the coil were left at the cliff-top.

Dangling like a spider several hundred feet above the surging breakers, he could do nothing but pray that the rope would continue to take the strain and that his companion was strong enough to haul him to safety. Fortunately, the anchorman was equal to the task. Foot by foot, he won back the rope until, at last, the fowler was standing by his side on safe ground.

The *ribe* (gin), consisting of a running noose made of horse-hair, was a very effective method of catching birds such as razorbills or fulmar. Gin-making was one of the favourite pastimes of the girls. A girl about to marry felt well pleased if she received a few pounds of horse-hair as her dowry.

A line of gins attached to heavy stones was laid on ledges popular with birds such as razorbills and guillemots. Once its leg was caught by the noose, a bird could not escape. Martin gives an account of an incident which demonstrates the effectiveness of the gin:

> As he was walking barefoot along the Rock where he had fixed his gins, he happened to put his Toe in a Noose, and immediately fell down the Rock, but hung by the Toe, the gin being strong enough to hold him, and the Stones that secur'd it on each end being heavy: the poor Man continu'd hanging thus for the space of a Night on a rock twenty Fathom height above the Sea, until one of his Neighbours, hearing him cry, came to his rescue ...

Norman MacQueen using a fowling-rod

26. Climbing

Furnished with the requisite ropes and other appliances, four or five of the cragsmen approached the edge of the cliff. One of the most agile of the party – a vigorous, bright-eyed islander of about thirty years – taking one of the ropes in his hand, in order to steady his movements and having the other firmly secured round his waist, was gradually lowered down the perpendicular face of the precipice by two of his comrades. Uttering a shrill Gaelic cry, he descended barefooted, skipping and singing as he went, and occasionally standing out nearly at a right angle from the beetling cliff! Arriving at the narrow ledges where the fulmar and the puffin sit in supposed security, a long stick resembling a fishing-rod, with a noose at the extremity, was let down to him from above, which he cautiously extended, making the noose fall rapidly over the head of the bird, the fluttering victim being immediately captured … It is difficult, by means of verbal narration, to convey anything like a verbal idea of the sensation produced by the wonderful performance which I have endeavoured to describe … To anyone who has witnessed the daring procedure of the St Kilda cragsman, the most startling feats of a Blondin or a Leotard appear utterly insignificant.

(George Seton, 1878)

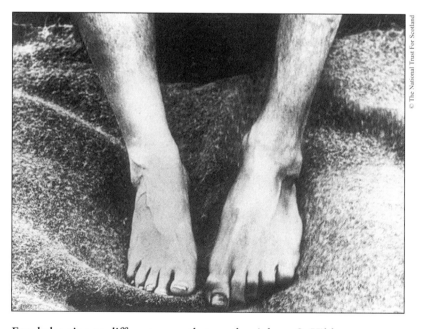

Feet belonging to different men; that on the right, a St Kildan

It is not possible to see St Kilda and its subordinate islands, or to form any idea of the prowess of the natives as cragsmen, without climbing. A good many of those who have written about the island have obviously not been mountaineers, and have often contented themselves with sitting in a boat and watching the natives ascending the rocks, or have given thrilling accounts of the difficulties second-hand. When Mr Seton says that, if the most venturesome member of the Alpine club were to witness the daring procedure of the St Kildan cragsmen, he would be compelled to hide his diminished head, he is obviously overstating the case; but, on the other hand, when Mr Dixon states that beyond the celebrated stacks there are comparatively few cliffs that a tolerable climber could not explore unaided by a rope, he unquestionably errs in the other direction. ... I may fairly claim to be a tolerable climber; but I should say that there are comparatively few cliffs that I should care to explore without the assistance of a rope. The St Kildans never wear boots when climbing, and I very soon found that I must imitate them in that respect.

(Norman Heathcote, 1900)

27. Birds of St Kilda

From the time the seabirds such as the razorbill and the gannet began to reappear out of the ocean in February, until they returned again to their mysterious haunts in October/November, the cliffs of St Kilda held an inexhaustible supply of food for the human population The principal staple food of the St Kildans was provided by four different species of bird: fulmar, gannet, puffin, razorbill and, to a much lesser extent, the guillemot.

The guillemot was the first to appear, in the New Year, when the days were still short, and before the storms of the 'Black Months' had abated. At a time of the year when the inhabitants of other crofting areas went hungry, the St Kildans were filling their cooking-pots with eggs and bird-meat – though not without first endangering their lives on cliffs which 'no sensible person from any other island would contemplate.'

In the entries that follow, SG = Standard Gaelic

> **tulmar** (SG fulmar)   In some districts of the Outer Hebrides the bird is known as *cearc-mhara* (sea-hen), *eun-crom* (stooped bird) or *mulcaire* (thick-neck).

The fulmar lays only one egg in the season, and as it is inclined to abandon its egg if anyone handles it, the St Kildans were careful not even to approach the nesting bird.

The cliffs were shared out amongst the families by lots. Harvesting the young birds began about the 12th August, when they were at their fattest. The season lasted for between ten and twenty days. Depending on the number of able-bodied men in the community, the harvesting was done by men working in groups of between four and six. The lower nesting-shelves were cleared by fowlers who scaled the cliff from boats. The upper shelves were harvested from above. When a fowler took a bird from its nest, he dispatched it by dislocating its neck. He then twisted the head round so as to prevent the precious oil in its stomach from draining away though its nostril. Bundles of the dead birds were lowered by rope to a boat or sent aloft where women and teenage children waited to empty the oil into the stomachs of gannets preserved from the previous season. When the day was over, women carried the dead birds and the oil-sacs back to the Village, where they got to work at once, plucking the birds and gutting them ready for salting. No sooner had the fowlers secured their boat ashore and prepared their climbing-ropes for the following day than they joined the women at the plucking, gutting and salting – work that often lasted well into the night.

When a fowler received his share of birds, it was usual for him to pluck the fattest and present it to his wife as a token of his love for her. The present was called an *eun-creige* (rock-fowl). Martin says:

> *The Bachelors do in like manner carry the Rock-Fowl to their Sweethearts, and it is the greatest present they can make, considering the danger they run in acquiring it.*

Fat from the boiled fulmar mixed with that from the guga was called *gìbean* and eaten with bread or porridge. A St Kildan who became ill while staying in Harris claimed that his illness was caused by the absence of *gìbean* in his diet.

While MacAulay was on Hiort, a local man gave the following assessment of the value of the fulmar:

> *Can the world exhibit a more valuable commodity? The Tulmer furnishes oil for the lamp, down for the bed, the most salubrious food, and the most efficacious ointment for healing wounds ... To say in one word: deprive us of the Tulmer and St Kilda is no more.*

After living for more than fifty years in Australia, Calum MacQueen, who emigrated in 1852, could remember the reliance of the islanders on the fulmar:

> *Most of the oil was used for lamps but much of it was sold, at one shilling per gallon to the factor. The oil from the old Fulmar was not so plentiful but was more valuable being used for lotion; it brought a shilling a bottle. They did not care to kill the old birds. They laid only one egg in the nests in the cliffs. We never gathered the eggs of this bird; a fine was inflicted for this. We got from the young Fulmar feathers and oil ... The oil was clear like kerosene but darker. If the Fulmar saw you coming, he would spit the oil at you. Some would spit a pint of oil in this way.*

© Cherry Kearton (S.S.S.)

After the Evacuation and the cessation of the annual cull, the fulmar population exploded, so that colonies became established on cliffs in different parts of the Outer Hebrides. Before the First World War, few fulmar were to be seen on the east coast of Lewis. Now they are so numerous that those failing to find nesting-places on the cliffs do so in the chimney-pots of ruined houses.

sùlaire – gannet (solan goose)

The gannet returns to St Kilda in February and leaves in October/November. During the nesting season, some 65,000 pairs occupy the cliffs of Boreray and its stacks (Stac an Àrmainn and Stac Lì). As soon as the gannet arrives, it begins to build its nest using materials such as grass, seaweed, bits of wood, rags and wool. The nesting-sites are so overcrowded that it is difficult for all the birds to find nesting materials. Consequently, they will thieve beakfuls of material from their neighbours at every opportunity. Usually the bird sitting on its nest will not stir even if it is approached by a human being and feels itself to be in danger.

Fowling practices changed from one generation of St Kildans to another. In the seventeenth century, for example, it was customary for gannets' eggs to be taken on Boreray and on Stac an Àrmainn, but not from Stac Lì. When the eggs from the first laying were taken, the gannet produced a second egg. The result of the islanders' predations, the 'guga'* harvest on those two places was delayed by several weeks.

làmhaidh (SG. làmhaidh or coltraiche) – razorbill. It is estimated that about half of the world's population nest on sea cliffs and boulder beaches in Scotland, Ireland and the north of England. They nest in colonies, often sharing territories with guillemots and kittiwakes. Data from the Seabird 2000 survey suggest that there were only about 2500 razorbills on St Kilda, a decrease of 33 % since the previous census. When the breeding season is over, the birds migrate to places as far distant as the Bay of Biscay and the Mediterranean Sea.

budhaigir/buthaigir (SG buthaid) – puffin. An estimated 140,000 pairs nest in burrows on St Kilda, the largest colonies being on Soay, Boreray and the Dùn. Harvesting them was mainly women's work! The St Kildan dogs were adept at catching them and were credited with being able to hunt independently of their masters.

When I last visited Lachie MacDonald in Glen Nevis, being en route for Lewis, and asked him if there was anything I could bring back from 'Tìr nan Òg', his reply was, 'Bring me back a *buthaigir* so that I can taste him roasted one more time!'

---

* the mature nestling of the gannet, though not sufficiently fledged for flight

gearrabhall – great auk, or garefowl. Until the middle of the eighteenth century, when it became extinct, the garefowl used to visit St Kilda to breed. It was as big as a goose, and laid only one egg which was as big as that of the ostrich. At the start of the nineteenth century it became fashionable to eat the eggs and use its feathers to decorate hats.

In the 'Account' written by Sir George MacKenzie in the seventeenth century, he mentions that among the birds harvested by the St Kildans was the *gearrabhall*.

> *... There be many sorts of these fowls; some of them of strange shapes, among which there is one which they call the Gare fowl, which is bigger than any goose, and hath eggs as big almost as those of the Ostrich. Among the other commodities they export out of the island, this is none of the meanest ...*

On 3rd June 1844 the last two adult birds and their egg were taken at the Isle of Elday, off Iceland, by an expedition of fourteen men who had been hired by an Icelandic bird collector. As the men approached, the garefowl did not show

> *the slightest disposition to repel the invaders, but immediately ran along under the high cliff, their heads erect, their wings somewhat extended. They uttered no cry of alarm, and moved, with their short steps, about as quickly as a man could walk.*

Both birds were dispatched and their egg taken. Members of the expedition returned to Elday in 1846 and again in 1860 looking for garefowl, but none was seen. For fifty years or more after the presumed extinction of the garefowl, some people were still reporting sightings of the species in different places. The *Oban Times* of 11th July 1896 reported that Donald and his son Alexander Ferguson claimed to have seen a pair of birds at St Kilda similar in shape to the razorbill, but twice its size. Sadly, the *gearrabhall* had been 'the goose that laid the golden eggs', a species which the St Kildans helped to exploit to extinction.

The following list of birds, in alphabetical order, are residents of, or visitors to, St Kilda but were not hunted by the islanders for their food value.

aisealag (SG luaireagan) – stormy petrel

buna-bhuachaille – red-throated, black-throated and great northern diver

Rarely seen at St Kilda, those birds are very elusive and spend as much time underwater as on the surface. According to Carmichael's *Carmina Gadelica*, *neither its nest nor its young has been found ... In Glen Elg, there's the curious belief that it hatches under water, an egg under each wing, and takes a year in hatching.*

In fact, both red-throated and black-throated divers nest in Scotland close to the edges of moorland lochs. The great northern diver, known also as the loon, is the largest of the three. It breeds in Iceland, Greenland and across the whole of North America and is seen on most British coasts as a winter visitor.

druid – starling

drùdhan don (S.G. dreathan-donn) – wren

The St Kildan wren is much bigger than wrens found elsewhere, and in the summer can be heard warbling in different parts of Hiort.

faoileag an sgadain – herring-gull

A herring-gull setting down near a house was regarded as a bad omen, signifying a forthcoming death. The young is called a *sgliùrach* or *odharag*.

feannag – hooded crow

Usually only two pairs breed on Hiort. There were many more at the beginning of the nineteenth century. When Rev Neil MacKenzie was resident minister (1829-43), he enquired one day why a certain old woman had not attended the Sunday service. He was told she had stayed at home to keep the crows away from her home. New laid thatch was always attractive to crows, which were prone to make holes in the straw while scrabbling for seed. When the minister next met the old woman, he asked her why she had not asked God to keep the crows away from her house.

"Because," she replied, "I knew He would not."

"How did you know that?"

"Because I asked Him before and He did nothing about it."

fitheach – raven

Usually two pairs breed on Boreray. Like the crow, it feeds on carrion, which is plentiful on St Kilda during eight months of the year. Occasional fatalities among the sheep population were the raven's main provider from November till March. Sighting the bird near houses was thought ominous, as they were believed to have the second sight. Of a man arriving unexpectedly at mealtime, the St Kildans would say, "Tha fios an fhithich aige" (He has the raven's intuition).

ruiteag/ruideag – kittiwake

The smallest variety of seagull found on St Kilda. The cries of a nesting colony resemble those of young children released into a school playground.

sgarbh – cormorant

St Kildans would not refuse to eat the meat of the cormorant or shag, but these were low on their list of favourite foods.

tuliac/arspaid (SG farspag or arspag) – lesser black-backed gull.

In 1764, MacAulay describes the *tuliac* as being as big as a gannet, with a white breast, bluish back and black wings. The islanders hated this bird because of its voracious consumption of eggs and young chicks. In order to reach its nest, they were prepared to risk their lives on the cliffs. Having taken the eggs, they drained them in the hope that the brooding birds would spend the season sitting on empty shells. They believed that, excepting the sea serpent, no creature would eat the eggs of the *tuliac*. Whenever they got hold of a member of that detested species, they tortured it by gouging out its eyes, then tied its wings together before releasing it in the sea.

While working in the Minch, fishermen of my acquaintance witnessed a black-backed gull swallowing a kittiwake which was lying injured in the sea. Recent surveys suggest that there are fewer than 200 on St Kilda.

sgràbaille (SG sgriab/sgràbaire) – Manx shearwater

A.R. Forbes in *The Gaelic Names of Beasts, Birds, etc.* gives … *the fat young (fachach) used to be given in payment of rent annually to a landlord, and that in great quantities.* This appears not to have been the case on Hiort.

trìlleachan (SG gille-brìghde) – oystercatcher.

The name *trìlleachan-tràghad* is also commonly used in Lewis. According to the Western Isles Natural History Society's magazine, *Curracag*, Number 14, only fifteen pairs nested on Hiort in 2001. In that year, fifteen adult birds were seen being taken by bonxies (great skuas) in the vicinity of Village Bay.

tunnag a' mhara (SG lach-mhara/tunnag-mhara) – eider duck

Seabird. In 2000 around fifty pairs were recorded as nesting on St Kilda. Mallard, teal and wigeon pass through on migration. Several other species are winter visitors, including goldeneye and scoter.

THE BIRD CALENDAR

	Gannet	Fulmar
December		
January	Individual scouts approach the coast	
February	The flocks arrive about the middle of the month	Newly returned to the cliffs, they are hunted during twilight or at night
March	Fowling begins in earnest with the killing of adult birds. De-feathered and split along the backbone, they were then gutted and having been washed in sea-water, many were stored in cleits to be dried by the wind.	
April		
May	From mid-May to the beginning of July, teams of girls went on egg-gathering excursions to Soay, Boreray and Stac an Àrmainn. It is said that a proportion of the eggs were well past their 'sell-by date' before they were eaten!	Lays one egg
June		
July		
August	GUGAS The first crop of gugas is ready	FULMAR On Boreray the nestling is ready for reaping
September	The Stac Lì gugas are reaped	
October	The second Boreray crop is taken	
November	The gannet returns to the ocean	The fulmar returns to the ocean

THE BIRD CALENDAR

	Puffin	Razorbill
December		
January		
February		Return to their traditional nesting sites; caught during twilight or at night.
March	Returns from the ocean in mid-March. It is estimated that, at one time, the population was about a million. The population has decreased by about half.	
April		Lays eggs
May	Lays eggs	
June	Hatches Fowlers' season begins end June	
July	Fowlers' season lasts well into July	Hatch
August		
September		Fledglings leave
October		
November	Last puffins return to the ocean	

© G. W. Wilson (S.S.S.)

Sharing the catch – more than a thousand fulmar

28. The Price Paid for Fowling: Eight Elegies

Most of the St Kildan poems collected by the Rev Neil MacKenzie (1829-43) were elegies composed in memory of family members killed while fowling. Though none of the elegies could be considered masterly *bàrdachd*, they all capture the sense of helplessness and grief felt by the bereaved.

a) Dha Mo Chuileana Gaolach

This song was composed by Margaret, daughter of Ruairidh Mòr, whose husband and brother lost their lives during a fowling expedition. She devotes the final verse to the loss of her brother.

Bheir mi toiseach mo thuiridh	I dedicate the beginning of my lament
Dha mo chuileana gaolach –	To my loving 'pups' –
An dithis bha tapaidh,	Two clever persons
'S bha air leacaig nan sìneadh.	Now prostrate on the slab.
Chan e clann rinn mi fhàgail	They were not children
Ach fir dhàicheil dheas, dhìreach;	But men who were upright and capable;
Gu ma geal a gheibh an anam	May their souls be received pure
Ann an gleannan na saorsa.	In the glen of freedom.
Fhir nach d' bhagair mo bhualadh,	A man who would not raise a fist to me,
'S nach d' chuir gruaimean air m' inntinn,	Who never caused me anxiety,
Dh'aithnichinn t' iomradh air bàta	I could recognize your style of rowing
Tighinn far thonnan a' chaolais.	When returning from the rough seas of the strait.
Ga h-iomradh 's ga h-èigheach,	At rowing and calling the beat
'S tu bu bhinn leam bhith 'g èisteachd;	You were the best to listen to;
'S mòr an teist aig an tuath ort,	Great is the steward's regard for you,
'S bu tu ruagair nan caorach.	The most expert at rounding the sheep.

Dh'aithnichinn bris-cheum do choise,
'S bu leat an toiseach a dhèanamh,
Gun luaidh air m' òganach tapaidh –
B' e fàth nan creach thu bhith dhìth oirnn.

I recognized your approaching footstep,
A sound you once enjoyed making,
Without mentioning my fair child –
My tragedy is that you've gone.

Chaill mo mhàthair a fradharc
'S chaidh a roghainn a dhìth oirr';
Chuir thu maill air a h-astar
'S cha dìrich cas-bheinn an fhraoich i.

My mother has become blind, made so
By the loss of her favourite child;
She walks now but slowly
And cannot climb the heathery brae.*

b) Bàrdachd Banntrach Shomhairle

While Sorley and his daughter were climbing a cliff in pursuit of razorbills, a great wave swept them away and they were never seen again. The following elegy was composed by Sorley's widow.

'S goirt a dh'fhairich mi bhliadhna
'S cha b' e biadh a bha 'n air' orm;
Cha b' e crodh air na blàraibh,
Ged a dhràbhadh iad seachad,
Ach mi bhith 'g amharc, 's gur cruaidh,
Far na sguabadh a-mach sibh;
Ach gur muladach tha mi
Ann am àros, 's tha sac orm,
'S gu bheil mise fo mhì-ghean
'S mi dìreadh na cas-bheinn.

Harrowing the year has been.
Lack of food has not been the problem;
Not the cattle on the moors,
Even if they had gone astray,
But when, though reluctantly, I look
At where you were swept out;
I am so sad at home
Heavily burdened,
Feeling depressed
As I climb the steep ben.

* a metaphor for her grief

c) Oran Màiri Nic Shomhairle

This song was composed by Màiri after she received the news that her husband had been killed while hunting for razorbills.

'S tric mi 'g amharc 's gur cruaidh leam,
Far na sguabadh a-mach thu –
Far na choinnich an t-aog thu
'S nach do dh'fhaod thu thighinn dhachaigh.

Difficult though it is for me to do so,
I often look at where you were swept out
Where death met you
And you were forbidden to come home.

Chaidh mi 'n iomall nan càirdean
'S tha mis' an-dràst' gun chùl-taice:
'S gur mairg a nì bun às
    an t-saoghal,
Ged chinneadh caoraich is mairt leis.

I avoided my relations
And am now without support:
Pity the person who depends (only) on
    wordly goods,
Though prosperous with sheep and cattle.

B' fheàrr bhith tric air na glùinibh
Gul an ùrnaigh bheir ceart leis
Na bhith le moit no le àrdan –
Chuir Dia mu làr e, 's bu cheart sin.

Better that he often kneels
To pray with contrite sincerity
Than to be conceited and proud –
For God will lay him low, and rightly so.

Fhuair mi roimhe 'n tùs m' òige
Am fleasgach còir a bha tapaidh;
Is o nach b' airidh mi fèin air,
Thug Mac Dhè uam e dhachaigh.

In my youth I found him,
The man who was kind and clever;
And since I was not worthy of him,
The Son of God took him home.

d)   Call na h-Inghinn

Composed by a father after the death of his daughter

Chan e uisge nan gleannta	The flood-water of the glen is not
Dh'fhàg mo cheann-sa cho tinn	What has caused me this grief;
Ach na thriall uam	Rather do I grieve for those who have
dhachaigh.	journeyed home
Air an astar nach till	To a place whence none can return.
Ged bhiodh fuachd ann is frasan,	Though there be cold weather and rain,
Cha ruig thu fasgadh mo thaoibh;	You will not come to shelter by my side;
Seachd beannachd do mhàthar	May your mother's seven-fold blessings
Gad chumail sàmhach, a laoigh.	Eternally soothe you, my child.

e)   Goirt Mo Thuireadh

This lament was composed by a widow who had lost her husband while bird-hunting.

Ach, Rìgh, 's goirt mo thuireadh –	O Lord, painful is my lament –
Ged 's goirt, 's èiginn dhomh fhulang,	But however painful, I must suffer it,
Ged dh'fhalbh mo chraobh mhullaich fèin.	Though I've lost my ridge-beam.
Thug siud leagail air m' inntinn	It has down-beaten my mind
'S chaidh mo bheadradh a dhìth orm;	And my confidence has deserted me;
'S truime m' inntinn na pìob chaidh gun ghleus.	My mind is heavy-laden, out of tune.
Is nach mi bh' air do chùlaibh	Would that I had been in support of you
An uair dh'fhàillig do dhùirn thu,	When your hands failed to keep hold
Is acfhainn làn lùiths bhith ad dhèidh.	Of your strong climbing gear.
'S mi chuireadh ri t' fhastadh	I would have helped you hang on
No dhìobradh mo phearsa,	Till my own strength was expended
Is cha bhiodh deò neairt agam fèin.	And I could hold no more.

Na h-earb à gaol an fhir-phòsta,
Ach dealachadh cho òg rinn
Mo chridhe leònadh gu m'eug.

Never trust the love of the husband,
For he may be fated to leave us so young;
My heartbreak leads me to my death.

Ge nach b' àrd thu on talamh,
Bu docha leam na fear-bail' thu,
Ged bhiodh tu falamh o sprèidh.

Though you were of lowly stature,
I preferred you to a farmer,
In spite of your stock being few.

Ge nach b' chraobh a bha àrd thu,
Bu chraobh mhath a chum stà thu –
Dh'aithnichinn thu à gàrradh leat fèin.

Though you were not high-born,
You were a person of worth
Whom I recognized as outstanding.

Gur fliuch cluasag mo leapa
An dèidh mo chur 's mi tighinn dachaigh –
'S iomadh tè bha na dalta dhomh fèin.

Tear-stained is my pillow
Each time I leave or come home –
Many are those (females) who comfort me.

The Rev Mackenzie tells us that the same woman lost her second husband when he drowned in the loch* while trying to make it to the shore during a violent storm.

'S tric mi 'g amharc gach là,
A rùin, an roilig do bhàis –
'S ann a-muigh air an tràigh
Chaidh an cunnart oirbh.

Every day, my love, since death
Called you, I frequently look out
To see where on the ebb
Danger came to you.

Thu bhith muigh gu fliuch fuar
Ann an iomall a' chuain,
'S gun ann ad fhàrdaich, a luaidh,
A' fuireachd ort.

To think of you out there cold and wet
At the bounds of the ocean,
While your household, my love,
Awaits you.

Do chlann bheag air mo sgàth
'S nach urr' iad do stà –
Bhith gan iomain gu càch
Gur duilich leam.

Because of what happened, your babes
No longer have your support;
Being forced to place them with others
Makes me very sad.

* Village Bay

Cò sheall anns a' ghrèin	Who has ever looked at the sun
No cheangail orra brèid	Or ever donned clothes
Nach bitheadh mo sgeula-sa	And would not consider my situation
Duilich leo?	To be unenviable?
Bhith faicinn an t-sliochd	To see your offspring
Rinn i àrach fo crios	Who were raised under your authority
Aig tè eile gun mheas	Now cared for by a woman disinterested
Gur duilich leath'.	And not fully committed to them.
Làmh dhèanamh an stà,	The hand that was ever busy,
Thoirt an fhraoch chùm an làir,	Who'd fetch heather as floor-cover,
Cha bhiodh tu ad thàmh	And always found idleness
'S cha b' fhurast' leat.	Difficult to bear.
Ormsa thàinig a' chlaoidh;	I am exhausted;
'S cha b' e roinn chur am mhaoin	It is not the division of worldly goods
Seo tha mise ga caoidh	That I grieve
Gu muladach.	So forlornly.

f) Bàrdachd Màthar a Chaill a Mac san Dùn

A father and son visited the Dùn in the Spring with the intention of catching razorbills. The father acted as anchorman while the son descended on the rope secured round his chest. Feeling his movements restricted by the rope, the boy cast it off. A flight of razorbills arrived in his vicinity and he began to capture and kill them. He was excited by having so many birds about him that he became careless and plunged headlong into the sea. The father, watching from the cliff-top, could only watch as his son struggled in a losing battle against the current.

Mi gun suigeart is mi gun sòlas	I am without joy, without peace,
'S mo leanabh uam feadh nan gòlaibh;	For my child is at the mercy of the waves;
Ach tha mo dhùil an Rìgh an Domhain,	But I hope that the Lord of the Universe,
Gun d' ghlac do Mhaighstir còir ort,	The kind Master, took you,
Mur do phill do pheacadh mòr thu.	Unless your great sinfulness excluded you.

Mo cheist a' ghruaidh a bha bòidheach
Gus na rinn an t-aog do leònadh;
Dh'fhàg thu t' athair dubhach brònach,
Cha dìrich cas-bheinn an fheòir e;
Ach ged 's mise dh'àraich òg thu,
'S i tha truagh dheth do bhean-phòsta –
Dh'aithnichinn t' fheannag, 's cha bhiodh
                sgòd oirr'.

Your earthly form was so beautiful
Until death wounded you;
You have left your father grief-stricken,
He'll not climb the steep, grassy ben;
Though I'm the one who raised you,
The one who'll suffer most is your wife –
I could always recognize your
                faultless spadework.

g)   Mairbhrainn le Anna Mhaol Dòmhnaich

The sheets belonging to the Rev Neil MacKenzie included these two pieces which were in the handwriting of some other person. The first lament is for her brother and the second (which is difficult to interpret) for her two sons. They are given below as written except for small changes made to make them conform to present-day orthography.

Bidh mo bhràthair air thùs –
Gum bu chomain siud dhuinn,
Gum bu shilteach do shùil
                mum chràdh.

I mention my brother first
As is only proper;
Tearful your eyes, as you recognized
                my pain.

Dè, cha deach mi a-steach,
'S ann, a ghaoil, na do theach,
On là thugadh thu mach às marbh.

Lord, I haven't entered
Your house, my love,
Since your remains were carried from it.

Mi mam Dhòmhnaill ùir òig,
Bheathaich mi thu glè òg,
Gur e Ruairidh thug bròn seach
                càch.

I am the mother of young Donald,
I fed you when you were young;
Roderick brought me more grief than the
                others.

Gura mis' th' air mo chlisgeadh
'S mi ri leughadh do litreach;
Gad a ghlèidh mi mo
                ghibhtean,
Fhuair mi fios air a' bhròn.

I am upset
After reading your letter;
Though I have (only just) retained my
                senses,
Having taken in the news of this sorrow.

Tha mo cheist an t-òg spèiseil –
Cha do rinn thu riamh eucoir;
Bu tu beannachd nam feumach
A rèir 's na bha 'd phoc.

My subject is the well-regarded youth –
You never caused trouble;
You benefited the needy
As much as you possibly could.

Tha mo cheist an t-òg fearail;
'S tric a fhuair mi a cheanal
Agus seudan gun d' cheannaich
On fhear tha Shìol Leòid.

My subject is the manly youth
Whom I found to be so charming
With compliments to win one
From the scion of Clan MacLeod.

Cò bhean no cò mhàthair
Rinn gillean riamh àrach
Nach creid mar a tha mi,
'S mi air fàgail mo dheò.

Which wife or mother
Who ever raised sons
Can fail to understand my condition,
For I have lost my reason.

The same woman composed the following verses for the same man.

Tha mo cheist an Leòdach
Gu math dhan tig an còta –
Na fhuair mi dha do shòlas
Na adhbhar-bròin domh 'n tràth seo.

My subject is the MacLeod
Who looks so well-dressed in his coat;
But however much he pleased me,
He is now the cause of my woes.

Làmh gheal bu mhath gu sgrìobhadh,
Gum b' àlainn anns an ruidhl' thu;
'N àm tarraing dhut na fìdhle,
Cò 'n t-aon neach bheireadh bàrr ort?

A dab hand at writing,
Wonderfully light-footed in the reel;
And when you played the fiddle,
No-one could surpass you.

Gur mis' a' mhàthair mhuladach,
An-còmhnaidh ris an turraban,
Smuaineachdh air m' uireasaibh –
Thuit buileach orm an gàrradh.

Such a sad mother I am,
Permanently reduced to weeping;
When I think of my loss,
It's as if a wall has collapsed on me.

Cha ghàrradh a rinn clachairean
Dh'àireamh mi san fhacal ud
Ach àilleachd nam fear maiseach
Chuir mi 'n tasgadh uam an càradh.

A mason-built wall was not
What I meant with those words,
But the image of my beautiful lad
Whom I had to lay to his eternal rest.

h) Òran Catrìon' Òig

The Rev MacKenzie was able to discover only a fragment of this song, which, it is said, was composed around 1780.

Is olc leam mar thachair,

Cèile mo leapa …

Air a ghlacadh gun airidh (?)

Their gach tè rinn mo
      ruigheachd

Gur ro righinn leam fèin
      d' èirigh;

Cha … fhada is tha mi

Am laigh' an taobh an taighe
      gun èirigh.

Cha dèan leighean slàn mi

Ged bhiodh làmh rium
      na ceudan.

'S ann tha m' dhùil ri dhol dhachaigh

Gu maitheanas an Dè mhòir.

'S gur truagh nach taitneach mo bheus riut;

Cha tèid air fhalach an cùil mi,

Is mo dhroch cùis dhomh ga stèidheadh.

I deem it so tragic,

What happened to my husband …

Who was caught unawares.

Every woman who comes to visit me
      remarks

On how difficult it is for me accept
      your fate;

………

Constantly lying housebound without
      stirring.

Doctors could not possibly cure me

Though they were to attend me in their
      hundreds.

My thoughts are to my going home

To the forgiveness of the great God.

Alas, my ways may have offended thee;

I shall not seek a hiding-place,

For my plight is inevitable.

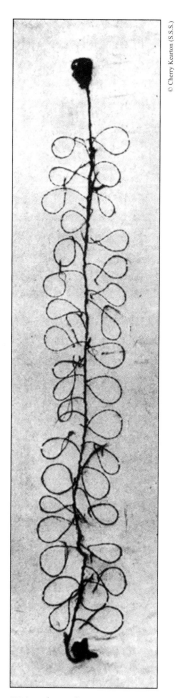

© Cherry Kearton (S.S.S.)

Using horsehair, women made gins by which birds
such as razorbills were ensnared

29. Geingeach and *Sgoth*

Three steep-sided stacks stand like steeples in the narrow sea passage between Hiort and Soay. The *Stac Bhiorach* (Sharp-Pointed Stack) is 240 feet high. Next in height is Soay Stac at 200 feet. *Stac Dhona* (the Wicked Stack), though only 87 feet high, proved to be the most difficult to climb. When it was decided that a fowling-party should collect eggs from the nests at its summit, the best climber of his generation was given responsibility for leading the assault. A fowling-party working those three stacks consisted of at least eight men: four for climbing and at least two to keep their boat in position near the foot of the stack, and two to receive the bags of eggs lowered by the 'harvesters'. The leading climber's job was to secure a rope by which three others could ascend. According to Martin, the stack was well named.

> ... it is reckoned no small piece of gallantry to climb this rock, especially that part called the thumb, which is so little, that of all the parts of a man's body the thumb only can lay hold on it, and that must be only for the space of one minute; during which time his feet have no support, nor any part of his body touches the stone, except the thumb, in which minute he must jump by the help of his thumb, (the agility of his body concurring to rise him higher at the same time) to a sharp point of the rock, which when he has got hold of it, puts him out of danger, and having a rope about his middle, which he casts down to the boat, by the help of this he brings up as many persons as are designed for fowling at this time; the foreman, or principal climber has the reward of four fowls bestowed upon him over and above his portion; perhaps one might think four thousand too little to compensate so great a danger as this man incurs; but he has the advantage of it, of being recorded among their greatest heroes ...

In 1698, Sir Robert Murray's description of his ascent of the *Stac Bhiorach* was one of the first reports of rock-climbing in Britain. It also explains the role of the *geingeach,**
the athletic climber who lead the fowling-party:

> ... a man having room but for one of his feet, he must climb up ten or sixteen fathoms high. Then he comes to a place where, having but room for his left foot and left hand, he must leap from thence to another place before him which, if he hit right, the rest of the ascent is easier, and with a small cord which he carries with him he hales up a rope whereby all the rest came up. But if he misses that footstep (as often times they do) he falls into the sea and the company takes him in by the small cord and he sits there until he is a little refreshed and then he tries it again.

* perhaps the St Kildan pronunciation of *cinneach* – a fearless, reckless male

Having embarked on a *sgoth,** the crew and passengers were fully conscious of the risks they were taking. Apart from the *Dìollaid* from which they had launched their boat, there was no other place in the whole archipelago where they could bring the boat ashore. If a south-easterly wind and a rough sea developed while the *sgoth* was on an outing to one of the offshore islands or stacks, the travellers would have had to content themselves with sheltering, until conditions improved, in Glen Bay or in the lee of Boreray. If, after a day or two, cold and hunger forced them out of their shelter in a bid to get back home, they were bound to run into danger.

Having rounded *Rubha Cholla* and entered Village Bay, the *sgoth* would be trapped by the wind and the waves. In such a situation, it would have been unwise to approach the *Dìollaid*, the shelf of rock from which they had embarked. Rowing against the weather is exhausting work which cannot be sustained for more than a few hours. To slow their progress, the St Kildans relied on their *mogais* – their anchor which, though of ancient design, proved effective through the generations. Attached to the boat by a strong cable, the *mogais*, which consisting of a bag of stones, sometimes ruptured. Deprived of their anchor, the crew would not have had any alternative but to steer for the *Dìollaid*.

Landing the *sgoth* in heavy seas was a community effort. The eldest man on board offered a prayer to God pleading for mercy. Two cables were prepared, in readiness for the moment the keel grounded. Ashore there were similar preparations. The women and the children formed a line heading towards the sea, with the strongest individuals at the front. Similarly, the men were in line, with the strongest in the van, each holding the man in front by the waist. Much depended on the daring of the man at the head of the line, for he was expected to walk into the sea, if necessary, to get hold of the painter – the cable attached at the prow. As soon as the keel grounded, the second cable, which had been passed round the stern, was thrown to the women ashore. With each successive wave, the *sgoth* was lifted and, simultaneously, pulled ashore. It was a dangerous operation and one which needed physical strength on the part of the whole community, and also a great deal of luck. If one of the two cables snapped, there was a strong possibility that the *sgoth* would capsize.

* The St Kildans used *sgoth* as the generic term for 'boat'. MacBain gives *sgoth* as being from Norse *skúta* – 'a cutter, small craft'

30. Òigear a' Chùil Duinn

This song is believed to have been composed by Marion Morrison a few years after the Napoleonic Wars. Marion and a young man who briefly visited the island fell in love, but, alas, when the suitor returned to Hiort to take Marion to be his bride, the islanders mistook his yacht for a naval vessel come to press men into service.

Mo ghaol òigear a' chùil duinn,
Dhan tug mi mo loinn cho mòr,
Dh'fhuilinginn dhut pòg san anmoch,
Ged bhiodh càch ri seanchas oirnn;
Mo ghaol òigear a' chùil duinn,
Dhan tug mi mo loinn cho mòr.

My young brown-haired sweetheart,
Whom I esteemed so highly,
I'd let you kiss me in the gloaming,
Though that gave rise to folk's gossip;
My young brown-haired sweetheart,
For whom I feel so passionately.

Gura mise tha gu h-uallach
On a thàinig an duin'-uasal,
Le mo ribinnean mun cuairt dhiom –
Cumaidh iad mo ghruag air dòigh.
Mo ghaol òigear a' chùil duinn,
Dhan tug mi mo loinn cho mòr.

I am released from care
Since the aristocrat arrived,
So I've donned my ribbons
To keep my hair looking pretty.
My young brown-haired sweetheart,
For whom I feel so passionately.

Dhòmhnaill uallaich MhicGhillÌosa,
Bha uair a bha thu a' strì rium,
Ach on thàinig an tighearn' Ìleach,
Sguir(idh) mi dhed bhrìodal beòil.
Mo ghaol òigear a' chùil duinn,
Dhan tug mi mo loinn cho mòr.

O, handsome Donald Gillies,
There was a time when you courted me,
But since the Islay lord arrived
I ignored your flirting.
My young brown-haired sweetheart,
For whom I feel so passionately.

Beul sìos air luchd na farchluais;
Luchd nam breug, chan iad as fhasa –
'S mi gu siùbh'leadh fad' air astar
Dh'èisteachd cantanas do bheòil.
Mo ghaol òigear a' chùil duinn,
Dhan tug mi mo loinn cho mòr.

Eavesdroppers are such pests;
The tellers of lies are no easier to bear –
I would happily travel far
To listen to your sweet words.
My young brown-haired sweetheart,
For whom I feel so passionately.

Ò, nam bithinn-sa cho fìnealt'
'S gun dèanainn litir a sgrìobhadh,
Rachadh fios thugaibh a dh'Ìle
Nach b' e 'n fhìrinn thug iad oirnn.
Mo ghaol òigear a' chùil duinn
Dhan tug mi mo loinn cho mòr.

Mo ghaol òigear a' chùil duinn,
Dhan tug mi mo loinn cho mòr,
Dh'fhuilinginn dhut pòg san anmoch,
Ged bhiodh càch ri seanchas
      oirnn;
Mo ghaol òigear a' chùil duinn,
Dhan tug mi mo loinn cho mòr.

If I were as sophisticated
As to be able to write a letter,
I would send a message to Islay
To tell that what they said of us was untrue.
My young brown-haired sweetheart,
For whom I feel so passionately.

My young brown-haired sweetheart,
For whom I feel so passionately,
I'd let you kiss me in the gloaming
Though that would give rise to folk's
      gossip;
My young brown-haired sweetheart,
For whom I feel so passionately.

31. Fair-haired Marion

From the seventeenth century, when Martin visited St Kilda, writer after writer mentioned the good looks of the St Kildan women. After his visit to Hiort in 1756, MacAulay wrote,

> *The women are most handsome; their complexions fresh and lively as their features are regular and fine. Some of them, if properly dressed and genteely educated, would be reckoned extraordinary beauties in the gay world.*

Alasdair Alpin MacGregor, the only journalist on Hiort at the time of the Evacuation, was unequivocal in his praise:

> *The women of Hirta are beautiful women. Life may have been a hard struggle ... but toil and inclement weather have produced a race of women that is tall, handsome and extraordinarily intelligent. ... The womenfolk, clad in the dark blue dresses and brightly coloured shawls and kerches, would charm you. For knitting, spinning and weaving, there is not the like of them in all the Isles.*

The story behind the last song appears to be as follows. Marion Morrison, who lived on Hiort in the 1820s, was considered to be exceptionally beautiful. A 'Laird of Islay' who visited the island fell in love with her and, after a brief courtship, proposed marriage. It was arranged that in the following summer he would return and carry Marion off to Islay, where she would become his wife.

True to his word, the Laird returned in the following summer, but did so in style! The sight of his grand yacht anchoring in Village Bay caused the St Kildans to panic. His retinue wore uniforms and the row of mock guns along her sides suggested that the yacht was a naval vessel.

The Battle of Waterloo which ended the wars with Napoleon Bonaparte was fought in 1815, only a few years before the Laird's visit. With stories of the wartime press-gangs still fresh in their collective memory, the St Kildans melted away to caves and cleits in remote parts of the island.

The men of Islay made their way through the Village but found the houses cold and empty. From the *Lag Bho Thuath* to the *Cambair* and from *Conachair* to *Ruabhal* they searched, but, in spite of their loud calls, they found only cattle and sheep grazing unattended. When the search failed to find a living soul, the Laird led his men back to the shore and returned to his yacht. At last, all was silent. When the clamour made by the strangers died away, the St Kildans ventured out of their hiding places. They were in time to see the Laird's yacht leaving Village Bay.

The romantic story of Marion Morrison so fascinated John Sands that he included an imaginary pen-sketch of her in his book of 1875. But who was the girl whom he calls *Mòr Bhàn* (Fair-haired Marion)? Her name does not appear in the census of 1831 nor in the records of the church. Was she perhaps a visitor from one of the other islands? Some modern writers claim that her name, in fact, was Marion Gillies and that her suitor was Robert Campbell, a landowner in Islay.

In his book, *St Kilda, Past and Present*, George Seton lends credence to the story:

> *The day after my return from St Kilda (3rd July, 1877) I had an interview at Obbe with Donald MacKinnon, precentor in the parish church of Harris, who is a native of St Kilda and whose brother still lives on St Kilda ... a few small guns, the sight of which so alarmed the inhabitants that they took refuge among the rocks, and the faithful suitor ... was obliged to depart, a disappointed bachelor! The girl composed a 'Lament' in commemoration of the event, the tune of which the precentor hummed. He heard her sing the air, and distinctly remembers her appearance, and her 'long flowing hair'.*

Mòr Bhàn, (Fair-haired Marion) as portrayed by John Sands

32. Rè an t-Samhraidh

(Words by CF; traditional Hiortach tune)

Rè an t-samhraidh bha mo dhùil ris,

Mo ghean sùrdail 's mi ga fheitheamh;

Sùil gu deas a dh'fhaicinn siùil

Mu Rubh' an Dùin, tighinn dlùth ri fearann;

Rè an t-samhraidh bha mo dhùil ris,

Mo ghean sùrdail 's mi ga fheitheamh.

Cha b' e gleusadh fear na fìdhle

A rinn inns' mo ghràdh bhith tighinn

'S cha b' e ceilear dheas na pìob'

A thog ruidhle fàilt' e ruighinn;

Cha b' e gleusadh fear na fìdhle

A rinn inns' mo ghràdh bhith tighinn.

All summer, I was expecting him,

Joyous while I waited for him;

My eye ever southward to see a sail

Rounding the Dùn, and approaching land;

All summer, I was expecting him,

Joyous while I waited for him.

It wasn't the fiddler's tune

That announced my darling's arrival

Nor the skilful playing of the bagpipes

That aroused the welcoming reel;

It wasn't the fiddler's tune

That announced my darling's arrival.

Thog fir sùil-bheachd sgairt le fiamh
Gun robh na nàimhdean air an stairsnich,
Bagart creich le daga 's lann,
Is theich sinn crom ri fasgadh cladaich;
Thog fir sùil-bheachd sgairt le fiamh
Gun robh na nàimhdean air an stairsnich.

Bha mo ghràdh a' ruith nan gleann,
Mac-talla meallta ris a' freagairt,
'S a chlaisneachd geur ri guth na h-òigh
A thug a bòid gum biodh i leth ris;
Bha mo ghràdh a' ruith nan gleann,
Mac-talla meallta ris a' freagairt.

Chualas faram chnag is ràmh,
Is leig mi ràn nuair thug mi 'n aire
Gun robh mo ghràdh gu bhith à fàir'
'S a bhratach àrd 's e tilleadh dhachaigh;
Chualas faram chnag is ràmh
Is leig mi ràn nuair thug mi 'n aire.

Dh' fhàg e còirean Hiort gun ghò,
Tighearna òg nam pògan meala,
Dh'fhàg e òigh a' sileadh dheòir
An creachadh dòchais chaoidh bhith maill' ris;
Dh'fhàg e còirean Hiort gun ghò,
Tighearna òg nam pògan meala.

Nàile, mise a tha caoineadh
Beatha gaoil mu sgaoil
    le sochair,
Oir chuireadh aontrachd orm le faoineas
'S mi nis às aonais laoich is tochair;
Nàile, mise a tha caoineadh
Beatha gaoil mu sgaoil le sochair.

A watchman's fearful call
Warned that enemies were on the threshold,
Threatening with pistol and sword,
So we fled headlong to hide by the shore;
A watchman's fearful call
Warned that enemies were on the threshold.

My darling searched the glens,
Echo mocking him with answers,
As he listened for the maiden's voice
Who had promised always to be his;
My darling searched the glens,
Echo mocking him with answers.

The rhythm of the oars in rowlocks was heard,
And I cried out when I realised
That my darling was pulling away,
His banner high as he sailed homewards;
The rhythm of the oars in rowlocks was heard,
And I cried out when I realised.

None could blame him for leaving Hiort,
The young nobleman of the honeyed kisses,
But he left a maiden weeping tears,
Thinking I'd never again be with him;
None could blame him for leaving Hiort,
The young nobleman of the honeyed kisses.

Woe is me that I'm left lamenting
That my life's love has been lost through
    folly,
For I've been abandoned through folly
Now with neither suitor nor dowry;
Woe is me that I'm left lamenting
My life's love lost through folly.

33. Housing

From the ferocity of the gales in winter and spring, it is not difficult to imagine that the original islanders lived in earth-houses. An example of such a dwelling was opened up by John Sands when he visited the island in 1877. It was known locally as *Taigh an t-Sìthiche** and had been buried beneath a potato patch. It consisted of a central chamber approached by a tunnel, with a roof of stone slabs flush with the ground. The walls of undressed stone allowed for several smaller compartments for sleeping** and for storage. Below a two-foot layer of peat and ashes, Sands unearthed a flagstone floor which drained into one corner of the central chamber. Buried in the peat he found the carcasses of fulmar and gannets. He also found limpet shells which had been cooked on a fire, and stone implements including an axe and a hammer.

Yet another earth-house was discovered on sloping ground some thirty yards to the north of the cemetery. Excavated in 1926, it was found to have a floor like that in *Taigh an t-Sìthiche* but with a drain (presumably for sewerage) running downhill underneath the flagstones. Its overall design and construction was similar to that of the Staller's House on Boreray and to the other earth-houses discovered in Uist and Lewis.

© School of Scottish Studies

The ruin of a family home inhabited pre 1834

* The House Belonging to the Sìthiche, i.e. to a male member of the Little Folk; mistakenly translated to English as 'The Fairy House'

** Until the middle of the 1930s, most of the people in the Outer Hebrides lived in *taighean-dubha* (black-houses) – thatched dwellings which had thick stone walls and the fire for cooking and heating on a hearth in the centre of the living room. A feature of the oldest of those dwellings was the *crùb*, a compartment providing sleeping accommodation for three or four persons.

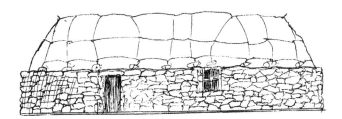

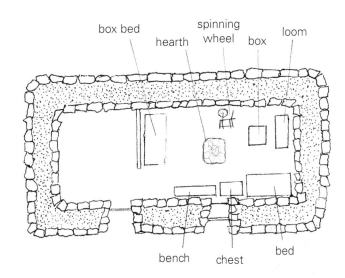

box bed hearth spinning wheel box loom

bench chest bed

Drawing based on Captain F.W.L. Thomas's plan of Betty Scott's black-house around 1860

So long as the floor remained above the water-table, a dwelling such as *Taigh an t-Sìthiche* would have provided warm, sheltered and relatively secure accommodation. Biting gale-force winds are common on St Kilda, particularly, but not exclusively, during the winter months, so that living underground had its advantages. On the other hand, living in dark and dismal accommodation without ventilation or daylight must have been very unhealthy.

Over the centuries the island dwellings slowly 'surfaced'! Until the Street was built in the late 1830s and 40s, the St Kildans lived in abject conditions, in dwellings which were partially underground.

When MacAulay spent time on Hiort in 1764, he found that the houses were different from those of the other islands in the Outer Hebrides, not least in that their roofs were flat. The islanders believed that, by not being lofted, their houses were better able to withstand the violent squalls of winter. The walls, eight or nine feet high, were constructed of undressed boulders without any form of binding such as lime or mortar. The thickness of the walls allowed for sleeping cubicles to be constructed within them. Overlaid with big flat slabs of stone, each *crùb* was designed to accommodate between two and four persons, depending on the number of persons in the family, and was accessed from the living-room. The entrance to a *crùb** was very low and narrow, so that anybody wishing to go to bed had to get down on all fours and crawl into the darkness of the wall. The floor of the *crùb* was covered with deer-grass, heather or straw – whichever was available, according to the season.

* The word *crùb* is also a verb meaning 'to bend down'.

A *fallan* (partition) divided the house into two rooms. On entering the house by its only doorway, one found oneself in the larger of the two rooms. Here the family's two or three head of cattle were tethered against the wall during the worst of the winter and spring weather. The second room in the house served as the family's living-room and kitchen.

The fuel used for cooking and heating the living-room was dried peat which, when burnt, produced a large quantity of ash. When mixed with manure and rotted seaweed, peat-ash became a valuable fertilizer and was regarded as particularly good for the growing of barley.

It was the duty of the females of the family to spread the ash evenly over the living-room floor, then cover it with a thin layer of what MacAulay describes as 'a rich friable sort of earth'. Over that mix the islanders scattered *smùr na mònadh* – the dust produced when dried peat crumbles. Finally, they splashed water all over the room and pounded the mix until it became a hard floor. This procedure, repeated every few days, had the effect of both gradually raising the level of the floor and reducing the headroom of the living-quarters.

© Slain Whitaker (S.S.S.)

In the spring, the houses were emptied of the odious contents accreted over the previous twelve months. Creelful after creelful was carried on to the fields on which the barley was to be sown. The work of emptying the house of pungent manure from the *bàthaich* (byre) and from the living-room *òtrach* (compost-heap) had the effect of returning the headroom of the living-room from four or five feet to the original eight or nine. Members of the household who wished to retire to bed no longer had to descend some four feet from the risen floor of the living-room to reach the floor of the *crùb*.

Until after the First World War (1914-18), the standard of housing in much of the Highlands and Islands was only minimally better than on Hiort. The black-houses in Lewis, for example, were certainly larger, but the cattle, sheep and poultry were, again, all under the same roof as the humans. However, in the dwellings on Lewis and other islands of the Outer Hebrides, the accommodation for the animals and humans was separated by a *fosglan* (lobby); also, the family's living-quarters consisted of a large living-room-cum-kitchen and one or two capacious bedrooms.

Until the First World War, housing conditions for Britain's working-classes were primitive by today's standards. Diseases such as tuberculosis, chickenpox, rubella, measles and whooping-cough were common. In the city of Glasgow, for example, the vast majority of the population lived in cramped tenement accommodation, often with several families sharing one toilet.

34. Chaidh Mi 'n Iomall nan Càirdean

Anna, daughter of Finlay MacDonald, composed this elegy as a tribute to her brother and sister, who died with only a short time between them.

'S gur mise tha gu dubhach
A' siubhal an t-aon là,
O chaill mi mo phiuthar
A bha subhach is faoilidh,
Bha gu maiseach ciatach,
Bha gu fialaidh ro dhaoine;
Cha leig mis' thu air dìochuimhne
Ged liathainn san t-saoghal.

I am downcast
Living from day to day,
Since I lost my sister
Who was happy and generous,
Who was pretty and good-humoured
And welcoming to visitors;
Though I live into old age,
I shall not forget you.

O dh'fhalbh ad mhnaoi òig thu,
'S e mo bhròn-sa mar thachair,
'S chan eil deò ann am sheòrsa
...
Mar tha smuaintean a' bhàis
H-uile là tighinn a-steach orm;
Chaidh mi 'n iomall nan càirdean
O là chàireadh an leac ort.

Your dying such a young woman that
It is difficult for a person of my nature
To come to terms with it,
...
Thoughts of death
Invade my mind each day;
I've avoided my friends
Since the day you were buried.

Chì thu, Rìgh, mar tha mise,
'S mi gam chlisgeadh 's gam chiùrradh,
Mar tha mi 'g ionndrainn na gibht ud
Tha fon lic air a dùnadh;
Chaidh mi 'n iomall nan càirdean,
Mar tha 'm bàs air mo spùilleadh;
'S tric nam chridhe-sa sàthadh –
'S e mo bhràthair-sa b' fhiù siud.

Lord, you see how I am,
Upset and sore-hearted,
Missing that gift
Now enclosed under a slab;
I've avoided my friends
Because I feel worn down by death;
Often my heart is pierced –
Caused by what happened to my brother.

Bu tu sguid-fhear na guailne
An àm gluasad a' bhàta;
Fear ruigheachd a' chruaidheachd,
Bhiodh tu shuas air ràmh–braghad;
'S gum bu bhinn thu ag èigheach
An àm èirigh na bàirlinn;
Bha thu foinnidh, deas,
      treubhach –
Gur mairg cèil' rinn thu fhàgail.

Gnùis an àigh, cha bu bheag orm
Thu thighinn thugam air chèilidh,
Mar bu mhiannach leam tachairt
Thu thighinn dhachaigh là fèille.
Bu tu an sòlas rod chàirdean,
'S mòr a' bheàrn thu gan trèigsinn;
Och is och, mar a tha mi,
'S mi gur n-àireamh le chèile.

You were the bearer of shoulder-weight
When the (beached) boat was being moved;
The one who pulled the anchor cable;
The one up on the fore-oar and who
Determined the rhythm of the oar-song
When the grey-backs came at you;
You were determined, competent and
      diligent –
Pity the spouse whom you have left behind.

Your cheerful countenance I enjoyed
When you came to visit me,
Something I always looked forward to
Was when you'd return on a feast-day.
You were the joy of your relations,
Great is the gap you've left us with;
Alas, that I should have come to this,
Grieving for the two departed.

© Robert Milne Collection

Margaret MacDonald No 8

35. Survivors of the *Charlotte*: 1839

In the eighteenth century, at least two ships were wrecked on Rockall, a stack only half the size of Soay Stac. Situated some 150 miles west of St Kilda, it has been likened to

an iron nail driven into the middle of a huge expanse of grey silk.

In spite of its relative insignificance in the vastness of the ocean, ships collided with it from time to time.

In 1839, the *Charlotte*, a vessel sailing out of Hull, collided with Rockall and was so badly damaged that the passengers and crew were forced to take to a lifeboat. It took the lifeboat a week to reach St Kilda. Approaching the west of Hiort late in the evening, the *Charlotte*'s captain the crew brought the lifeboat into the calm waters of Glen Bay. They sheltered overnight in a large sea cave and in the morning, being short of food, stepped ashore on *Leacan an Eathair* – a shelf of rock at the foot of a tall cliff. Unfortunately, the cliff was so steep that no-one was able to climb to the top. The survivors of the *Charlotte* became weaker and more pessimistic by the hour, and would have surely died there, had they not been spotted by a young lad who was in the *Gleann Mòr* herding cattle.

Leaving the cattle, the lad ran back to the Village to report what he had seen. It happened that most of the island's able-bodied men were out fowling, but fortunately, Donald MacKinnon, a precentor from Harris, happened to be visiting Hiort. With the lad who had spotted the survivors leading them, Donald MacKinnon and a group of volunteers set off for the *Gleann Mòr*.

As the youngest and fittest of the group, Donald MacKinnon was the one lowered by climbing-rope to *Leacan an Eathair*. The fugitives were in a sorry state – frightened, cold and hungry. One who had a broken leg was the first to be hauled aloft. In turn, they were all brought to the cliff-top. Last to arrive at the top was Donald MacKinnon, who, unlike the St Kildans, spoke English fluently. The strangers were led up through the *Gleann Mòr* to the *Blàid,* and then down towards the Village, where women and children stood at the doors of their houses wondering how eighteen visitors could be found accommodation in their already cramped homes.

The Rev Neil MacKenzie welcomed the strangers and assured them that they would be given food and shelter. The St Kildans were noted for their hospitality, and by evening every one of the strangers was settled with an island family. When the fowlers returned to base, eight of them returned to the *Gleann Mòr* and salvaged the *Charlotte*'s lifeboat.

Most consideration was given to the man whose leg was broken. After a meal, he was carried on a litter to the manse, where the Rev Neil MacKenzie set his broken bone in splints. The minister was experienced in treating similar injuries suffered by the islanders while working on the rocks.

The orthopaedic patient was carried to his adoptive home and gently put to bed in a *crùb*. However, the dark, cramped, overcrowded conditions of the *crùb* were not to his liking and he complained loudly all through the night. Over the next few days, his condition improved, and in due time he was able to thank everybody who had taken care of him. He confessed to the minister that during his first night on Hiort when he was deposited in the *crùb*, he thought he had been lowered into a well as a punishment for his ill temper!

The St Kildans patched up the lifeboat, which had sustained some damage when it was abandoned at the *Gleann Mòr*. Once the weather turned fair, the eighteen survivors of the *Charlotte* re-boarded her and, accompanied by Donald MacKinnon, set sail for Harris.

When they reached the Isle of Pabbay in the Sound of Harris, they gifted the lifeboat to Donald Mackinnon, who sold it for £9, a sum which he sent to the people of St Kilda. But in spite of Donald MacKinnon's generous gesture, the St Kildans became increasingly disappointed, as the months went by, that their erstwhile guests did not fulfil their promises to 'repay them handsomely with money and gifts'. They often quoted the Gaelic proverb:

Cha bhi cuimhn' air an aran-eòrna ach fhad 's a tha e anns an sgòrnan.

Gifted bread is forgotten as soon as it passes the gullet.

TOWARDS THE CLIFF EDGE (1852 onwards)

The community's mainstay broke in 1852 when most of the island young decided to emigrate to Australia. After that exodus, the remainder of the population found it difficult to sustain the island economy. The young men whose energy and expertise as cragsmen and fishermen had ensured that the stores were replenished each year with bird-meat, eggs and fish were almost all gone. So also was the light-heartedness and vitality which had once made the life on Hiort tolerable. Little was now heard but pessimistic expressions of doom and concerns about the Hereafter. In the end, the community was overwhelmed by infant mortality and a growing reliance on charitable support from the outside world.

36. Hogmanay Old Style

In 1752, the Gregorian Calendar replaced the old Julian Calendar, which had the effect of shifting the old pagan festival of Hogmanay (*A' Challainn*) forward by twelve days. In the Gaelic-speaking districts of Scotland, the *Callainn* continued to be celebrated, but on the twelfth day of January – the New Year by the old reckoning. Thus, the Gaels had a double whammy – Hogmany on 31st December and the *Callainn* on 12th January! In his *Carmina Gadelica*, Alexander Carmichael gives the following description of how Gaels of the nineteenth century celebrated the *Callainn*:

> *One man is enveloped in the hard hide of a bull with the horns and hoofs still attached. When the men come to a house, they ascend the wall and run round sun-wise, the man with the hide shaking the horns and hoofs, and the other men striking the hide with sticks. The appearance of the man in the hide is gruesome, while the din made is terrific. Having descended and recited the runes at the door, the Hogmanay men are admitted and treated to the best in the house. The performance seems to be symbolic, but of what it is not easy to say, unless of laying an evil spirit. That the rite is heathen and ancient is evident.*

Carmichael gives a version of the runes under the title *Cairioll Callaig* (Hogmanay Carol). It is centuries old and appears to have been adapted to make it acceptable to the Catholic Church. The following is an excerpt:

Nis tha mis air tighinn dhur dùthaich	I am now come to your country
A dh'ùrachadh dhuibh na Callaig;	To renew to you the Hogmanay;
Cha leig mi leas a dhol ga innse –	I needn't tell you about it –
Bha i ann ri linn ar seanar.	It existed in our forefathers' time.
Dìrim ris an àrd-doras,	I ascend by the door lintel,
Teàrnam ris an starsach,	I descend by the doorstep,
Mo dhuan a ghabhail dòigheil,	In order to say my rhyme
Modhail, mòineil, maineil ...	Mannerly, slowly, carefully ...
Bean an taighe, is i as fhiach e,	The housewife is the one who deserves it,
Làmh a riarach oirnn na Callaig:	The dispensing hand of the Hogmanay:
Sochair bheag a bhlàth an t-samhraidh,	A small gift from the bloom of summer
Tha mi 'n geall air leis an aran.	Is what I crave to have with the bread.

Tabhair duinn e ma dh'fhaodas;	Give it to us if that's possible;
Mura faod, na cùm maill oirnn;	If you may not, don't detain us;
Mise gille Mhic Dè san doras –	I am the servant of God's Son at the door –
Èirich fèin is fosgail domh e.	Arise and open it for me.

The rhyme (or runes) was generally known as *Duan na Callainn* – the Hogmanay Chant. However, on Hiort it was known as *Nuallan na Callainn* (The Hogmanay Bellow) and, because the community was so small, it was recited at half the houses of the Street on alternate years. The boys from the western half of the Street would visit the houses of the *Taobh Sear* – the East End. The following year, the boys from the Taobh Sear would visit the houses of the *Taobh Siar* – the West End. Every household due to be visited baked a *bonnach Callainn* (Hogmanay bannock) which was presented to the visiting troupe. The bannock was sometimes as big as the grindstone of the quern and took as much as half a stone of barley meal in its making. After reciting the *Nuallan* and receiving the bannocks, all the boys of the community retired to some hideaway to enjoy the *Callainn* feast. On the following day, the revellers announced to the community which of the bannocks they considered to be the tastiest. Usually, the 'best bannock' was the biggest!

Nuallan na Callainn

Thàinig mise seo gur h-ionnsaigh	I have come to you
A dh'ùrachadh dhuibh na Callainn;	To renew to you the Hogmanay;
Cha ruig mi leas sin innse –	I needn't explain what it means –
Bha i ann bho linn mo sheanar.	As it has been since my grandpa's day.

Thèid mi deiseal air an fhàrdaich	I'll go clockwise round the house
Is teàrnaidh mi aig an doras;	And I will descend at the door;
Gabhaidh mi null uimpe mar as còir dhomh	I'll continue round the home as I should,
Cùlaibh caol-druim fear an taighe.	Round the back of the man of the house.

Craiceann Callainn na mo phòca,	With the *Callainn* skin in my pocket,
'S math an ceò a thig on fhear ud –	And what smoke will come from that –
Chan eil neach a gheibh fhàileadh	Everybody who gets a whiff of it
Nach bi gu bràth dheth fallain.	Will forever feel its health-giving benefit.

Gheibh fear an taighe na làimh e	The man of the house will take it in his hand
Is sparraidh e a cheann san teallaich;	And shove its end in the fire
Thèid e deiseal air na pàistean,	He will go clockwise round the children
Ach gu h-àraid gheibh a bhean e.	But his wife will be especially favoured.

Gheibh a bhean e – 's i as fhiach e –
Làmh-riarachaidh na Callainn.
Leis an tart a th' air an
        dùthaich,
Chan eil dùil againn ri drama –

Rud beag de thoradh an t-samhraidh,
Tha mi 'n geall air leis an aran;
'S mòr tha siud a th' againn ri fhaotainn;
'S ma dh'fhaodas sibh, na cumaibh maille.

For she's the one who deserves it –
The dispensing hand of the Hogmanay.
Considering the drought that is upon the
        land,
We don't expect a dram –

Just a wee amount of summer produce
That I hope to get with the bread;
We have a great deal to collect;
So if you don't mind, please don't delay.

37. Ancient Stones

There are man-made stone structures all over Hiort and Boreray. Each one of those provides us with clues to the changing world in which the St Kildans lived. Some are of great antiquity.

Taigh na Bana-Ghaisgich – The Heroine's House, translated to English as the Amazon's House, a building situated near to the Well of Virtues in the *Gleann Mòr*.

According to folklore, the building was the home of the *Bana-Ghaisgeach* (Heroic Woman), who in the Young Age went hunting deer on horseback over a plateau said to have linked St Kilda to the Isle of Harris. By the early 1690s, women tending cattle in the *Gleann Mòr* used it as a summer residence, and for that reason it became known as *An Àirigh Mhòr* – The Big Shieling. Martin, who saw it whole, said it was

> *in the form of a circle, pyramid-wise towards the top, having a vent in it, the fire being in the centre of the floor ... The body of the house contains not above nine persons sitting; there are three beds or low vaults that go off the side of the wall, a pillar between each bed, which contains five men.*

As had happened in the case of the Staller's House on Boreray, the *Àirigh Mhòr* was partially demolished early in the nineteenth century, by islanders who took stones from its walls to build cleits.

Altraichean – Altars

On top of the *Mullach Geal* are a great number of monoliths piled up as if by some giant. One of those blocks rests like a lintel on two others. Referring to this 'lintel' in 1848, Sands says:

> *... the stone in question is probably one of the altars on which offerings were made to the unknown gods – a heathen custom which continued long after the inhabitants had become Presbyterians. Several of these altars existed and were regarded as sacred even so late as 1759*

Bàtaichean cloiche – 'Stone boats'

They are said to be the oldest memorials on Hiort. Archeologists have discovered up to twenty of these curious shapes in the *Lag bho Thuath*, the corrie high above the Village, between *Oiseabhal* and *Conachair*. They were built in ancient times, perhaps to represent the passage of the souls of the dead into the Hereafter.

Cill Chrìosda – Christ Church

The cemetery, near the site of the old church, was known as *Cladh Chille Chrìosda*.

Clach-oidhche – Night-stone

This was a lamp of ancient design and consisted of a stone hollowed out so as to contain fuel. The wick was a small piece of *còsach* (fibrous peat) floating on the fuel. The *clach-oidhche* was also known as *clach-shoillse* – 'a light stone'. By the 1870s, the *clach-oidhche* had been replaced by the *crùisgean* (cruzie), which consisted of one or two open fuel-pots made of iron and suspended by an iron hook.

Clach na Gruagaich – The Gruagach Stone

It is situated about 200 yards to the north of the Village and to the left of the road leading to the summit of *Conachair*. At one time all the people of the Western Isles propitiated the *Gruagach*, a friendly spirit associated with a large boulder close to where cattle were regularly milked. On Hiort, it was the custom to pour milk at the Stone every Sunday, from May until August. The *Gruagach* Stone was also known as *Clach a' Bhainne* (The Milk Stone).

The Gruagach Stone

Clach an Eòlais – The Stone of Knowledge

It was also known as the *Clach-àine,* and stands close to the cemetery. In olden days, the islanders believed that anyone standing on it on the first day of the quarter would be endowed with the Second Sight during the three months that followed.

Clach Èiteig – a quartz stone

This was a round or oval quartz stone associated with the raven, a bird much admired for its wisdom.

Young men of St Kilda used to steal an egg from a raven's nest, boil it, and then return it to the nest. It was claimed that the parent bird, hoping to revive its dead egg, would respond by going in search of a *clach-èiteig* which it added to its clutch. Such a stone, discovered in a deserted raven's nest, was highly prized and was worn by women as an amulet. In 1858, a pale pink quartzite pebble discovered in the floor of the *Àirigh Mhòr* may have been treasured as a *clach-èiteig* long ago.

Clach-shiull – Mashing-stone

A stone used for breaking shells such as limpets and winkles. The mashed bait was then thrown into the sea to attract fish. The word *soll* – broken bait – comes from ON *sollr* – ('swill').

The Lag bho Thuath Stones are arranged as if to represent the gunwale of a boat; hence the term 'stone boat'

This slab of rock is known to visitors as 'Lovers' Rock'. it is said that it was traditional for any young man wishing to marry to prove his bravery by going to the outer rim of the rock and, looking seaward, stand there on one foot. However, the Hiortaich we knew said that it was unnecessary for the island's young men to carry out such a pointless exercise.

It is probable that this stone in the wall of House 16 was originally part of the fabric of one of the island's churches.

38. Cumha na banntraich Hiortaich

Gur mis' tha fo ghruaim,
'S tric snigh' air mo ghruaidh;
Cha chaidil mi uair gun dùsgadh;
Anns an tulach ud shuas
Dh'fhàg mi m' aighear 's mo luaidh
Fo lic dhaingeann nach gluais 's nach tionndaidh.

Mo thruaighe mi fèin
Gun fhear taighe nad dhèidh,
Gur dubhach dhomh cèis do ghiùlain;
Làmh thùrail an àigh,
Bu mhath d' fheum anns gach àit' –
Cha bu lapach thu 'n dàil no
        tùirneil.

I feel downcast;
Tears often stain my cheek;
Each time I sleep, I wake with a start;
On the hillock up yonder
I laid my hero, my love, to rest
Under a flagstone that will never stir.

How unfortunate I am
Without anyone to replace you;
How awful to see the burial casket;
A joyful man who had an inventive talent,
Who was so useful in the community –
Who was never reluctant or slow to
        respond.

Mi faicinn leam fèin
Do chuid uidheam ri stèill,
Làmh a dhèanadh an fheum gun dùil ris;
'N ciste chaol an dà thaobh
Chuir mi tasgadh mo chuim,
'S chan fhidir i caoidh no ionndrainn.

Ach, a Thì as mòr glòir,
Neartaich fhèin a shliochd òg
Tha gun taca, gun stòr an cùl riuth';
'S tric mi smuaintinn leam fèin
Air grad-theachd Mac Dhè
Is a' ghiorrad gu 'm pill sinn còmhla.

In solitude, I look upon your work-gear
Hanging idly by the wall,
And remember that diligent creative man;
Now hemmed in between two boards
The love of my heart who is unaware
Of my weeping and my deep sense of loss.

But I beseech thee, great God of glory,
Strengthen his little ones
Who are cast without store or support;
Often I think to myself
That the Son of God may soon come
And hasten the time of our reunion.

© James Smith

The Feather House seen from the church window

39. The Rev Neil Mackenzie: 1838

The Rev Neil MacKenzie, born at Sannox in the Isle of Arran, was translated to St Kilda in 1830 – the first minister to be resident on Hiort in one hundred years. In the summer of the following year, aged forty, he left the island briefly to marry. His bride, who had been brought up in Glasgow, was unable to speak Gaelic, and for the following thirteen years had little opportunity of conversing with anyone except her husband. None of the islanders was able to speak English. While on Hiort, Mrs MacKenzie bore six children whom George Atkinson described as

> *fine rosy-cheeked children with clean hands and well-washed faces ... and bare little feet.*

In the summer of 1830, the first year of MacKenzie's incumbency, MacLeod of MacLeod, the proprietor of St Kilda, sent his master mason and workers to build a church and a manse at the south-eastern end of the Village. The manse, comprising four rooms, came to be known as *An Taigh Mòr* (The Big House) – an appropriate appellation as all the other dwelling-houses on the island consisted of two apartments: one for the family and dogs and the other for the cattle. The church, with Gothic windows and a slated roof, was built immediately behind the manse at a cost of £600. It measured thirteen feet by eighteen and had two doors – a main door used by the congregation and, close to the manse, a smaller door reserved for the minister.

MacKenzie was intelligent, energetic and dedicated to improving the living conditions of his flock. He concerned himself with their material as well as their spiritual welfare. One of his most pressing concerns was the islanders' poor housing conditions and lack of personal hygiene. He impressed on them the importance of their having basic essentials such as beds, tables and chairs, which would enable them, both literally and metaphorically, to live above the level of the dogs. He persuaded the islanders to change some of their traditional crofting practices – by, for example, building *Gàrradh a' Bhaile* (the Village Dyke), the drystone dyke separating their arable ground from the marginal ground on which the cattle and sheep grazed during the summer and autumn months.

In the following passage, written about 1837, MacKenzie gives a graphic account of the islanders' housing conditions.

> *Of their most ancient houses several still remain entire. They are circular or nearly so, and roughly built. The walls are six or seven feet thick with spaces for beds left in them. These bed spaces are roofed in with long slabs, and the entrance from the interior of the house is about three feet by two feet. The walls are not arched, but contracted gradually by overlapping of the stones to nearly a point ... The outside is covered with earth and rubbish and appears like a green hillock. In some places they are almost entirely underground. The houses which they occupied when I came to the island were larger and more oval shaped. The walls were seven or eight feet thick, about six or seven feet high, and the same height all round. The beds were in the thickness of the walls as before. There was also the same absence of a window. The only opening for*

light was a small circular opening at one end, where the thatch joins the wall, left for the exit of smoke. The door aperture was near the end and faced east. It was higher than that in the former houses and had a wooden door with wooden hinges and lock. A partition of rough stones about four feet high, called fallan, divided the abode of man and dog, from that of the cattle. There was a light wooden roof resting on the inner edge of the wall, covered with a thickness of about eighteen inches of straw, simply laid on, and not in layers as ordinary thatch. When beaten flat and uniform it was secured by numerous straw ropes called siaman ... The cattle occupied the half of the house next the door, and the manure was not removed until taken to the fields in spring. In the other portion dwelt the family, and there all the ashes, and the dirty water, and other things far worse, were daily spread over the floor. This was covered every few days with a layer of peat dust. Before the time for removal to the fields in spring the mixture was often higher than the side walls, so that at times a visit to a parishioner was quite an adventure. Owing to the great thickness of the wall the house door was at the end of a tunnel, and owing to the lowness of the door space one could not stand upright. In front of the doorway and extending well into the tunnel, was a hollow into which were thrown all the portions of the bird not used for food, the entire carcasses of those not edible, and all and every abomination you can think of. Stooping low, you groped your way over this till you reached the door. Inside the door, you had to climb over the manure among the cattle, which, on account of the presence of a stranger, and the barking of dogs, and the shouting of your friends above, soon got very excited. Amidst the confusion and the excitement you were helped along and over the fallan. Here you had to creep along on hands and feet, and it was only in the centre of the space that you were able to sit upright. Carefully creeping along in almost total darkness, you made your way to the top of the steep slope which led down to the bed opening. Down this you went head foremost, nothing visible above but your legs, while you prayed.

Sir Thomas Dyke Ackland, an Englishman, first visited Hiort when he was twenty-five years of age. During his stay, he made a series of beautiful water-colours and pen-sketches, a number of which are reproduced in David A. Quine's book, *St Kilda Portraits*. Aged forty-seven, Ackland re-visited the island in 1834 and was so shocked by the St Kildans' living conditions that he left twenty guineas with the minister, to be gifted to the first family to build a *taigh-geal* (white-house). Though reluctant to demolish their old dwellings, the islanders began to waver and were finally won over after one householder decided to take the plunge.

Whereas the original Village was a cluster of *taighean-dubha*, the new houses were built in an arc, as a street. The size of the houses was limited to the roofing timbers available. A few of the features of the old dwellings were retained: the roofs were thatched with barley straw and some of the houses had a bed built into the wall. Nevertheless, the new houses were better designed. Each had one or two small windows and a doorway higher than that of the old. The door to each house was fitted with a wooden lock, purchased by the Rev Neil MacKenzie, using money donated by Sir Thomas Dyke Ackland and other well-wishers. No longer was the *òtrach* allowed to compete with the humans for accommodation in the living-room, but it was given a prominent place at the front of the house. As before, the byre occupied one half of the house. In 1860, a hurricane caused a great deal of damage, and in the following year, John MacPherson MacLeod, the proprietor, provided money for the construction of mortared, gabled houses which proved to be a great improvement on those they replaced. They had two rooms, each with a fireplace and a window looking on the Bay. The houses built thirty years earlier were made into byres for the cattle, and barns in which croft implements and potatoes could be stored. Captain Otter, another visiting Englishman, purchased sufficient zinc sheeting to re-roof all sixteen houses. In the following decades, the zinc decayed, and was replaced with felt and tar. Thus, the St Kildans were living in 'white-houses' about fifty years before most crofters in other parts of the Outer Hebrides were able to abandon their black-houses.

The Rev Neil MacKenzie is best remembered for his brand of practical theology and for his deep interest in the cultural heritage of St Kilda. He left to posterity a priceless record of the islanders' songs and poems, a number of which are reproduced in this book.

© James Smith

A view of the Dùn from the village

Village Bay and the Dùn from Conachair

© James Smith

Aerial view of Village Bay with the Dùn bottom left and Soay top left

Boreray from Conachair; to the left, Stac Lì and Stac an Àrmainn

© James Smith

Approaching Soay Stac at low tide

Lady Grange's house

© James Smith

Cleits and drystone dykes in the Lag bho Thuath demonstrate the islanders' building skills

Birds for the pot, razorbills below and fulmar above

© James Smith

At the summit of Mullach Bì, with the sea 1100 feet below

Stac Lì, close to Boreray, is one of the main breeding sites of gannets

Some of the cliffs of Boreray rise to more than 1000 feet

© James Smith

Cleits near the Village

The Factor's House, known to the islanders as An Taigh Mòr – The Big House

Basking under the summer sun, the Dùn in the distance and in the foreground the Gaineamh – the stretch of sand which is annually washed away by winter storms

The Feather House in which the islanders' sacks of feathers used to be stored, ready for export

40. Boch oirinn Ò

'S truagh, a Rìgh, nach mi bha thallad, Ò,
Anns an tìr sa bheil mo leannan, Ò.
Boch oirinn Ò, boch oirinn, oirinn,
  Boch oirinn, Ò.

Anns an tìr sa bheil mo leannan, Ò,
Tìr nam beann, nan gleann 's nam bealaichean.
  Boch oirinn, Ò.

Tìr nam beann, nan gleann 's nam bealaichean,
Eòin air gèig is fèidh a' langanaich;
  Boch oirinn, Ò.

Eòin air gèig is fèidh a' langanaich,
Far am biodh na h-uaislean dan dual bhith
  barrasach.
  Boch oirinn, Ò.

Pity me, O Lord, that I 'm not yonder
In the land where my sweetheart is.
Boch oirinn O, boch oirinn, oirinn,
  Boch oirinn, Ò.

In the land where my sweetheart is,
The land of glens, bens and passes.
  Boch oirinn, Ò.

In the land of glens, bens and passes,
Birds on branches and deer baying.
  Boch oirinn, Ò.

Birds on branches and deer baying,
Where live the gentry born to be
  refined.
  Boch oirinn, Ò.

Far am biodh na h-uaislean dan dual bhith
    barrasach,

Rachadh don bhlàr 'n coinneamh
    nàmhaid mar dhealanach.

    Boch oirinn, Ò.

Rachadh don bhlàr 'n coinneamh
    nàmhaid mar dhealanach;

Bha mo leannan fèin ann, 's gur beusach
    fearail e.

    Boch oirinn, Ò.

Bha mo leannan fèin ann, 's gur beusach
    fearail e:

'S truagh nach mi bha seòladh thairis leat.

    Boch oirinn, Ò.

Where live the gentry born to be
    refined,

Who in battle would advance upon
    the enemy like lightning.

    Boch oirinn, Ò.

Who in battle would advance upon
    the enemy like lightning;

My own sweetheart was there, virtuous
    and virile.

    Boch oirinn, Ò.

My own sweetheart was there, virtuous
    and virile:

I wish that I were sailing across with you.

    Boch oirinn, Ò.

41. Enigmatic Diseases

Lockjaw

For many generations, infant mortality prevented the regeneration of the population. The chief reason for infant deaths was lockjaw, a symptom of tetanus which causes the muscles of the jaw to contract violently and the teeth to clench. Caused by umbilical sepsis, the disease was so prevalent among new-born babies that it became known as *tinneas nan ochd latha* (the eight days sickness) – eight days being the average life-span of the victims.

Studies of neonatal deaths in certain Icelandic parishes between 1790 and 1839 also showed a high rate of mortality due to tetanus. Scientists concluded that 'farming and, especially, fowling contributed to infection at birth'.

Between 1830 and 1880, four out of every five babies born on Hiort died – eighty-four in all. Some islanders had come to accept the deaths as divine intervention, proof that God was ensuring that the population would not exceed the island's capacity for food production. When Emily MacLeod, a sister of the proprietor, visited the island in 1877, she was distressed to meet a woman who had borne twelve babies, of whom only one had survived. In spite of the islanders' fatalism and their stubborn adherence to traditional methods, she was convinced that they could be persuaded to allow a trained nurse to assist at births. The only way forward, she argued, was for a young St Kildan woman to accompany her to Skye to learn English, and from there to go to Glasgow to be trained as a nurse. None of the young women on Hiort was willing to accept the offer. Rejection of her suggestion did not deter Emily MacLeod. She visited the island several times but continued to be thwarted in her efforts to introduce measures which would reduce infant mortality. In the end, in 1884, she sent a fully trained nurse to Hiort at her own expense. Regarding the newcomer as an intruder, the island women steadfastly rejected the nurse's overtures and prevented her from attending at births. Newly-born babies continued to die of tetanus infection.

George Murray became schoolmaster of St Kilda in 1886. Aware of the prevalence of tetanus on the island, he became anxious when ten year-old Annie Ferguson, one of his brightest pupils, became seriously ill. Fearing the worst, he noted her symptoms in his diary:

> *She returned not in the afternoon and now her life is quite despaired of. What she suffered since Friday is terrible to think on. She is affected exactly the same as the infants who are seized with it. The muscles of her body appear to be in a state of lasting rigidity, while at the end of every three or four minutes, paroxysms of spasm occur followed by intervals of comparative ease and a desire to sleep, till she is suddenly aroused by the excruciating pain which attends the paroxysm. She cannot rest in the same position five minutes but must be turned from side to side or kept sitting or standing.*

Five days later he wrote:

> *Every limb and part of her body is affected. Her very toes are bent downwards ...*
> *Offered to give her an injection, but the people are so very curious that they will*
> *have their own way do what you will. I remonstrated but to no purpose.*

Ten days after the schoolmaster's first entry, Annie died.

> *It was to us nothing less than a great wonder how she stood it so long ...*
> *so great had been the pain that the body was entirely out of shape. What*
> *a warning to us all!*

Though he was sympathetic to the islanders' plight, their intransigence must have greatly shocked George Murray. After less than two years on St Kilda, he demitted his post in 1887.

In 1889, the Rev Angus Fiddes* became the island's resident minister. Extrovert and strong-willed, he determined to discover the cause for the continuing loss of life among the island's young. During his holidays, he travelled to Glasgow to learn about midwifery. While there, he sought advice from Professor Reid of Glasgow University, who, from the minister's description, identified the disease as neonatal tetanus, an 'infection resulted from contamination of the severed cord due to unsanitary delivery conditions'. By the time he returned to St Kilda, the Rev Fiddes was confident that he had the knowledge and the means by which the Eight Days Sickness would be defeated. He had learned the identity of the disease and acquired a supply of the antiseptic powder that would save the island's babies.

It was traditional for the local midwife to smear a new-born baby's umbilicus with fulmar oil which, following an age-old tradition, had been stored in the preserved stomach of a gannet. The Rev Fiddes suspected that the fulmar oil was contaminated with tetanus bacilli and appealed to the midwife to use, instead of fulmar oil, the antiseptic powder which he had brought from Glasgow. His appeal fell on deaf ears!

It so happened that a new nurse arrived on Hiort about the time that the old midwife died. By then, the Rev Fiddes had managed to persuade the women in his congregation to reject fulmar oil in favour of the antiseptic powder. Once the nurse was allowed to assist at births, the deaths stopped.

The last case of neonatal tetanus on Hiort was in 1891. The Rev Angus Fiddes retired in 1903.

---

* Laying of the foundation-stone of the Free Church at Torridon, 1887: The proceedings on Thursday were opened by singing the Old Hundred, after which the Rev Angus Fiddes, the probationer appointed by the Highland Committee of the Free Church to minister to the Torridon people, offered up a most impressive Gaelic prayer. Mr Fiddes then, in the name of the crofters, cottars, household, and workmen at Ben-Damph, presented Mr Darroch with a beautiful silver trowel and mallet ...

The Boat-cold

In the nineteenth century, writers amused their readership with references to what they suggested was a peculiarly St Kildan disease – one which, they believed, arose from the incurable paranoia and pessimism of the islanders. They rejected the islanders' claim that they suffered from the illness only after they were visited by strangers. On Hiort, the illness was called *cnatan nan gall* (the foreigners' cold). Non-islanders referred to it ironically as the 'boat-cold'.

The St Kildans' fear of infection was justified for they had little natural resistance to diseases common on the mainland. They had never forgotten how smallpox had devastated their community in 1729, nor how a cholera epidemic had killed some of their number a century later.

In 1764, MacAulay wrote that he could vouch for the fact that, on the third day after his arrival, some people had symptoms of a violent cold and that, within eight days, all the islanders were suffering from the illness, some of them with fever and headaches. *Cnatan nan gall* began with shivering accompanied by a headache and congestion of the nasal passages and throat. After a day or two, sneezing and coughing developed. The Rev Neil MacKenzie recorded that, between 1830 and 1846, six people died of the illness.

The islanders believed that the illness brought from Uist and Harris was worse than that from Glasgow or Liverpool. One respected physician accepted that the illness was real but ascribed it to the food and lifestyle of the islanders. Other physicians believed that it was carried to Hiort by an easterly wind.

As late as 1907, the noted teacher and diarist Alice MacLachlan wrote:

> All the *baile* (village) have the steamer cold, the last day or two very badly. They say it came by the last boat. It seems so funny! They believe implicitly in this. Everybody has it and all the School is in a constant cough and sneeze …

It took until about one hundred years ago for doctors to understand what really caused the illness. At that time, medical research discovered how illnesses were spread by viruses and bacteria. Doctors then understood how the incidence of boat-cold at St Kilda coincided with the arrival of visitors. In other areas of the world, people living in remote communities suffered similar problems when visited by outsiders. Tristan de Cunha, off northern Africa, and the island of Muriori, five hundred miles from New Zealand, were two other islands on which the inhabitants suffered outbreaks of the common cold when ships visited them.

No wonder that an age-old, St Kildan superstition, regarding the rare visit of a cuckoo, took on a new twist. For generations, the call of the cuckoo was believed to herald the arrival of a stranger. In the nineteenth century, it presaged the arrival of both strangers and the onset of the boat-cold! Looking at the various theories put forward to explain the outbreaks of the illness, we see that the theory put forward by the St Kildans themselves was closest to the truth. They held that the air of the island was naturally pure and unpolluted and that unclean air brought to the island by visitors was injurious to their health.

Happy enough provided cold and toothache could be avoided

Families await the return of the fowlers

42. Utopia

The inhabitants of St Kilda are much happier than the generality of mankind, being almost the only people in the world who feel the sweetness of true liberty: what the condition of the people in this golden age is feigned by the poets to be, that theirs really is; I mean in innocence and simplicity, purity, mutual love, and cordial friendship; free from solicitous cares, and anxious covetousness; from envy, deceit, and dissimulation; from ambition and pride and the consequences that attend them.

There is only one thing wanting to make them the happiest people in this habitable globe, viz. that they themselves do not know how happy they are, and how much they are above the avarice and slavery of the rest of mankind. Their way of living makes them condemn gold and silver, as below human dignity or human nature; they live by the munificence of Heaven, and have no designs upon one another, but such as are suggested by kindness and benevolence.

Martin Martin, 1697

If this island is not the Utopia so long sought, where will it be found? Where is the land which has neither arms, money, laws, physic, politics, not taxes; that land is St Kilda. No nation is without those vices except St Kilda. The taxman doesn't pursue him to the door of his church … His state is his city and his city is his social circle: he has the liberty of his thoughts, his actions, and his kingdom, and all his world are his equals. His climate is temperate and his island green.

Dr MacCulloch, 1819

43. Ochòin, a Thì, Nach Foir thu Mi

by Neil Ferguson, 184 (from the collection
of the Rev Neil MacKenzie)

Ochòin, a Thì, nach fòir thu mi	Help me, God, I beseech thee,
Om smuaintean gu faireachadh,	Move from (foolish) thoughts to awareness,
Mun tig an t-àm a thèid mi dhìth	Before the time comes when I shall die
'S nach bi ann tìm gu aithreachas.	Without my having time to repent my sins.

© James Smith

44. Opposition to the Gaelic Language

The Liturgy approved by John Knox was translated into Gaelic in 1567. About a century later, the Synod of Argyll published the first fifty Psalms of David in metre, and shortly afterwards the Confession of Faith. However, influential voices were raised against the publication of the Bible in Gaelic. The Scottish Society for the Propagation of Christian Knowledge (SSPCK) believed that, until the Gaelic language was rooted out, the people of the Highlands and Islands would continue to be backward and ignorant. In schools, teaching through the medium of Gaelic was forbidden. At the beginning of the eighteenth century, the SSPCK changed its policy in this regard and contributed to the translation of the New Testament which appeared in print in 1767. The complete Bible appeared in 1801.

All the twenty ministers and missionaries who were resident on St Kilda between 1704 and 1930 preached in Gaelic. From the middle of the eighteenth century, the islanders became steadily more interested in mastering enough *Beurla* (English) to exchange pleasantries with visiting yachtsmen and fishermen, and to enable them to sell their wares to tourists.

Following his visit in 1878, Seton wrote:

> *Mrs Vean informs me that when her father went to the island in 1830, the people were deplorably ignorant. Only one woman could read and write a little, and none of the women could hold a needle.*

MacAulay considered that the St Kildans spoke

> *a very corrupt dialect of the Gaelic, adulterated with a little mixture of the Norwegian tongue.*

In fact, Scottish Gaelic everywhere was (and is) similarly 'adulterated' – some would say, enriched – by numerous words derived from Norse. This is particularly true of words pertaining to fishing and sea-going.

In 1697, Martin mentions that

> *both sexes have a lisp, but more especially the women, neither of the two pronouncing the letters d, g or r.*

The so-called 'lisp' continued to be a feature of their language, even after the St Kildans left their island home and came to live on the Scottish mainland. Lachie MacDonald, one of the three native St Kildans whom I knew well, pronounced the word *làmhaidh* (razorbill) as 'waawy' and the word *ruith* (run) as 'luith'.

In 1878, George Seton encapsulated the Lowlanders' attitude to the Gaelic language in the nineteenth century:

> *A recent number of Chamber's Journal – to which every English-speaking section of the globe owes such deep obligations – contains an admirable article ... on the subject of the 'Gaelic Nuisance', to which I venture to call the attention of all those who are interested in the future welfare of the inhabitants of St Kilda. The writer points to Galloway on the one hand and to the Orkney and Shetland Islands on the other, as illustrative examples of the blessings which have flowed from the substitution of English for Gaelic and Norse respectively ... Even after the entire abolition of Gaelic, Professor Blackie need have little fear as to the survival ... of 'provincial peculiarities and local diversities.' ... An intelligent and accomplished Lowlander, whose official duties imply a residence in one of the largest of the Western Isles, very recently informed me that ... he had been forced to the conclusion that the people among whom he lived were afflicted by two 'curses' – one of which I forbear to mention in the present connection, the other being the perpetuation of the Gaelic tongue.*

Dòmhnall Òg (young Donald) by John Sands

45. Tàladh Cailin an Fhuilt Òr-Bhuidh'

This is a traditional St Kildan air; words are by the late Rev Iain MacLeod, Minister of the Parish Church, Oban.

Fàil-èilidh horò, fàil-èilidh horò,

Aghaidh bhòidheach air a' phàiste;

Falt òr-bhuidh' mo ghràidh-sa,

Fàil-èilidh horò, fàil-èilidh horò;

Caidil sàmhach gus a-màireach,

Gràdh blàth an uchd màthar;

Fàil-èilidh horò, rirò-ririnn-èile;

Caidil sàmhach, a ghràidh!

Caidil socair, chailin bhàn!

Fàil-èilidh horò, fàil-èilidh horò;

Tha bò-bhainn' tighinn bhon àirigh

Le bainne math blàth dhi;

Fàil-èilidh horò, fàil-èilidh horò;

Thig maorach à tràigh dhi;

Thig biadh à muir-làn dhi;

Fàil-èilidh horò, rirò-ririnn-èile;

Caidil sàmhach, a ghràidh!

Caidil socair, chailin bhàn!

Fàil-èilidh horò, fàil-èilidh horò;

Leis na gluaisean, leis na dùisgean;

Mo luaidh-sa mo ghaol-sa,

Fàil-èilidh horò, fàil-èilidh horò;

Bi sàmhach gun cùram;

Fàil-èilidh horò, rirò-ririnn-èile;

Caidil sàmhach a ghràidh!

Caidil socair, chailin bhàn!

Fàil-èilidh, etc.

Lovely face of the child;

The golden hair of my loved one,

Fàil-èilidh, etc.

Sleep soundly till the morrow,

A darling, warm on the mother's lap;

Fàil-èilidh, etc.

Sleep soundly, my love!

Sleep softly, fair lassie!

Fàil-èilidh, etc.

The milk-cow is coming from the shieling

Bringing her warm milk;

Fàil-èilidh, etc.

Shellfish will be brought from the shore;

Wholesome food from the high tide;

Fàil-èilidh, etc.

Sleep soundly, my love!

Sleep softly, fair lassie!

Fàil-èilidh, etc.

So restless, so sleepless;

My love, my darling,

Fàil-èilidh, etc.

Be you quiet, without care;

Fàil-èilidh, etc.

Sleep soundly, my love!

Sleep softly, fair lassie!

46. Laoidh Fhionnlaigh Òig

This hymn was composed by Finlay Òg MacQueen in 1842 and preserved by the Rev Neil Mackenzie.

Bha sgeula air fhoillseachadh
Air machaire nan coilltichibh,
Is buachaillean na h-oidhche
Ghabh oillt is crith-fheòla.

The story unfolded
On the plain of forests,
And the shepherds at night
Took fright and shook with fear.

"Na gabhaibh an sgàth dheth!"
'S e thubhairt na h-aingle;
"Tha slàinte air foillseadh."
Bha seinn tighinn à Glòir ann.

"Don't be afraid of what you see!"
Said the angel;
"Redemption is revealed to you."
Heavenly music was heard.

"Is rugadh an tràth s' dhuibh
Ann am baile Dhaibhidh
An Slànaighear gràsmhor
San stàball neo-dhòigheil.

"At this time is born
In the city of David
The gracious Saviour
In a humble stable."

"Gu ceartas a dhìoladh
'S gu saoradh o phiantaibh;
'S an lagh a choilìonadh
Mar dh'iarradh on òige."

"To establish justice
And to free from pain;
And to fulfill the law
As promised since yore."

Bha reulta na h-oidhche
Mar chomharra cinnteach
'S i falbh le a soillse,
Ro Dhraoidhean an dòchais.

The night star
As a certain sign
Travelled with its light,
Guiding the Wise Men.

Bha thrusgan cho suarach
'S e paisgte mu chuairt da,
'S cha sheòmar duin'-uasail
A fhuair E gu còmhnaidh.

Modest was the cloth
In which He was swaddled,
Nor did a gentleman's abode
Give Him shelter.

Cho luaithe chaidh inns' do	As soon as news was given
Luchd-àitich na tìre,	To the local people,
Bha 'n cridhe fo mhì-ghean,	They were appalled
An Rìgh gun bhith dòigheil.	That the King was in such a state.
Thàinig guth anns an oidhche	A voice in the night came
Gu Iòsaph: "Gabh greum air	To Joseph: "Prepare
Is falbh leis an naoidhean –	To leave with the baby –
Tha nàimhdeas cho mòr da!"	For there is great danger!"
Bha 'n sgeul ud cho prìseil,	That story was so precious
Cha d' fhan i san tìr sin;	That it did not remain in that land;
Tha i 'g imeachd sna h-Innsibh	It is spreading in India
'S h-uile mìr den Roinn-Eòrpa.	And all over Europe.
Is thàinig i 'n taobh sa,	It arrived here,
Cha d' fhàgadh air chùl i:	For it was not ignored:
Tha slàinte ri fhaotainn	But gives comfort (health)
Do dh'aois is do dh'òige.	To old and young alike.
Cha dèan beatha no bàs e,	Neither life nor death
No nì eile 'n làthair –	In this world
Ar sgaradh gu bràth	Can ever separate us
O Àrd-rìgh na glòire.	From the High-king of glory.
Chan fhaca 's cha chuala,	Never seen, never heard,
Chan urrainn neach luaidh air –	Nobody can ever describe
'N sonas tha shuas ann	The happiness that reigns there
Don t-sluagh a gheibh còir air.	For those who are worthy of it.

47. A Trouserload of Eggs!

There are numerous accounts of the islanders' hospitality to survivors of shipwrecks. By contrast, others of their folktales told of how they dealt with visitors who arrived intending to steal what they regarded as their property. The following tale, based on an incident which, according to Martin, took place in 1695, was heartily appreciated by local audiences. It demonstrates the natives' sense of ownership of the archipelago's natural resources.

The weather at the beginning of June was fair. Six men took a boat out to the Dùn for the purpose of collecting eggs. They secured their boat in Geodha nan Ruideag (Kittiwakes' Gully) and started to work. While there, they saw a well-appointed ship sail into Village Bay and anchor half a mile from the village.

Passengers and crew could be seen on deck, enjoying the fine scenery of Hiort.

Ashore, the locals were offended by the strangers' reluctance to engage with them and considered it ill-mannered that they should choose to watch the village from afar through binoculars. It so happened that the six egg-collectors on the Dùn were not reaping as bountiful a harvest as they would have wished. They had finished at the Seilg-Gheodha (Hunt Gully) and had reached above Gob na Muice where they expected the harvest to be better. But instead of hearing the chiming of a thousand happy kittiwakes sitting on their nests, they came upon three strangers helping themselves to property which the islanders considered to be theirs. One of the strangers was sitting at the oars of a cock-boat. The second stranger was robbing nests on the cliff-face. The third, bare-bottomed, was using his tarpaulin trousers as a receptacle for the eggs collected.

"Now," whispered an elderly St Kildan, "it seems typical of strangers who refuse to give us the time of day to try to steal the very food from our mouths."

"Just so!" said another. "But, as we know to our cost, the world is made up of *uachdarain* (top-dogs) and *iochdarain* (underlings). For once, we are the ones who are more elevated than the strangers, so let's show them our mettle!"

The tarpaulin trousers, brimful of eggs, were about to be lifted on to the strangers' cock-boat when thundering, sparking rocks began to fall from the cliff-top. Never did a cock-boat leave the Dùn so swiftly and never was seen such an energetic rower as that bare-bottomed fellow, who must surely have thought that St Kilda was in the throes of a mighty earthquake!

With their cargo of eggs secure in sheepskin sacks, the islanders returned to the Village in high spirits. In an era when the islanders' mode of dress was 'the girded plaid', the sailor's tarpaulin trousers were regarded as a trophy and a reminder that judgment and vengeance are most appropriate when meted out from above!

48. Calum MacQueen

Calum MacQueen, born on 25th December 1828, was known to the people of Hiort as Calum Fhionnlaigh Mhòir. His father was Finlay MacQueen and his mother Christina Ferguson.

According to Calum's autobiography, Finlay, his paternal great-grandfather, was 'probably from North Uist' and was regarded as being 'well to do' when he visited Hiort and fell in love with a local girl. Finlay and the girl were married and had a son, John (Calum's grandfather), who 'spent three years in college'. The identity of the college and the subjects studied are not given.

Calum's mother was Christina, daughter of John Ferguson, a St Kildan. She and Finlay MacQueen were married in 1822 at a ceremony conducted by the famous evangelist, the Rev John MacDonald of Ferintosh (the Apostle of the North).

At that time, the houses were huddled together as an unorganized group. Writing his autobiography in Australia, Calum recalled that, when he was aged eight, ten surveyors arrived on Hiort to divide into crofts the islanders' arable land, which in total consisted of around fifty acres. Lots were cast and the head of each family had to identify with the croft allocated by that method. He was also required to help with the building of a new house for each family. In this, the community was supported with material help from the Rev Neil MacKenzie, who had been given gifts of money for that purpose by Sir Thomas Dyke Ackland and other well-wishers. The crofts or lots were long and narrow and extended from the shore to Gàrradh a'Bhaile – the drystone dyke at the foot of the hills behind the Village.

© The National Trust For Scotland

The steward: a foreigner who wielded authority in the island

© Ewan Garth MacQueen

Calum MacQueen

Calum's father owned a few head of cattle and had more sheep than anyone else. In addition to his sheep on Hiort, he had about 200 sheep on Boreray. He owned six or seven horses, which he bred and sold locally. In summer, about twenty men used to visit Soay to get the wool from the large number of sheep free-roaming on the island. In the 1840s, the population of Soay sheep was reckoned to be between 1000 and 1400, all of which belonged to the proprietor. According to Calum, the animals were in poor condition and worth less than half the money paid for a good sheep reared on Hiort. The St Kildans were not required to pay the Steward for their first ten sheep they owned; but for more than ten were required to pay annually one shilling and six pence each. They also paid £5 annually if they had sheep on Boreray. Each household was allowed to own one cow free of charge, but for additional cattle the owners were charged seven shillings per head per annum. The families also had to pay thirty shillings for the use of their crofts, and between them £35 for the privilege of fowling.

Martin describes the St Kildan as living in

> *innocency and simplicity, purity, mutual love and cordial friendship …*
> *free of envy and deceit, and dissimulation.*

MacAulay is less effusive in his praise. He said that some of them were

> *rather free of vices than possessed of virtues.*

When it came to paying tax to the Steward, it was deemed acceptable to dissemble when reporting the number of sheep they owned. In their dealings with the estate, deceit was excusable, whereas swearing, fornication and stealing from one another was not.

Most of the family's income came from the sale of tweed woven within the home. Christina, Calum's mother, owned two spinning-wheels and spun the wool from the family's sheep. In winter, Calum's father used his loom to weave into tweed the yarn spun by his wife. Spinning and weaving were a cottage industry which kept the married couples of St Kilda busy in winter, but also in spring and summer when foul weather kept everybody indoors.

Because of poor weather conditions in winter and spring, fishing by boat was restricted to the summer and autumn. Species in abundance in the seas around St Kilda included cod, ling, pollack, bream, halibut, turbot, skate, mackerel and herring. The Steward bought salted cod and ling at 'four shilling a tail'. The islanders owned two herring-nets, a small and a large, which they set in the morning and collected in the evening. They netted only as much as they themselves could use. Long before the inception of steam-driven trawlers, fishing-smacks from Lewis, Harris and Uist visited the waters of St Kilda during spells of good weather. MacQueen recalls:

> *There were always fishing boats on our shores and they would only have to fish there for a couple of days until they were fully loaded.*

As in the other islands of the Outer Hebrides, *creagach* (fishing from the rocks) was a favourite pastime. *Carbhanaich* (bream) and *liùth* (pollack) were the two species most popular.

On his last visit in 1828, the Rev John MacDonald of Ferintosh baptised a number of children, including Calum, who could remember the occasion clearly:

> *I was able to walk down to the church by myself.*

Following the first visit of MacDonald of Ferintosh, there was a religious revival. In 1841 there was another

> *great revival, following which, little work was done by the islanders for two years.*

In spite of their regard for their minister, the islanders decided to join the Free Church.

Since the end of the eighteenth century, the policy of evicting the native people of the Highlands and Islands from their land – the Clearances – had continued in full swing. News of the harrowing events taking place elsewhere reached Hiort and gave rise to a great deal of anxiety. The St Kildans were a religious, law-abiding people who felt that they were, at all times, under scrutiny by the Almighty. In 1830, when the Rev Neil MacKenzie became their resident minister, they regarded him as 'God-sent'. They came to rely on him as their spiritual leader, teacher, doctor, adviser and friend. However, he was an employee of the Established Church, which was funded by wealthy landowners – the very people whose creation of sheep-farms and sporting-estates was the root cause of the Clearances. By contrast, the Free Church was born out of the suffering of the oppressed people. It was funded by them and its ministers were appointed by them. In the north and west of Scotland,what became known as the Disruption of 1843 involved a mass exodus of disaffected members from the Established Church.

MacKenzie remained faithful to the Established Church, which claimed to own the island's church and manse. Typical of many such conflicts in the Protestant churches of the Highlands and Islands in the course of our own lifetime, the quarrel caused untold unhappiness in a community which until then had operated as a clan of interdependent families.

On Hiort, there was a rumour that the families were about to be evicted. MacLeod, the proprietor, told his Steward to give the islanders an assurance that on no account, for debt or for anything else, would that ever happen. In spite of that, some of the older islanders felt under threat because of their having 'come out' – that is, having turned their backs on the Established Church. Calum MacQueen recalls,

> *... I remember the father of Ewen Gillies ... was excited over the land question and said he reckoned the people had made a mistake in coming out. He said, 'If it had not been for that, we would have been on our land from eternity to eternity.' Ewen Gillies was one of the principal movers in coming away. After he was gone, Malcolm MacDonald turned to me and said, 'Is that not an ignorant man?' On another occasion, he was speaking in this style and his son reminded him that he was the second to sign for the Free Church*

> *'Yes,' he said, 'but I did not know what I was doing ...'*

When Calum was about twenty-three years of age, a deputation from the Free Church visited Hiort for the purpose of appointing a teacher. The officials arrived in a yacht – probably one owned by the Marquis of Breadalbane, a member of the deputation. 'A Mr MacGilvray from Glasgow' (also a visitor) purchased all the tweeds on the island, giving two (old) pence per yard more than the price normally paid by the factor.

There were three candidates for the post of teacher: Calum Ferguson, Finlay MacQueen and Calum MacQueen. The first two were married men; the last was the candidate favoured by the island's elders.

Calum MacQueen was ferried out to the yacht to be 'examined'. He was asked to read a passage from an English Bible, and after he had done so, he was offered the post. After teaching the children for about a year, he relinquished his duties three days before he left for Melbourne, Australia.

© Ewan Garth MacQueen

The church and manse in Brighton

© Ewan Garth MacQueen

Calum MacQueen (seated) is third from the left, and on his left is is brother-in-law, Donald MacSween, who came from Raasay. Behind Calum is his son, the Rev Finlay MacQueen. This photograph was taken around 1910, when Calum was almost 82. His wife had died in 1905.

49. The Barque *Priscilla* – 1852

In 1852, seventeen ships left for Australia with approximately 2,600 passengers most of whom were from the Highlands. The *Priscilla* sailed from Liverpool on the 13th October 1852 with 302 passengers on board, thirty-six of them from St Kilda. The St Kildans' lack of immunity to viral infections was to prove catastrophic.

Among the passengers crowded below decks there was already a variety of diseases, including measles, scarletina, dysentery, mesenteric fever and gastric influenza. Within a few days of the *Priscilla*'s leaving Liverpool, there was an outbreak of measles which resulted in the death of about eighty passengers, mostly children and old people. Calum MacQueen and his mother were among those infected, but both survived.

In the space of three months, forty-one passengers died on the *Priscilla*, a proportion more typical of the loss of life on slave-ships carrying men and women from Africa to the sugar plantations of America. Of the thirty-six St Kildans, eighteen died – ten adults and eight children.

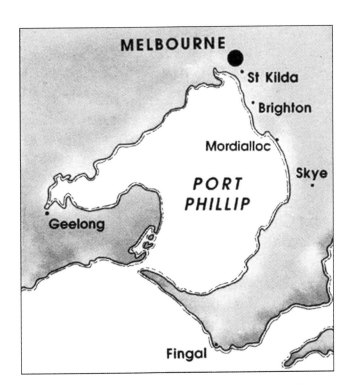

Those who left.

MacQueen

	Finlay (58)	survived
	Christina (50)	survived
	Calum (24)	survived
†	Rachel (19)	died of measles, 16 October
	John (13)	survived

MacQueen

†	Finlay (44)	died of dysentery 26 October
†	Catherine (44)	died of mesenteric fever, 30 October
	Donald (18)	survived
	Marion (16)	survived
	Catherine (12)	survived
	Anna (9)	survived
†	Neil (7)	survived
†	Finlay (4)	died of marasmus, 21 February, 1853
	Mary (1)	died of measles and dysentery, 2 December

Ferguson

	Calum (31)	survived
†	Catherine (23)	died of scarletina, 9 February, 1853
†	Mary (3)	died of dysentery and measles, 6 December, 1852

MacCrimmon

†	Donald (32)	died of dysentery, 14th October, 1852
†	Anna (32)	died of debility, 25 January, 1853
†	Marion 9)	died of dysentery and measles, 23 October, 1852
†	Mary (6)	died of dysentery and measles, 22 October, 1852
†	Donald (5)	died of dysentery and measles, 22 October, 1852
†	Christina (1)	died of dysentery and measles, 27 October, 1852

MacDonald

†	Roderick (47)	died of dysentery and measles, 11 October, 1852
†	Marion (48)	died of dysentery and measles, 14 October, 1852

MacDonald

	Neil (22)	survived
†	Catherine (51)	died of dysentery and measles, 17 October, 1852
	Ann (15)	survived

Morrison

†	Mary (57)	died of gastric fever, 9 October, 1852

Ferguson

	Hector (35)	survived
	Mary	survived

Gillies

	Ewen (27)	survived
	Margaret (28)	survived
†	Mary (1)	died of dysentery and measles, 3 December, 1852

† deceased

© Mary Evans Picture Library

Meal-time on board an emigrant ship

The suffering on board the *Priscilla* was unimaginable. During the first few weeks, many of her 302 passengers crowded below decks were seasick as the little ship ploughed through heavy seas and listed heavily in howling winds. She slowly sailed through the Irish Sea, southwards along the coasts of Wales and Devon, past the Lizard and then into the tumultuous currents of the Bay of Biscay. Passenger after passenger succumbed to disease, and their remains, in weighted sail-cloth, were discarded in the sea. Brief religious services were held for each one, but as the voyage progressed into the sub-tropics and then into the airless heat of the equatorial latitudes, the survivors became ever weaker and the memorial services ever shorter. Nonetheless, each morning and evening, the St Kildans continued the practice of holding family worship – *Gabhail an Leabhair* – at which a passage from the Bible was read and a precented psalm sung. In the disease-ridden gloom below decks, the sonorous delivery of the Gaelic reading and the defiant sound of congregational singing offered comfort to the living and the dying.

The *Priscilla* entered Port Phillp Bay on 19 January 1853. In all, forty-two passengers failed to reach their destination. Most of them died on the voyage; others at the quarantine-station. The majority of immigrants were government-sponsored, many of them from the Isle of Skye. The St Kildans were fare-paying passengers but were not given special consideration while on the *Priscilla*.

In September 1852, Donald and Anna MacCrimmon, both aged thirty-two, had left Hiort with their four children, looking forward to succeeding in a young country on the far side of the globe. Tragically, within days of leaving home waters, Donald and the four children died and were buried at sea. Only Anna saw the sunlit land of Victoria. But she was allowed to see it only from a distance. She was immediately detained on the *Lysander*, the quarantine ship anchored at Port Phillip Heads.

A mere shadow of the bright-eyed, happy young woman who had left her native Hiort, Anna had witnessed her husband and four children die within a fortnight of their leaving Liverpool. Her grief was such that she ate scarcely any food in the final weeks of the voyage. Six days after boarding the *Lysander*, she died of marasmus, a disease resulting from a lack of nourishment.

Finlay MacQueen, Calum's father, had been the owner of horses, cattle, sheep and a tweed-making loom, and had probably been the most prosperous man on Hiort. For the passage to Melbourne, he had paid '£120 or £130', a relatively large sum for a St Kildan.

In his autobiography,* Calum scarcely mentions his father, who must surely have deeply regretted selling his island property in exchange for a perilous voyage and an uncertain future under the blaze of the Australian sun. In spite of his physical strength and youthful thirst for adventure, Calum appears to have been dismayed by what he first saw of the 'Land Of Sunshine and Golden Opportunity':

> *At the Quarantine Station, we built mia-mias of ti-trees. I saw no buildings ... A marquee was sent from Melbourne ... I attended a service conducted by Dr MacDonald there and I conducted a Gaelic service after he had gone. There were about 1000 people there, mostly Highlanders. We came, after about five weeks, in the* Priscilla *up to Melbourne*

---

* Entitled *St Kilda Heritage*, edited by Kelman and Ewen G. McQueen, an autobiography of Calum MacCuithinn was published by the Scottish Genealogy Society in 1995

50. 'Goldrush'

By 1850, about 150,000 convicts had been transported from Britain to Australia. The peak year was 1833, when thirty-six ships transported nearly 7,000 persons. By the mid-1850s, the transportation of criminals to Australia had slowed down.

In January 1851, Dr Hermann Bruhn, a German immigrant, wrote to the governor of the state of Victoria, Australia, confirming that there was gold-bearing quartz on a sheep-farm owned by Donald Cameron at Clunes. James Esmond, who already had mining experience on the Californian goldfields, went up to Clunes with mining equipment and had little trouble in discovering a rich vein of gold. His discovery triggered a goldrush. As letters and rumours circulated throughout the world, huge numbers of men journeyed to Australia, eager to make their fortune. By the end of 1851, over 30,000 immigrants had arrived from Britain, Europe, America and China. In the decade following the discovery of gold, the population of Victoria grew from 76,000 to half a million, nearly half of Australia's population. The goldrush brought hundreds of diggers every week. Among them were gangs of criminals determined to become rich, but not necessarily by digging for gold! As the St Kildan immigrants were soon to discover, the maelstrom of aggression and lawlessness which they had entered was very different from the introspective, timorous little community which they had abandoned.

Margaret was the daughter of Ruairidh MacDonald, a church elder whose enthusiasm for the Calvinist doctrine of the Free Church made him a pillar of St Kildan society. In 1851, when she was aged nineteen, she married twenty-four year-old Ewen Gillies. A year later, the young couple sold their furniture and croft at No. 26 for £17 and, with the other brave thirty-four islanders, set off for Australia. They both survived the voyage on the hapless *Priscilla* and, after that, their detention in quarantine. Having been pronounced 'sound in mind and limb', they re-boarded the *Priscilla* and were taken up to the port of Melbourne.

As the *Priscilla* approached her destination, the passengers standing on the deck must have been surprised by the sight of five prison hulks moored at Hobson's Bay. The authorities did not have enough shore accommodation to house the sudden influx of criminals who had arrived, hoping to 'get rich quick'. An English immigrant who arrived in the same year wrote:

> *Our first sight of Melbourne from the vessel's deck had not given us a favourable impression. The buildings appeared low and mean, the country road looked barren and parched, and indeed the open parts of the bush land about Melbourne did not improve on a nearer view ... The streets looked very strange with poorly lit shops and crowds of people.*

While men were streaming out to the diggings at the goldfields, there was a chronic shortage of men willing to work on roads and building-sites. Mr Walstab, who owned a brickworks, met the immigrants at Melbourne and recruited a number of labourers, including three of the St Kildans: Ewen Gillies, Calum MacQueen and Calum Ferguson. His brick-making factory was at Brighton, a settlement some twenty miles from the port of Melbourne. Ewen Gillies was accompanied by his wife Margaret; Calum MacQueen by his parents and his thirteen-year old brother, John. Calum Ferguson was on his own, his wife having died at the quarantine station.

The three young men were kept busy splitting wood 'for brick burning, etc.' – hard, exhausting work in the heat of the Victorian winter, when average daily temperatures were about 20 degrees Celsius. Employment in the heat and smoke of the brickworks was better than the alternative – unemployment, and possibly destitution.

Of the three St Kildan labourers, Ewan Gillies, with his wife to support, was the unhappiest. Whereas Calum MacQueen and Calum Ferguson continued for six months to meet their employer's demand for productivity, Ewan was restive and inclined to swing the lead! Catching him sitting on a haystack one day when he ought to have been working, Mr Walstab called him bone-lazy and sacked him.

When the work at Brighton petered out, the St Kildans, including the Gillieses, moved to Mordialloc, about twenty miles south east of Brighton, and found employment with another brick-maker surnamed MacDonald, 'a splendid employer'. There they were taught how to make bricks, and by the time the work petered out they had produced 40,000.

Next, the three St Kildan labourers joined a squad of men draining a swamp called the Double Lagoon. They were paid ten shillings per day. As before, Ewen Gillies was unhappy with his conditions of employment but, as he proved, laziness was not his problem. Gold-fever had become an epidemic and Ewen, like most of the fit young men in Australia, had become heavily infected. It was only a matter of time before he gave in to the urge to buy a shovel and gold-pan and join the scores of thousands living in tent-cities in the bush. At last, he bade his employer and compatriots farewell and, with his wife, moved into Melbourne.* The rest of the St Kildan community heard nothing of Ewan Gillies for several years.

According to rumours circulating in Melbourne, men were returning from the diggings having become rich overnight. Ewen Gillies went out and bought tools, a tent and a few days' supply of food and headed off into the bush. It was to be his first sortie in a treasure-hunt that was to last most of his lifetime.

---

* Trying to cross some roads in summer sometimes proved to be dangerous. Occasionally, obstructions such as gullies, tree stumps and mud-pits, resulting from the traffic of bullocks and wagons in the dry season, caused fatal accidents. In 1856 the Argus newspaper reported that a man had struggled until he perished in six feet of water and slimy mud in Spencer Street. Reports of drowning in streets were not uncommon through to the 1860s. Thanks to the prosperity brought by the gold, some of Melbourne's most important public institutions were established in the 1850s and the foundations laid for three of its most impressive buildings: Victoria's House of Parliament, Melbourne University and the Melbourne Public Library

It is not known where in the diggings Ewan Gillies first tried his luck. The nearest settlement in the goldfield was at Ballarat*, and it is quite likely that he would have spent at least some of his time there. But wherever he pitched his tent, he soon discovered that men digging for gold had a heavy price to pay. Indeed, some paid with their lives.

After a few months taking care of their first child, Margaret Gillies was overjoyed when her husband walked into their home one day with a bag full of pound coins hidden in his backpack. Temptation to return to the diggings was strong, but reports of continuing violence and corruption on the goldfields persuaded Ewan that he should find a less hazardous way of making a living. Ewan may have heard that his friend Calum MacQueen had begun to invest in land. In any case, he decided to purchase a farm. After a few months, he discovered that the cash returns from the sale of vegetables was meagre compared with what could be earning at the diggings.

Margaret presented him with a second child just as Ewan ran out of money. He sold the farm and, leaving his wife and children with a sizeable sum of money, he set off for New Zealand in search of more gold.

Margaret waited for month after month hoping that her husband would return. After a year, during which she did not receive any letters from him, she began to doubt that she would ever see him again. Having been absent for two years, Ewan suddenly reappeared and was flabbergasted to find that his wife had remarried.

During Ewen Gillies's absence from the St Kildan community, Calum MacQueen was married to Mary MacSwain**, who, together with her family, had emigrated from the Isle of Raasay. The newly-weds returned from Mordialloc to Brighton and bought a block of land. Having fenced his land, Calum built a house which had four rooms. Its exterior was of weatherboard, 'lined with lathes and filled in between with clay. Roof was shingles'.

* The diggers objected to having to pay the state a licence fee whether or not they found gold and they deeply resented the brutal way in which that state law was enforced. Rumours circulated of corrupt goldfields officials. The tension came to a head on the Ballarat Diggings in 1854 when soldiers attacked and killed twenty-four of the diggers who were determined to work independent of state interference. When a local publican was acquitted on a murder charge, the diggers were convinced that the verdict resulted from the corruption of the magistrate. They burned the publican's hotel to the ground. The posting of additional troops in Ballarat did not quell ill-feeling. Instead, it inflamed the diggers' sense of injustice. They burned their licences and built a flimsy stockade to protect themselves from sudden attack. Feeling confident that the authorities would not send soldiers to fight against them on a Sunday, many of the diggers went home on the Saturday evening of December 2, 1854. At dawn on the following day, troops swooped on the poorly defended stockade and killed twenty-two diggers. Four soldiers were also killed. The skirmish heralded one of the most important turning-points in Australia's short history.

** The MacSwains (or MacSwans as they were called before they emigrated) came from the Isle of Raasay. Calum MacQueen's grandson Malcolm visited Raasay in 1912 while awaiting a boat to take him to St Kilda. The editors of MacQueen's autobiography say, 'He was told that the MacSwans could trace back their ancestry to the Norwegian King who, many hundreds of years previously, had annexed the Raasay and Skye. In 1851, 129 people left Raasay in a single day. Apparently, not all the people went willingly. The MacSwans told of the people being put by force into the boats going to the mainland though 'clutching to the grass on the hillside to save themselves.' The present-day MacSweens of the Harris acknowledge Raasay as their ancestral home and Suaibhne as the patronymic of Clann 'ic Suain.

As already stated in the part of his autobiography dealing with his experiences in Australia, Calum MacQueen rarely mentions his father, who, one suspects, never recovered from the experience of the passage and his subsequent detention at the quarantine station.

One can imagine that, as he sat with his wife in the marquee that was, temporarily, their home, Finlay MacQueen yearned for the cool, showery Atlantic winds of Hiort and the loud chatter of the fowlers as they set off for the stacks to 'steal birds'. On the other hand, he and his wife may have felt relieved that they had escaped the oppressive, relentless debate of St Kildan church politics and the pervasive anxiety that stemmed from them. Finlay died in 1854 and was buried in the English Church cemetery at Brighton.

Whether or not Ewan Gillies tried to renew his friendship with his St Kildan compatriots is not known. It seems that he left Victoria in high dudgeon. He sailed from Melbourne on a voyage that took him to San Francisco in California. No doubt he was well aware that, in 1848, a goldrush had started in that state. Surprisingly, however, when he arrived in the USA, he did not set off into the hills with his panning equipment. Instead, he joined the Union army and fought in the Civil War. When they were off duty, the soldiers who sat with him drinking in saloons stirred his mind with stories of men who had gone into the foothills of the Rockies and returned with a fortune in gold. They were all tempted to follow suit.

On duty one night, in 1861, Ewan slipped away from his unit and, risking being caught as a deserter, travelled west to California and joined the throng looking for the Sacramento River, and particularly, the place where the gold had first been discovered. He found that thousands of men suffering from gold fever had preceded him and were lining the banks of the river and its tributaries, panning for nuggets. Ewan worked in the wilds for many months and found so many gold nuggets that, when he returned to the town of Sacramento, he began to worry that his good fortune might bring him to the attention of the authorities. He realized that, with the army making an example of deserters, the wisest thing to do was to leave California altogether. With a sizeable haul of dollars, he sailed from San Francisco to Melbourne and went in search of his former wife and his children. He engaged a lawyer and sued his wife for desertion. Surprisingly, the court found in his favour and gave him parental control of his children. Without further ado, Ewan went to a shipping office and booked a passage for himself and his children on a ship bound for Glasgow.

In 1871, Ewan and his children returned to St Kilda. The islanders took the three newcomers to their hearts. Nonetheless, it is unlikely that the children were happy with the prospect of living on Hiort in a climate and on a diet very different from those to which they were accustomed. After only a month on Hiort, Ewan and his children bade farewell to the islanders and boarded a smack which took them to the Isle of Skye. Thence, they made their way to Glasgow, where they stayed only briefly before sailing to the USA.

Once his children grew to adulthood, Ewan Gillies began to feel the urge to return to his native heath. In 1884, aged fifty-seven, he landed back in St Kilda and found that there were few left who cared to remember him. He dressed differently from the islanders and he was happier speaking English than Gaelic. He had become full of himself and, in the eyes of the young islanders, unbearably opinionated. In short, he had become a *Gall*! He spoke so much about his adventures in the Golden State of California that they nicknamed him

California, a pejorative term which passed into St Kildan lore as a definition for anybody who was bumptious and happier to tell than to listen. But there was one girl on Hiort who was not bored by California's stories. She was sixteen years of age and was captivated by his descriptions of *Tìr an Òir agus nam Measan* ('The Land of Gold and Fruit'). They fell in love, were married, and sailed away to the USA, never to return.

Footnote Calum MacQueen put down roots in Victoria. In 1888, *The Metropolis: Its Providers Past and Present* describes his achievements as follows:

> *Mr MacQueen has eleven acres of land at South Brighton, twenty seven acres at Cheltenham managed by his son, and 117 acres at Colac, let under lease for three years. His suburban property is very valuable as he has spared no trouble in the cultivation of the land and the planting of trees. He has made fruit-growing a speciality and, a few years ago, took first prize at the Dandenong show.*

© J. Sands

51. Partial Recovery

After the emigration to Australia, the population of St Kilda was reduced to a little over seventy. The burden of gathering birds and eggs from the cliffs was left to a few. From day to day, the islanders awaited news from the emigrants, but for many months, none came. Not surprisingly, when news of the catastrophe finally reached them, the St Kildans were inconsolable. They retreated indoors and spent days by their firesides grieving the loss of their kinsfolk.

Ten years after the exodus to Australia, the community was struck by yet another tragedy. In 1860, a wealthy visitor arranged for a large boat, called the *Dargavel*, to be presented to the St Kildans. It was a gift intended to encourage the islanders to develop their fishing skills.

In April 1863, the *Dargavel* left Hiort with seven men and one woman on board. When last seen from the top of Oiseabhal, the boat, under sail, was making excellent progress towards her intended destination in North Uist. In the evening the wind changed direction from west to south and increased in strength.

The goods which the *Dargavel* was carrying were, in terms of the St Kildan economy, very valuable: cloth, salt fish and other native produce which the islanders hoped would fetch £80 at Balranald. Some of the travellers also carried paper money which they wished to exchange for gold coins. Nothing was heard of the fate of the boat until mid-May, when three English fishing-boats anchored in Village Bay. The local people gathered round to watch as the skippers of the fishing-boats played quoits on the *Gaineamh*, the sandy strip at the west end of the bay. As ever, the islanders wanted news of the outside world, particularly news of the fate of those who had departed on the *Dargavel*. It so happened that there was one Gaelic-speaking crewman on one of the smacks, and he came forward to report that articles of clothing from a sunken boat had been washed up on the shore at Mealasta in Lewis. The shock of hearing the news, so casually delivered, caused the St Kildans present to give vent to their grief by wailing and wringing their hands – a show of sorrow which moved the visitors to laughter.

The visitors' callous disregard for the St Kildans' anguish caused a great deal of anger both on the island and elsewhere. Duncan Kennedy, the resident catechist, who had spoken to some of the crewmen, had not noted the names of the fishing-boats. However, the St Kildans themselves maintained that, although one of their crewmen spoke Gaelic, the fishing-boats were definitely out of London.

When James McRaild, the Factor, visited the island, he brought articles of clothing which had been recovered from the cave at Mealasta. They proved to belong to those who had travelled on the *Dargavel*. The sight of the clothes 'torn as if in a struggle', persuaded some of the St Kildans that their fellow-islanders had been murdered. Sir John MacLeod, at that time the proprietor of the island, initiated an investigation at Uig, in Lewis, but nothing to suggest foul play was ever discovered.

Three of the seven men lost on the *Dargavel* were married and, in addition to their widows, left seven children. The other four, in the prime of life, were skilful fowlers. They were survived by mothers, sisters and other dependent relatives. The woman who had perished was forty-nine year-old Betty MacDonald, nee Scott, a native of Lochinver in Sutherland, who had gone to Hiort as a young girl to be a servant to the Rev.Neil MacKenzie. She was married to Calum MacDonald of No. 8 and was the only islander who could speak English. According to Seton, she was

> *in other respects intelligent and superior and was sometimes called the 'Queen of St Kilda'.*

The value of the cargo on the *Dargavel* suggested that, by 1861, the islanders had begun to recover from the loss of a third of its population nine years earlier. The recovery continued into the 1870s, as is shown by Sands's table of St Kildan exports for 1875.

		£	s	d
Cloth	227 yards of 47 inches and a thumb	25	10	0
Blankets	403 yards of 47 inches and a thumb	27	0	0
Fulmar Oil................	566 gallons	45	6	0
Tallow.....................	414 lb	6	12	0
Black Feathers	1494 lb	26	5	0
Grey Feathers	1179 lb	17	10	0
Cheese....................	646 lb	11	9	0
Fish	1080 marketable	31	10	0
One year-old cattle	20 head	60	0	0

52. The St Kilda Mail

The Gulf Stream Drift originates in the Gulf of Mexico and crosses the Atlantic to wash the coasts of Europe as far north as Iceland and Norway. Known to the St Kildans as *Casair a' Chuain* (The Ocean Current), the Gulf Stream Drift brought to their shores many different kinds of flotsam, ranging from wreckage of sunken ships to *cnothan bhachaill* (Moluccan beans)* which had travelled more than 2,000 miles across the Atlantic from the tropical lands around the Gulf of Mexico.

In mid-January, 1877, the Austrian ship *Peti Dubrovacki* foundered near St Kilda. Nine members of her crew landed at Hiort and were given shelter by the inhabitants. As a result of having ten extra mouths to feed, the islanders' store of food began to run alarmingly low and starvation became a frightening prospect. John Sands, who was revisiting the island at the time, was puzzled by the provenance of a certain kind of reed used by the St Kildans in their looms. On being told that the reeds had come with *Casair a' Chuain*, he concluded that the same ocean current might carry a message to Uist. He fashioned a small 'canoe which he had hewn out of a log'. In a pickle-jar that fitted perfectly into the hold, he enclosed a message appealing for immediate help. With nothing else to do, the sailors marooned on the island helped Sands to caulk the deck and to ballast the canoe with iron nails. A hot iron was used to print the words 'Open this' on the deck. Finally, Sands rigged a small sail on what was, in effect, the first issue of the 'St Kilda Mail' and launched it on the 5th February. It was discovered on a sandbank at Poolewe on 27th February, five days after the *Jackal* arrived at Hiort to take the shipwrecked mariners and John Sands back to the mainland. News of the emergency on Hiort had reached the authorities nearly three weeks before Sands's canoe was discovered at Poolewe. It was carried by a lifebelt from the *Peti Dubrovacki* which the ship's captain had launched from Hiort on 30th January. A bottle carrying a message addressed to the Austrian Consul was attached to to the lifebelt. It arrived at Birsay in Orkney nine days later.

Three months after the rescue, the Factor's smack brought to the island a cargo of foodstuffs, including oatmeal, tea, sugar and salt. The cost of those provisions was deducted from a donation of £100 which the Austrian government had donated in appreciation of the islanders' kindness to their citizens.

From 1877 until 1930, the Gulf Stream Drift and the prevailing south-westerly wind continued to carry St Kildans' letters to the west coast of the Outer Hebrides and, occasionally, far beyond. Together with money to cover postage, the letters were most often carried inside a jar which was secured in a hollow carved out of a roughly-shaped wooden boat and caulked with archangel tar. To catch the wind and speed the letter to its

---

* The 'Mary's nut' (Caesalpinia bonduc), native to Florida, is occasionally found on the western shores of Britain, from Cornwall in the south to Lewis in the north. Known to Gaels as *Teàrna Moire* ('the Virgin's Charm of Deliverance'), it was in bygone centuries highly prized, particularly in Catholic communities. Three of those nuts strung round the neck as a charm were commonly worn by young women. In June 1883, a Mary's nut was found in a fulmar's nest on St Kilda and is in the National Botanic Museum, Dublin.

uncertain destination, a short length of rope was used to attach the boat to a *labaid* (inflated sheep's stomach).*

As St Kilda was the property of a private individual (MacLeod of Skye), the government refused to use HMS *Jackal*, based at Stornoway, to deliver mails to Hiort. In 1878, the surveyor in charge of the Scottish division of the GPO suggested to his superiors in London that arrangements should be made to ensure that there were mail deliveries to the island in spring and in the autumn; a third delivery could be by the Factor during his rent-collecting visit in summer. The suggestion was ignored. The delivery and collection of St Kildan mail continued to depend on the goodwill of ships' captains. By 1895, the Post Office was paying £500 to the owners of the passenger-ships the *Dunara Castle* and the *Hebridean* for providing fortnightly deliveries of mail during the summer months. For nine months of the year, the St Kildans were unable to communicate with their families and friends abroad except by the haphazard, uncertain method devised by John Sands.

The inception of steam-trawlers provided a solution to the problem. From about 1890, trawlers from Fleetwood and Aberdeen regularly visited St Kilda to exploit the rich fisheries of the archipelago. It was in the interest of the owners of those vessels to allow the captains to befriend the islanders and to help them whenever possible. The trawlers frequently anchored in Village Bay, sometimes to shelter from northerly gales or to give the crew an opportunity of mending gear. Steam trawlers operating inside the legal limit were reviled by communities dependent on inshore fishing. By contrast, they were seen by the St Kildans as dependable, generous friends. During the nine months when the *Dunara Castle* and the *Hebridean* withdrew from the scene, the GPO relied increasingly on Aberdeen trawlers to provide a postal service, free of charge.

In 1899, the GPO sanctioned the establishment of a sub-post office on Hiort. At first, it was housed in a room in the manse and the Rev Angus Fiddes, the minister, was appointed sub-postmaster with a salary of £5 per annum, plus bonuses. In 1906, a rural post and delivery service was introduced, with Neil Ferguson as postmaster with a salary of £10 per annum, plus £2 15s in bonuses. Sending a postcard stamped and franked on St Kilda became something that all tourists wished to do. As often as a steamer anchored in Village Bay, there was a queue of tourists at the door of the corrugated iron shack that bore the legend 'Post Office' over its door! It is said that when the population was evacuated in 1930, Neil Ferguson was the richest man on the island.

In spite of the introduction of the GPO's postal service, letters continued to be sent by the less reliable St Kilda Mail. For the most part it served to satisfy the demands of the tourists and, indeed, continued to do so until the day of the Evacuation.

---

* Heavy weather frequently carried away the marker buoys of great-lines. As late as the 1930s, a lost buoy was sometimes replaced with a *puta labaid* consisting of an inflated sheep's stomach affixed to a circular wooden lid and tarred overall.

53. Euphemia MacCrimmon

The origin of the MacCrimmon family is uncertain. One theory is that they were of Irish extraction and for several generations lived on Hiort. Members of the family are thought to have crossed from Hiort to Harris, where, according to the Bannantyre MS, they were landlords. From Harris members crossed to Skye and settled at Boreraig, two miles south of Dunvegan Head. The supposed connection with Ireland is based on the fact that there are Crimmins living in the Cork area.

Effie MacCrimmon (*Eibhrig NicCruimein*) was highly intelligent and, in the tradition of the Highland *seanchaidh*, had an inexhaustible fund of songs, *bàrdachd* and traditional tales which she could recite at the drop of a hat. One of the many tragedies of the people of Hiort is that some of their resident ministers and visiting clergy discouraged the people from recalling their cultural heritage.

Alexander Carmichael (1832-1912), born in the island of Lismore, joined the Civil Service and was influential in numerous organizations aimed at improving the lot of the people of the Highlands and Islands. In his spare time, he compiled a record of the traditions, superstitions and beliefs of contemporary Gaels. He travelled throughout the Highlands and Islands collecting hymns and incantations, which are published under the title *Carmina Gadelica*.

© Society of Antiquaries of Scotland

Euphemia MacCrimmon

Carmichael went to St Kilda in 1865, and while there, he heard about a remarkable woman who lived alone in a *taigh-dubh*. Her name was Eibhrig NicCruimein, (Euphemia MacCrimmon) and one can imagine his excitement when he heard that, so far as local history, *bàrdachd* and songs were concerned, Euphemia was more knowledgeable than anybody else on Hiort. When the minister heard that Carmichael the folklorist was going to visit Eibhrig, he objected.

> *'I don't want you to have her dredge up all these old foolish things,' he declared. 'She should be allowed to continue preparing her mind for her eternal home.'*

In spite of the minister's misgivings, Carmichael did visit Euphemia, but when he did, he was followed by a host of inquisitive adults, barking dogs and noisy children. Alasdair entered Euphemia's home and soon realized that he was in the presence of a very remarkable person who was glad of the opportunity of meeting *an srainnsear* (the stranger) and entertaining him.

One of the legends she recalled was regarding the name of a rock in the sea passage between Hiort and Soay:

> *A son of the king of Lochlann was wrecked on a rock a little to the west of St Kilda. He came ashore in a small boat and, while he was drinking out of a water-brook a little west of the present church, those who were then the inhabitants of St Kilda came on him and caught him by the back of the neck, and held his head down in the brook until he drowned.* The rock on which he was wrecked is called Sgeir Mac Rìgh Lochlain ('The Rock of the son of the King of Lochlann') until this day.*

At seventy-six years of age, Effie seemed to be able to remember every piece of poetry and story she had ever heard.

'*A laochain*,' said Effie, "you have come to the right house if you want to hear Gaelic songs and Gaelic stories! My mother and father composed a love song for each other while they were courting, long before I was born. Unfortunately, my father died shortly after he and my mother were married. He went with my grandfather to catch birds. Being young and active, he was the one below on the end of the rope killing the birds. The rock on which my grandfather was standing at the top of the cliff crumbled and both men plunged into the sea. The seabirds they had tied round their waists kept them afloat, but they were soon blown out to sea and lost. They were two whom I would have loved."

---

* If we assume that the story was inspired by an historical event, the incident may hark back to the ninth century, when the Norwegian king, Harold the Fair-haired, sent his cousin Ketil to re-establish Norse authority in the Outer Hebrides. Ketil was successful in his campaign, but after a time declared himself King of the Isles. In the end, the native people rose against their Norse overlords and slew them and their supporters.

Carmichael sang one verse of a St Kildan song he had heard many years previously. Effie smiled.

That, she said,

> *is a verse from the Còmhradh (Conversation) that my mother and father composed for each other when they were courting.*

I've often told my friends, said Carmichael,

> *that I would willingly walk forty miles just to learn the whole of the Còmhradh.*

Later he wrote:

> *Though [the songs are] not old, they have a charming simplicity and intense feeling. They are some of several which the writer took down on 22nd May, 1865 from the recitation of Eibhrig NicCruimein, cottar, aged eighty-four years, who had many old songs, stories and traditions of the island. I would have got more of those had there been peace and quiet to take them down, but this was not to be had among the crowd of naval officers and seamen and St Kilda men, women and children, and even noisier than these, St Kilda dogs, mad with excitement and all barking at once. The aged reciter was much censured for her recital of these songs and poems, and the writer for causing the old woman to stir the recesses of her memory for this lore; for the people of St Kilda have now discarded songs and music, dancing, folklore, and the stories of the foolish past. We were silenced but not subdued, and I fear that one of us was – 'Even in his penance Planning sins anew'.*

Footnote The family of MacCrimmon were renowned pipers and were hereditary pipers to the MacLeod chiefs at Dunvegan. The first MacCrimmon piper mentioned in the annals of the MacLeods was Dòmhnall Mòr (1570-1640), who was a piper and composer of great renown. He is credited with having evolved the new musical form known as *pìobaireachd* (pibroch) and which was a sophisticated form of theme and variation. One of his best known compositions is *Cumha MhicCruimein* (MacCrimmon's Lament). His son Pàdraig Mòr (1595-1670) was, in turn, regarded as the greatest piper of his generation. He composed *Cumha an Aona Mhic* ('Lament for the Only Son') but his best known work is *Cumha na Cloinne* (Lament for the Children), which he composed after seven of his eight sons died of fever in the one year. At the death of the revered MacLeod Chief Ruairidh Mòr, he composed his famous song of sorrow, *Tog Orm Mo Phìob* (Give Me My Pipes) The music of the bagpipes was not written down, but was transmitted orally by an intricate system of vocables called canntaireachd. Iain Dubh (1730-1822) was to be the last MacCrimmon of the Boreraig college. When Macleod withdrew part of his endowment, MacCrimmon left Skye in disgust. He later returned to the island and died in Glendale.

54. Courtship Conversation

The courting couple's Còmhradh (Conversation) is an expression of the composers' exuberance and vitality. It is an exultant song, reflecting the joy of being in love on a small island which, at that time, had a unique lifestyle. The *bàrdachd* of the song is inventive, making use of the island's rich specialist vocabulary, some of which was peculiar to eighteenth century St Kilda.

beidearach – *beadarach* – beloved

bligheadh – *bleaghadh* (*bainne*) – yielding milk; some cows would yield their milk only to familiar milk-hands; *a' cleith a' bhainne*: refusing to yield the milk

buit – *buthaid* – a puffin; the name usually used by the St Kildans was *buthaigir*

cuat – a lover, sweetheart

cugar – a tomcat

farchaill – (*farch-chiùil*) – a lyre

lur – delight, pleasure

luran – a beloved youth

Mhoire – Virgin Mary. The song was composed around 1780, some fifty years before the arrival of the first resident minister in a century.

smùirean – a turtle dove

Esan:

Bhuam chas-chrom, bhuam chas-dìreach,
Bhuam gach mìs is cìob is uan;
Suas mo lon, nuas mo rioba –
Chuala mis' an gug sa chuan!

Buidheachas dhan Tì, thàine na gugachan,
Thàine 's na h-eòin mhòra cuide riu;
Cailin dubh ciar-dubh, bò sa chrò.

Sèist

Bò dhonn, bò dhonn, bò dhonn bheidireach,
Bò dhonn, a rùin, a bhligheadh am bainne
    dhut,
Hò rò rù rà rì roideachag,
Cailin dubh ciar dubh, bò sa chrò!
Na h-eòin a' tighinn, cluinneam
    an ceòl!
Na h-eòin a' tighinn, cluinneam
    an ceòl!

Ise:

Nàile, 's e mo chuat am buachaill
Bhagradh am bata 's nach buaileadh!
Cailin dubh ciar-dubh, bò sa chrò, etc.

Esan:

Mhoire, 's ì mo rùn an cailin,
Ge dubh a cùl, is cùbhr' a calann!
Cailin dubh ciar dubh, etc.

He:

Away the bent-spade, away the straight spade,
Away each goat and sheep and lamb;
Bring up my rope, bring down my snare –
I have heard the gannet in the ocean!

Thanks be to God, the young birds are come,
Accompanied by the mature birds;
Dark dusky maid, a cow in the fold.

Chorus

Brown cow, brown cow, beloved brown cow,
Beloved cow that would release her milk
    to you,
Ho rò rù rà rì playful maiden,
Dark dusky maid, a cow in the fold!
The birds are approaching, let me hear
    their music!
The birds are approaching, let me hear
    their music!

She:

Truly, but my lover is a herdsman
Who would raise the stick but never strike!
Dark dusky maid, a cow in the fold.

He:

Faith, the lass is my secret love,
Though black her curls, her form is fragrant!
Dark dusky maid, etc.

Ise:

Is tu mo luran, is tu mo leannan,

Thug thu thùs dhomh 'm fulmair meala!

Cailin dubh ciar-dubh, etc.

Esan:

Is tu mo smùirean, is tu mo smeòirean,

Is mo chruit-chiùil sa mhadainn bhòidhich!

Cailin dubh ciar-dubh, etc.

Ise:

M' eudail thusa, mo lur 's mo shealgair,

Thug thu 'n-dè dhomh 'n sùl 's
        an gearrbhall.

Cailin dubh ciar-dubh, etc.

Esan:

Thug mi gaol dhut 's tu nad leanabh,

Gaol nach claon gu 'n tèid mi 's talamh.

Cailin dubh ciar-dubh, etc.

Ise:

Is tu mo chugar, is tu mo chearban,

Thug thu 'm buit dhomh 's thug an .
        gearr-bhreac

Cailin dubh ciar-dubh, etc.

Esan:

Mo shùgradh sùl thu 's mo shùgh
        sòlais,

'S m' fhairchill bhinn thu 'm beinn a' cheòthaich.

Cailin dubh ciar-dubh, etc.

She:

You're my lovely lad, you're my sweetheart,

The first to give me the honeyed fulmar!

Dark dusky maid, etc,

He:

You're my turtle-dove and my mavis;

You are my harp in the sunlit morning!

Dark dusky maid, etc.

She:

You're my treasure, my hero and my hunter,

Yesterday you gave me the gannet and
        the auk.

Dark dusky maid, etc.

He:

I loved you from your childhood days,

Love that will not wane till I am in the earth.

Dark dusky maid, etc.

She:

You're my hero, you're my basking-shark,

You gave me the puffin and the
        pied guillemot.

Dark dusky maid, etc.

He:

The smile of my eyes, my drink of
        happiness,

My sweet-sounding lyre on the misty ben.

Dark dusky maid, etc.

Ise:

Tì ghad chùmhnadh, Dùl ghad chòmhnadh,

Spiorad Naomh a bhith chùl do luin!

Cailin dubh ciar-dubh, etc.

Sèist

Bò dhonn, bò dhonn, bò dhonn bheidireach,

Bò dhonn, a rùin, a bhligheadh am bainne
dhut,

Hò rò rù rà rì roideachag,

Cailin dubh ciar dubh, bò sa chrò!

Na h-eòin a' tighinn, cluinneam
an ceòl!

Na h-eòin a' tighinn, cluinneam
an ceòl!

She:

May God keep you, Heaven protect you,

The Holy Spirit behind your rope!

Dark dusky maid, a cow in the fold!

Chorus

Brown cow, brown cow, beloved brown cow,

Beloved cow that would release her milk
to you,

Ho rò rù rà rì playful maiden,

Dark dusky maid, a cow in the fold!

The birds are approaching, let me hear
their music!

The birds are approaching, let me hear
their music!

Island knitters relaxing in the open air

Planning the next communal activity – the so-called St Kilda Parliament

55. The Rev John MacKay

In 1866, thirteen years after news of the *Priscilla* disaster reached the island, the Rev John MacKay from Lochalsh in Ross-shire arrived to minister to the islanders. He found the older islanders suffering from the *lionn-dubh*, that deep depression that overcomes close-knit communities when loved ones lose their lives. The new minister believed that, with his own unshakeable faith and wide knowledge of Scripture, he could assuage the St Kildans' dejection and sense of hopelessness, and inspire them with the Bible's promise of Salvation and Eternal Glory.

During his time on Hiort, the Rev MacKay often held services on every day of the week excepting Saturday and Monday. Attendance at his services was obligatory for his entire flock, except for the infirm and for mothers nursing children under the age of two. On Sundays, MacKay held three services: *An Ciad Searmon* at 11 a.m., *An Dara Searmon* at 2 p.m. and *A' Choinneamh* at 6 pm. Sands reckoned that the congregation spent six and a half hours in church every Sunday. Each service included the singing of two or three Psalms led by a precentor. With such a small congregation, the quality of the singing was not always pleasing to the ears of strangers who happened to be within earshot. MacKay's cynical arch-critic Robert Connell likened it to the 'baying of hyenas'.

The minister's cavalier treatment of Alexander Carmichael was in marked contrast to that of John Sands, some ten years later. Carmichael, the Gael, had come to Hiort to discover evidence of the islanders' creative genius; Sands had come with a less defined brief – that of learning about the islanders' lifestyle. The following is John Sands's account:

> *There, posted like a sentinel on a rocky bank close to the sea, his whole aim is to keep the devil out of the island. Absorbed in his duty, he forgets the loneliness of his situation ... he is content with plain fare and drinks none, is attentive to the infirm, and shares in a stealthy way what luxuries he has with them. Personally, I am indebted to him for numberless acts of friendship – kindness continued from first to last. He pressed me to live in his house and, when preferring freedom and the bagpipes, I declined his invitation, he did his utmost to render me comfortable in my own quarters. Taking him for all in all, the Free Kirk has few soldiers she has more reason to be proud of ... Nowadays, the whole population are members of the Free Church. They attend public worship three times every Sunday, and hold a prayer-meeting (which is conducted by the elders) every Wednesday night. The Sunday is indeed a day of intolerable gloom. At the sound of the bell the whole flock hurry to the church in single file, with dejected looks and eyes bent on the ground. They seem like a troop of the damned, whom Satan is driving to the bottomless pit. ... Surely religion, which promises eternal life and everlasting joy, should make believers more cheerful and not more miserable than benighted heathens who have no such consolations ... The poor St Kildans contributed £20 to the Sustentation Fund of the Free*

Church and coupled with the unprofitable way in which their trade is conducted reminds one of the passage in Scripture: 'That which the palmer-worm hath left, hath the locust eaten' (Joel i. 4) 44.

After a short time on the island, MacKay appointed elders, who automatically rose in status above the rest of the people. Their appointment led to jealousy and division, not least because they were charged with responsibility for reporting individuals suspected of wandering off the straight and narrow. Robert Connell was scathing in his condemnation of MacKay:

> *... a weak-minded pope and prime minister rolled into one, who rules the destiny of the island, and has reduced religion into a mere hypocritical formalism, finding no place in his creed for self-reliance or any of the manlier virtues ... It is nothing to Mr MacKay whether the poor people starve their crofts or neglect the fishing so long as his own silly fads are observed.*

The Rev John MacKay left Hiort in 1889, having been in his position for twenty-three years. During that time, knowledge of the Bible became the yardstick by which a person's worth was measured. To the detriment of all else, religion came to dominate the islanders' way of thinking and their way of life.

© R. C. MacLeod of MacLeod 1892 (S.S.S.)

The Rev John Mackay

56. Work Tools

When John Sands visited Hiort in 1875, he found that traditional agricultural implements had been replaced by ones similar to those used in other crofting areas. For the most part, his description of St Kildan croft implements and practices shows that there was little difference between the agricultural methods of St Kilda and those of the rest of the Outer Hebrides. One exception was that 'wooden rakes were more popular than harrows', a claim difficult to believe, as harrows with iron teeth were in use elsewhere many centuries earlier. The observation suggests that this may have been one area in which the method of preparing the ground for cereal crops had regressed from the seventeenth century, when, as Martin reported,

their harrows are of wood as are the teeth in the front also.

The old *cas-chrom*, he observed, had been stored away in the rafters, having given way to the standard spade. As in other parts of the Outer Hebrides, the main crops were oats, barley and potatoes; these were supplemented by kale and turnips grown in small walled enclosures called *iodhlainn*, on the lee side of the houses. Sickles rather than scythes were used to reap the oats. As was the custom elsewhere in the Outer Hebrides, barley was harvested by pulling the stalk out of the ground by the root. The barley was then bound into sheaves (*sguaban*) and left for about a week standing on the field in stooks (*adagan*) – twelve sheaves to the stook. It was believed that, during that period, much of the energy in the stalk was drawn up into the grain. On a dry day the sheaves were carried from the fields and stacked in a cornyard or stored in a nearby cleit. The barley lost much of its moisture during its months in storage. Whether it was stored in a cornyard or cleit, mice always took a share of the food bonanza.

Hunting for fulmar (John Sands)

In winter, work on the barley continued, but indoors. To separate the grain from the stalk, the St Kildans used a flail (*sùist*), an implement consisting of two rods, one shorter than the other, and connected by a short piece of cord.

At one time, this method of threshing was in vogue all over Europe. The threshing done, the precious grain was gathered and carefully stored in receptacles which ensured that it would remain safe from mice and mould. What remained of the stalks of the barley was also valuable. The sheaves were unbound and cut in half, the root end to be used for thatching and the other as cattle feed.

Apart from the proportion set aside for planting in the following spring, the grain of the barley and oats was ground into meal. Barley-meal and oatmeal were a staple food of the islanders.

Before milling could begin, the characteristic 'beard' of the barley had to be removed; that was done during the 'malting' or roasting process. An iron pot, half full of the grain, would be hung over a fire. When steam began to rise from it, the grain would be vigorously stirred. Contact with the hot metal caused the beard to shrivel. Having lost its moisture, the grain would gradually change in colour from golden yellow to mahogany brown.

Some St Kildans employed a different method of malting. They repeatedly plunged heated stones into the pot and then withdrew them to allow the grain to be stirred. The age-old tool used for milling both barley and oats was the quern.* John Sands reported seeing

> *a half-naked woman squatting on the floor rotating the up-stone of the quern with tremendous energy while another fed grain into the socket.*

The oatmeal and barley meal were baked into large roundels or made into porridge. Meat was sometimes added to the bubbling porridge to produce a thick broth.

In the nineteenth century, only the local minister had matches, which, as often as he lit one, were regarded as objects of wonderment. In every house a peat fire burned continuously on the hearth. If a fire became extinguished, a member of the family would hurry to the nearest house to get a burning peat by which the dead fire was rekindled. When a company of men and women went on a fowling expedition to the islands, they always took with them a supply of food and a kettle containing burning peat.

Covered with ash and damp turfs, a peat fire will continue to smoulder for many hours and glow with renewed vigour when uncovered and exposed to a draught. On long fishing expeditions, fishing-boats from the other islands of the Outer Hebrides carried an iron pot containing a 'sleeping' peat-fire (*teine tasgaidh*) – a practice not without risk.

'*S fheàirrde braich a breacadh* (a quern is the better of having its furrows deepened). A reprimand improves the conduct of one inclined to break rules, be without discipline etc.

---

* The quern was developed around 1000 BC. It consists of a pair of flat circular stones that fit one on top of the other, with the grain sandwiched in between. By using a stick placed in a hole near its outer edge, the upper stone is turned around the central axis, thus reducing the grain to the powder we call meal. An additional hole enabled new grain to be added. A major improvement was the introduction of furrows on the grinding surfaces radiating out from the centre to the outer edge. These were partly to help spread the grain evenly over the grinding surfaces and also to introduce cooling air into the grinding process. The furrows also help move the resulting meal to the outside edge.

57. Excursion to Boreray by John Sands

Young women and girls were multi-skilled. In common with their contemporaries throughout the Highlands and Islands, they were expected to spin wool, waulk tweed, carry manure in creels from the *òtrach* to the fields, grind oats and barley, pluck birds, milk the cows and sheep, make cheese, as well as bear children and look after them. The menfolk were kept equally busy throughout the year. In winter they wove cloth and tailored clothes. From February to October, they spent most of their time working the crofts, repairing their houses, attending to their animals and engaged in the demanding pursuits of fowling and fishing.

In his book, *Out Of This World*, John Sands, who spent six weeks on Hiort in 1875, describes his visit to Soay and Boreray in the company of fowlers – all of them female.

© James Smith

Boreray

On the 15th of July, a boat took a number of young women to the island of Soay to remain there for three weeks to catch puffins for the sake of their feathers which are sold to the factor for six shillings a stone. On the following day another detachment of damsels (seven in number) was carried to the island of Boreray for the same purpose; and I went with them, and returned with the boat and men. On our way thither we went round by the cliffs on the north of St Kilda, where the crew dropped their long-lines* into the sea and left them there.

In honour of the ladies, I took the pìob-mhór with me, and, sitting in the stern sheets, played some tunes, to which the men kept time with their oars. The day being calm and sunny, the crew soon became heated with their work, when the girls took their bright-coloured handkerchiefs and covered the heads of the men. They also arose from the bottom of the boat, where they had been demurely squatting, and helped the men to row – partly, I fancied, to give vent to their suppressed spirits. A jolly and picturesque crew!

Boreray is three and a quarter miles to the north of St Kilda. It rises to a height of 1072 feet above the sea and is one and three quarters in length. It is faced on all sides with cliffs, some of them very lofty; but it grows less precipitous as it ascends, and the top is covered with grass which affords pasture for a considerable number of sheep belonging to the natives. The west end of the island rises into rocky peaks. Boreray is a great resort of the Solan geese, thousands of which were flying over our heads. We landed on a sloping cliff on the south-east. One man as usual, secured by a rope, leaped from the heaving boat on to a jutting rock, and another followed, and, crawling up the cliff, sat and held the line firmly. The girls in succession then jumped into the arms of the man at the foot, who lifted them on the slope, where, by the help of the rope, they attained a level spot. Some of the men went with them to help carry their baggage, and I scrambled up with the others. By winding and hazardous ways we ascended to a height of perhaps five hundred feet, where there was a sort of natural terrace, on which stood a number of cleits or primitive-looking stone cellars used for storing birds, peats, etc. The girls were all laden with straw bags filled with stores, and one carried a kettle of burning turf in a basket on her back. They complained a little of being blàth *(warm), but stepped up the perilous ascent like goats, without the slightest symptom of fatigue or fear. 'Custom has made it to them a property of easiness'.*

* Thin rope often several metres long at intervals bearing hooks to which bait such as half herrings were attached

Whilst we all sat resting on the grass for a few minutes, the dogs had already started to catch puffins, sniffing and scratching their holes, and seizing the birds when they fluttered out. Whilst the sagacious animals pawed at one hole, they kept a watchful eye on the burrows adjacent, as if they expected the puffins to issue from them. In a few minutes some of the girls were walking about with a dozen birds dangling from their girdles. 'Look!' said a fair-haired damsel to me, as she took a live puffin from her dog, and giving its neck two gentle turns, as if it had been a stopper in a scent-bottle, held it up for my inspection, whilst with a smile of health and the joy that springs from perfect health, sparkled in her bonnie blue e'en; 'Tha e marbh – chan eil e duilich' – 'The bird is dead - it is not difficult,' – thrusting the dislocated head under her belt, away she bounded for fresh game. But although the women are useful auxiliaries, the men do not altogether depend on them, but set snares by which each will bag several hundred in a day. A few yards from where we rested, the puffins were sitting on the grassy hillside in countless numbers, and the air was alive with them and Solan geese. Although subjected to such wholesale destruction, the sea-fowl are said to be increasing – possibly in an inverse ratio with their human enemies.

I was told that there was an old hut across the hill, in which these unprotected females would reside during their stay of three weeks. Martin says, ' In the west end of the isle is the Staller's house which is much larger than the Female Warrior's ….' This is probably the house in which the young women were to live.

Of all the occupations for females, this of catching birds seems to me the strangest. It has very likely been followed from a great antiquity. I noticed that some of the girls had their Gaelic Testaments with them, and was told they would have family worship as when at home.

They wishing me 'Beannachd leat', some of the young ladies expressed a fear that a yacht would call at St Kilda in their absence, and that I would go away in her and they would see me no more: for which compliment, I played 'Cumha Mhic an Tòisich' and the doleful airs, as our boat left the craggy shore. It was the first time, one of the men remarked, that the rocks of Boreray had heard the sound of the pìob mhór for two hundred years.***

---

* MacIntosh's Lament; incidentally, the music inspired part of the theme for Dvorak's New World Symphony.

** Punitive measures taken by the Government against the Highland clans after Culloden in 1746 included the banning of bagpipe music. John Sands's visit was in 1875-77.

58. Tourists and the *Dunara Castle*

In 1877, John McCallum, a Glasgow ship-owner, advertised ten-day cruises on the SS *Dunara Castle*, visiting 'The Romantic Western Isles and Lone St Kilda'.

The public responded with enthusiasm. The ship was equipped to carry forty passengers, each paying £9.

The *Dunara Castle*'s first visit to Village Bay marked the beginning of tourism, a development that was to have a major impact on the St Kildans' way of life. The sight of 'the steamer' dropping anchor in Village Bay caused great excitement ashore, for the influx of tourists gave the islanders an opportunity of selling their produce for cash: tweeds, knitted socks and gloves, and the 'blown' eggs of the guillemot, puffins and fulmar. Two other ships, the *SS Ambrosine* and the *SS Hebrides*, helped to swell the number of summer visitors. While the tourists were ashore exploring the village, the St Kildans were allowed to board the steamer and, with the money they had earned from selling their produce, to purchase luxuries such as biscuits, sweets and tobacco. Money became increasingly important to a community the economy of which, three generations earlier, was based mostly on barter.

The process of drawing St Kildans into a world which they had formerly regarded as remote and inaccessible began to accelerate, and continued to do so until the Evacuation some fifty years later.

Some contemporary writers complained that, too often, tourists sought to humiliate the islanders.

> *On a steamer day, they are seen, in one sense, to their best advantage and in another to their worst. They are seen to their best advantage in this way. A great part of their clothes is cleaned up in honour of the visitors as they like to appear externally as decent as possible. Then their houses get a little bit of a turn to harmonise with their persons. Again they are seen to their worst advantage in the way they generally act on such a day. Parties are very often, if not always, led to take a wrong view of St Kildan character during a stay of a few hours. The St Kildans are spoiled children. This is the only opportunity afforded them of 'turning a penny' and they are just over pressing in taking advantage of it. A few years back, visitors there used to scatter money right and left and the poor natives expect that it should run a little more freely now.*

> John Ross, 1889

> *The arrival of a vessel is now a more commonplace affair than it used to be and it consequently must give rise to less commotion, though even yet it is sufficient to send these poor invertebrate creatures into a fit of nervous excitement such as cool-headed Saxons have really no conception of.*

> Robert Connell, 1885

A few year back this singular people chopped up one of their boats into firewood. The boat was a gift from people in the South, and on the islanders being remonstrated with on the enormity of their conduct they coolly replied that the boat did not quite suit their purpose, and they had made up their minds to burn it, so that their kind friends in the South might have a better chance of giving them a better one ... (The four boats they have) are simply going to wreck in their hands, and one apparent reason is that they are common property. What is common property is nobody's business, and so the boats are allowed to lie and rot uncared for on the beach.

Robert Connell, 1886

I do not wonder that they dislike foreigners, so many of the tourists treat them as if they were wild animals at the zoo. They throw sweets to them, openly mock them, and I have seen them standing at the church door during service, laughing and talking, and staring in as if at an entertainment got up for their amusement ... Mr Connell, writing in 1885, also complains of their dirtiness and viewed with horror the thought of having to shake hands with them. Either he must have been very particular or they must have taken to washing during the past fifteen years, for we thought they were remarkably clean.

(Norman Heathcote, 1898-99)`

SS *Dunara Castle*

Tourists being brought ashore

59. Mrs MacLachlan's Diary (1906)

Peter MacLachlan, from the Isle of Mull, studied law at Glasgow University, but did not complete his studies there. He was one of a group of Gaelic-speaking students who transferred to Edinburgh University, where Professor John Stuart Blackie* had taken the Chair of Greek Philosophy.

After leaving university, Peter abandoned his ambition to emigrate to Canada and responded to a vocational calling for the Free Church. He had been strongly influenced by the evangelical fervour of Moody and Sankey and decided to become a missionary working in the Highlands and Islands. He married twenty-five year-old Alice Scroggie, who, though born in Haddington, East Lothian, had received her education in Lincolnshire and spent several years teaching small children in York.

© John Sadler

Alice MacLachlan

* John Stuart Blackie was among the best-known Scots of his day. He took a degree at Marischal College, Aberdeen, then studied at the universities of Gottingen and Berlin, where he developed, firstly, a lifelong love of the German language and, secondly, of the Greek language and antiquity. In 1839, he was appointed Professor of Humanity at Marischal College. Declining to enter the church, he took a law degree at the University of Edinburgh and joined the Scottish bar. In 1860, he achieved his ambition when he was appointed to the Chair of Greek at the University of Edinburgh. There he became well-known as a charismatic and popular lecturer on many subjects. He espoused the causes of educational reform and of the Gaelic language, and was largely responsible for raising the £12,000 needed to endow the new Chair of Celtic at Edinburgh. His death was the occasion for a national day of mourning and his funeral brought Edinburgh to a standstill.

The MacLachlans' first position was to the village of Garve, some fifty miles north of Inverness. Settling into married life, the young couple felt fortunate in having the manse at Garve as their home. However, in January 1906, they received a letter from the church authorities giving them the unwelcome news that the manse was to be surrendered to the Free Presbyterians (Seceders), a splinter group of the church. A Free Church official met with them at Dingwall and told them that they were to be translated to St Kilda.

Alice was an impressively tall, feisty woman but, though she had misgivings regarding their immediate prospects, she left Peter to decide whether or not to accept the posting offered. However, in her diary she noted her own reaction: What cheek!!!

The MacLachlans sailed to St Kilda in the summer of 1906. Alice's diaries (see *St Kilda Portraits* by David A Quine, 1988) provide a unique, first-hand account of life on Hiort at the beginning of the twentieth century. Susan MacLachlan, the daughter of the diarist, granted permission for a Gaelic translation of excerpts to be published in *Hiort: Far na Laigh a' Ghrian*. Permission to publish the following excerpts has been granted by the National Trust for Scotland, which now holds the diaries.

AUGUST 1906

Tuesday 14 ... Kate our servant is very nice and kind. One or two days we have been seeing the people, but we did not see them all. All the men were so busy at the fulmar hunting, while many of the women had also gone to carry home the birds. We went first to see Rachel McCrimmon* who is the only one who still lives in the same old house and would not have a new house. The hens just live in the same room. Peter found her most intelligent, and spoke very good Gaelic.

© School of Scottish Studies

Rachel MacCrimmon

* The last of the St Kildan MacCrimmons, niece of Euphemia

Tuesday 21 The men being still at fulmar catching, we went to the top of the highest hill, Conacher, Kate with us. The women and girls were there at the top and overtook us as we came home, with their load of birds. I rolled a bag of fulmar a long way down Conacher with my walking stick. Then on Wednesday we went and saw the rest of the folks, those who were not away at the fulmars.

Thursday 23 It was wet and windy so we stayed in and sewed my curtains and Friday did the same. We been very busy unpacking all our boxes and getting things in order. We have people coming to see us every day and all who come bring us a pair of fulmars, plucked and ready for the pot.

Saturday 25 This is a lovely fresh day. The Big Whaler came into the bay last night as we were going to bed and today they are unloading coal which they have brought for the people here. … The St Kildans have been busy taking coal all morning. The Captain of the Big Whaler has kindly given them five tons in a present and they gave him a suit of clothes. In the afternoon the men took home the coals. They went fishing and we got several presents of fish (caravanich)*.

Sunday 26 Went to both services and Sunday School. Children fearfully shy. Good congregations and singing slightly better than on last Sunday.

Tuesday 28 Wet all day. We were in all day until evening when we went out to the pier to meet a little boat which came from the whalers. We sent out milk to both boats and the Captain of the *Brymwolf* took us out in his little boat to see the whales, one was 65 feet long … It was jolly seeing the strangers.

Thursday 30 We were aroused at midnight by the whistle of the *Hebrides*. I was so excited I could hardly sleep for the remainder of the night. The first sirens sounded at 5.15 am and we jumped out of bed. The mails had been brought ashore at mid-night, and our letters, papers and parcels were on the parlour table. What an array! … We didn't feel a bit lonely. We will feel worse when the whalers stop. Later in the day, several of the younger St Kildans left with the *Johanna* for Scalpay, the Happy Hunting Ground. They won't return till next week.

Friday 31 Great excitement prevails, Three young fellows are going off by the whalers to Glasgow. They will go as far as Tarbert (Harris) by the whaler and then to Glasgow next week by the *Johanna*. The whole crowd were in the afternoon and wanted a bag from Duine which they got with great pleasure for the Glasgow trip. We gave them an order to bring back from Cooper's for us. We all went down to the pier at 8 o'clock to see them off. They went off in great glee – Norman McQuien, Neil Gillies and Ewen Gillies. There was lamenting at the pier and kissing any amount.

* *carbhanaich – bream*

SEPTEMBER 1906

Saturday 1st Simply a glorious day. Did a little cooking in the morning, but spent the whole afternoon out of door in the sun which was blazing hot. What an exquisite night. Duine call me out to the door and we went out as far as the pier. I have never in my life seen such a picture as the bay presented tonight. There was a full (or nearly so) moon. At the left hand Oshavale stood guarding the bay – on the other the towering heights of the Dune. Between, in a clear, cloudless sky shone the moon. It made a broad clear path on the rippling water, and the night was so bright together we could have stayed out for hours. It was altogether most beautiful.

Sunday 2

Monday 3rd Another glorious day. We were to have started school today, but it is the monthly meeting morning service so we do not have school that day.

Tues 4th Opened school at 10 o'clock this morning with twenty pupils, two pupils being absent. I went in during the morning but was only in for a little while when we heard the siren of a yacht so there was confusion. We made them sit still for a little and then dismissed them, as is usual in such events. We all rushed down to the pier and there was a lovely steam yacht in the bay. The men put out a boat, when to our disgust, the yacht turned and went steaming at full speed out of the bay. It was an awful shame, and the poor people here were so disappointed. … Duine and Kate went out to try the new scythe. Duine agreeably surprised. Kate is a grand hand with the scythe. I went, but to applaud.

Thursday 6 After school went into the field where Kate has been very busy cutting the hay. Duine and she cut alternately and I raked. It looked like rain so Kate carried the driest into the 'Clet'. This is the most ingenious method of drying the grass. These 'Clets' are loosely built stone houses with earthen roofs. The grass is kept in there and pushed in between the stones in huge quantities. The rain can't get near it and the wind whistles through the stones and quite dries it, although it might be quite damp when put in. The boys went fishing for red mullet and brought us some.

Tues 7 The 'Botoch' has just arrived … Three boats came in and all the men came home. None went to Glasgow as Mr Herlofson (Tarbert) dissuaded them on account of the weather. … The three Captains and the engineer all came ashore and had tea with us. We had great fun. The old Captain (at least, the father, for he is not old) teases Kate that he is to take her back to Norway with him for his wife is dead. This is a fib as his wife is alive and he has nine of a family. He speaks in broken English and Kate in Gaelic, and it is too comic.

Monday 17 Miserably wet day. Was in school in the afternoon. Had a scene with John Gillies as to who was to be master, or mistress rather. Kept him in and talked plainly to him. He stayed in for an hour and he finally said he was sorry. Went to see all the folks after that. Got quite a lot of red mullet tonight. Had it salted.

OCTOBER 1906

Thursday 25 Liner from N. Shields sent us a lovely little fish by Donald Òg yesterday. Liner left this morning. Men cutting 'feur' (grass) on Conacher. I don't like that as it is so dangerous. Lot of children kept in today.

Wednesday 31 After dinner, before school, went to watch them catching sheep (they call it ruagadh) on Oiseabhal, which is at the back of the Manse. When catching them Donald Gillies got a terrible bad fall over a stone, which pierced and cut his leg badly. Duine and I washed his leg and sent him home. Then school.

NOVEMBER 1906

Fri 2nd Men putting sheep on Dune. The old men went themselves with a boat and rescued a sheep which had fallen into the sea. Went visiting our two patients. Finlay MacQuien much better … worse at night.

Mon. 5th Church Service being the first Monday of the month, also 'ceisd' day. It was rather interesting. One man introduced a rather difficult passage from the Bible. First Duine spoke and then called on every member to say something on it, which they all did except two. Some spoke very well.

Tues. 13th Duine bad with toothache all night. Men went to Dune with a sick sheep. Rather windy and stormy day.

© A. M. Cockburn (S.S.S.)

Whale carcasses in Village Bay, 1928

Thursday 15   Just dressed when Kate came in to say she saw a steamer in the distance. I also saw it coming nearer and nearer. To our great joy we saw it making for the bay. It turned out to be the great Fleetwood boat and had our mails at last. What rejoicing and no wonder, the first letters since the beginning of September. Duine and I got nearly two dozen letters besides newspapers innumerable. Bride cake from Mrs McWalter (Newport) and parcel from Inverness. ... The boat waited for our letters. All are well at home.

Sunday 18   Terrible storm of wind and rain. Duine's face very bad but still he went out twice. … Duine's gumboil burst after supper and toothache went at once.

Wednesday 21   Children specially wicked today. Getting on well with counterpane.

Saturday 24   Simply awful day. Bed until after dinner, but still feeling very seedy and glad to get to bed. Duine so kind all these days, kinder than I am to him when he is sick I'm afraid but I am so nervous when he is ill and can't help it.

Monday 29   Time taken up all day with visitors. Donald Ferguson and Finlay McQuien have been in all day courting Kate. Ewen Gillies was here too, and we tease her, but we all suspect it is cupboard love with him, but the two botoch* are in earnest right enough and it is awful fun.

* *bodaich* – old men

DECEMBER 1906

Wednesday 5th   Most awful gale. Garden gate blown down and bedroom window smashed. Writing letter during morning to be sent off by real St Kilda Mail.

Friday 7   When we came home Callum was in. He had brought down a spinning wheel for me to practise on.

Saturday 8   Boys sent away St Kilda Mail as the wind was from the right direction.

Tuesday 25   Xmas Day on Hirta!!! Heavy snow all day. Busy in the kitchen all morning cooking Xmas pudding and roast fowl. Had capital dinner. Quite happy this Christmas with my dear Duine.

MARCH 1907

Mon. 25th   All the baile (village) have the steamer cold the last day or two very badly. They say it came by the last boat. It seems funny. They believe implicitly in this. Everybody has it and all the School is in a constant cough and sneeze.

Wed. 27th   Great excitement this morning during breakfast when the 'Knowsie' came in. She brought us our potatoes, toffee, sugared almonds, blacking. The Capt. brought me a bag of oranges and apples, 2 bts ginger beer and last but not least a big box of kippers from Stornoway. I shall never forget Capt. Wagner's kindness – never.

APRIL 1907

Mon. 1st   Lovely day. Ian Bahn and old Donald McQuien in ceilidhing and got great fun. Donald was in great form and was telling us heaps of stories about the island – pirates, etc. I wish I had had more Gaelic to understand better. He told us about men falling over the rocks at Soay – boys being stolen away from Boreray, and robbers coming to the island. His gestures were so funny and if any of the others dared to dispute anything he said he almost devoured them.

Mon. 22nd   Very blowy still. So many absent with bad colds. Chickens in second brood beginning to come.

Tues. 30th   My back is so bad I did not go out. Capt. Ritchie sent us a ling. Duine and I both broke the Sabbath by writing letters, about seed to Mr Laing, to County council, etc.

MAY 1907

Fri. 10th   … Neil Gillies got word that the 'Post' posted by sea on 8th Dec had reached its destination, but no particulars yet.

Tues. 14th   Very sorry to say Finlay MacQuien's dog killed and ate my little Soay lamb which was just a fortnight old. I am so cut up over it.

Sun. 19th   When we were in S.S. (Sunday School) a dog came and killed two of my hens,* both of them with chickens. Duine was in a fearful state. However, none of them (the chickens) were any the worse. D. nearly killed the brute.

Mon. 20th   Awakened by the siren of the *Dunara Castle*. Great excitement.

The MacLachlans' first baby (Susan) was born on 9th April 1909. Their tour of duty on Hiort ended in mid-May of that year.

A gannet (stuffed with feathers) held by Finlay MacQueen, the oldest man on Hiort

* It is possible that the 'the brute' mistook the hens for puffins!

60. The Loss of Loved Ones 1906-14

The late Neil Gillies was born on Hiort in 1896 and spent the last few years of his life in Garthamlock, one of Glasgow's deprived suburbs. He often came to our house at Lenzie either for an evening ceilidh or for Sunday dinner. In old age, he lived alone – a duck out of water except when one carried him in his thoughts back to his beloved Hiort. He died while his brother, the Rev Donald John Gillies, a minister of the United Presbyterian Church of Canada, was visiting him. The following is based on what I was told by the Gillies brothers and my good friend Lachie MacDonald, who passed away at his home in Glen Nevis in 1993. All three had been in school together on Hiort.

John Gillies and Annie, his wife, lived at No. 15 with their family of four. Neil and Donald John were their third and fourth children respectively. Neil described his father as 'a quiet, good-natured man' who, when he reached middle age, was made an elder in the church. He had a powerful tenor voice, and for a time, was the precentor who led the singing of the Psalms in church. As was the case in all of Hiort's households, the Gillieses conducted their family worship in the morning before going out to work, and in the evening before going to bed. After the evening service, it was customary for John Gillies to withdraw to the barn to spend time alone 'communing with the Lord'.

A deep-seated fatalism underlay the islanders' approach to everything they did. *Ma tha e an dàn* ('If it is pre-ordained') was a phrase often quoted. Everything that occurred in the course of their lives was predestined and inescapable. In the dangerous pursuits of fowling and herding sheep on precipitous cliffs, and fishing in the unpredictable waters of the archipelago, they relied on *an làmh nach caill a grèim* ('the hand whose grip never fails') – the protection of Christ the Saviour.

Through the generations, their religion remained pivotal to the life of the community. At the beginning of the twentieth century, the presence of Peter and Alice MacLachlan was important to the community, not least because they were both committed Christians, and also competent, enthusiastic teachers. Alice was a good musician and fond of sewing and spinning. Sewing was one of the subjects she taught in the school.

The late Rev Donald John vividly remembered Tuesday, 2nd October 1906, the day on which a fellow pupil lost his life. In the late afternoon, Norman Gillies became restless in class, and more than once was checked by the teacher for not giving his attention to his work.

> 'You're like a hen on a hot girdle, Norman,' said Peter MacLachlan. 'What's bothering you, Norman?'

> 'The big boys are going fishing, sir, and they promised they would wait for me.'

Thirteen year-old Norman sounded so unhappy that the teacher allowed him to leave. Released from the confines of the class-room, he ran outside and saw that the older boys were already disappearing over the shoulder of Oiseabhal. He hurried home for his fishing-rod and, without a word to his parents, set off in pursuit. Peter MacLachlan left his class briefly to keep an eye on Norman as he climbed the hill and smiled to himself as he remembered the carefree days of his own boyhood on Mull. When he returned to the classroom, he brought the day's lessons to a close. The children put their books away and together sang the hymn *Until We Meet Again*.

Having followed *An Stiogha* – the treacherous path that took him over the shoulder of Oiseabhal – Norman began his steep descent to the sea. He completed his journey without mishap, and when he reached the 'fishing rocks' of Rubha Cholla, began to prepare his hooks. As he turned to take up his rod, he slipped and fell into the sea. Alice MacLachlan records the event in her diary:

> As we were finishing our tea, we heard a great shouting and other confused noises. In a few moments the men were down, and in less time than it takes me to write this, they launched the boat. The women were screaming and wringing their hands. It seems that poor Norman Gillies (who had gone away from school a little earlier than usual to go to the Point of Coll to fish mullet) had fallen from the rocks into the sea. There was a fearful current there and although the only man there (Hugh Gillies) had flung him a rope, the current carried him out beyond it. Some of the bigger boys ran home to give the news. Norman MacKinnon went to the place on foot but only in time to see the boy sink. He was clinging to his fishing rod. He never made a sound.

Every time the schoolchildren sang the hymn *Until We Meet Again*, they remembered Norman with sadness. Nor could they ever forget the community's grief on that evening. The loss of Norman Gillies (known locally as *Tormod Fhionnlaigh*) brought home to the islanders how vulnerable they were. Once they fell into the sea, they had little chance of surviving. Unlike the seventeenth century islanders, whom Martin describes as proficient in both swimming and diving, nobody of that generation was able to swim.

A still greater tragedy was to hit the community three years later. Intending to spend the day working on sheep, five men set off for the Dùn, two miles across Village Bay. All was well until they were close to their destination. Although the five men were experienced in those waters and the sea unusually calm, their boat struck violently against a reef and capsized. Neil MacKinnon surfaced and managed to keep himself afloat by clinging to an oar. John Gillies also surfaced and, holding on to the keel of the boat, began to shout for help.

Sitting by the open window in the manse, Alice MacLachlan was the first to hear John Gillies's cry for help. In her diary entry for 22nd March, 1909, she says:

Monday 22 Glorious day. I'm still in bed ... Just like summer and so warm. Two boats left about 10 or a little after for Boreray to see about sheep, etc. and Kate told me when she came to tidy the room that five men, Donald McDonald, John Gillies, Neil McKinnnon, Norman MacQuien and his brother John, went to the Dùn in William's boat. Kate had gone out of the room and my window was left wide open as the day was so lovely. All at once I heard the most terrible cries from the Dùn and I called to Kate who ran out, and in turn gave the alarm that something had happened at the Dùn. Duine [Alice's husband] came from school in time to help old Angus, Finlay Mòr and Finlay McQuien, and in a very short time they got over to the scene of whatever happened. The suspense at home was awful; the women were all down and anguished weeping and wailing, I cannot describe. However, the boat came, and our worst fears were realized; worse than we ever imagined. Donald McDonald, Norman and John McQuien were all drowned. Neil McKinnon and John Gillies were rescued in a very exhausted condition. Donald MacDonald's body was found floating in the water but poor Norman and John had gone down gripping each other. The scenes are indescribable.

Duine up twice. A beacon was lighted at Berenahake [*Bearradh na h-Eige*] to make the men come home, as it seems they proposed staying to kill gannets. Poor Donald Òg and Ewen McDonald.

Tuesday 23rd I brought in the five men making Donald McDonald's coffin to tea and dinner. Gave Neil Ferguson coffee also; he will take some time to get right. This is an awful place.

10th February 1907 (*Strange Noises in the Night*) ... Kate telling of a curious sound (we put it down to an owl) heard by many people on Osahaval. They say that poor Norman's blood is still about the place and is calling out. The superstition is appalling.

Before the First World War, some islanders wore wooden clogs while working on the land. Many islanders believed that Donald MacDonald perished because he was wearing his clogs that day. Having been thrown headlong into the sea, he was unable to struggle to the surface owing to the buoyancy of his clogs. Neil Gillies assured me that, after that accident, St Kildans never again wore clogs to sea.

Seven years after the Dùn tragedy, another accident claimed the lives of two more young men: Iain MacDonald and Ewen Gillies. On 17th August 1916, the two friends went hunting for nesting fulmar on a cliff at the back of the Mullach Mòr, opposite to the *Brada Stac*. Iain, the anchorman, chose a position which had good footing and overhung shelves occupied by scores of plump, young fulmar still in their grey down.

Though the First World War had been declared two years earlier, none of the island's young men was called up for military service. A number of them were employed by the Admiralty as labourers to work alongside men from a garrison which had been established on Hiort. While the war had brought to the rest of Europe nothing but destruction and misery, it brought to St Kilda unprecedented prosperity and an opportunity of living in close proximity to groups of men from different parts of the British Isles. Iain MacDonald, who had been married for only a few weeks, was employed at the naval camp as a labourer and was delighted to be bringing home a regular wage. He had come to the cliff to catch fulmar, but particularly, to get an *eun-creige** to present to his young wife as a token of his love for her.

* Lit. a rock-fowl: a fowl in tiptop condition

Having secured the climbing-rope about his chest, Ewen began his descent. With the coil behind him, Iain paid out the rope at a steady pace. Owing to the strength of the wind, Ewan spent some time being swung like a pendulum across the cliff-face. Eventually the wind carried him to a point in the rock where he managed to get his feet against the cliff but failed to get himself on to a ledge. He pushed himself outwards but, on the backswing, the wind carried him forward so violently that his whole body was wedged tightly into a crevice. Even though he struggled with all his might, he was unable even to move his arms. One can imagine that he yelled as loudly as possible but his voice would have been unheard above the noise of the wind and the sea.

At the top of the cliff, Iain waited patiently to hear some instruction shouted from below or for the *lon* to slacken to indicate that Ewen had managed to gain a footing on a ledge. Minutes passed. When nothing was signalled from below, Iain became increasingly concerned but continued to hold the rope taut. After a while, he began to slacken the rope slightly and then tighten it again to see if there would be any response from below. Nothing.

According to Lachie MacDonald, the young men of Hiort had, by 1916, lost the climbing skills of their forebears. Working for a regular weekly wage had changed their approach to fowling, so that they were no longer as well prepared mentally or physically to cope with its dangers. Perhaps, also, they had been less careful than they ought to have been in checking the condition of their climbing-rope. There were no witnesses to what actually happened, but it was widely accepted that Iain MacDonald would have become tired of waiting for a signal from his friend and decided to heave with all his might. If the rope had not been properly tested before being taken to the cliffs, it may have snapped, throwing Iain off balance, so that he plunged off the cliff.

As the evening sun disappeared behind the Mullach Mòr, the families in the Village began to worry that yet another fatal accident had occurred. In the morning, men and women searched behind the Mullach Mòr while others followed the cliffs from Conachair out to the Cambair. Late in the afternoon they returned, having failed to find the missing fowlers.

Several days later, a naval officer using binoculars to survey the coastline spotted the body of Ewen wedged in a crevice from which he had been unable to escape. He had died of hypothermia. Later in the day, a team from the garrison retrieved the body and carried it to the Village. Iain's body was never found.

61. Iorram air Niall Dòmhnallach

His niece composed this lament for Neil MacDonald, who lost his life while hunting fulmar. (From the Rev Neil MacKenzie Collection, 1830-43.)

dùcan – dùthchasach – of noble birth

faicill – caution; consciousness of danger

air faicill – on guard; on Hiort also meant engaged in a hazardous activity

bràthair mo mhàthar – uncle (my mother's brother)

'S ann Dihaoine ron Dòmhnach	It was on Friday before the Lord's Day
Fhuair sinn sgeula gun sòlas;	That we received the sad news.
Bhith caoidh an fhir òr-fhuilt	I grieve for the golden-haired man
Thug deòir air mo ghruaidh.	Who has brought tears to my cheek.
'S truagh nach bu mhi bh' air ceann t' acair	I wish that I'd been your anchor-man
Nuair chaidh thu às t' fhaicill –	When you embraced danger –
Dhèanainn dìcheall air t' fhastadh,	I would have done my best to buy you time,
Fiù do sheachnadh on uair.	Even to alter your destiny.
Tha do phàistean gun taice,	Your children are without support,
A' chuid tha làidir is tha lag dhiubh,	The oldest are but infants,
Mu chas dèanamh an tapaidh	(He) whose feet were ever active
'S nach bu lapach san ruagadh.	Was never slow at the (sheep) gathering.
Tha do bhean air a ciùrradh	Racked with pain by her grief,
O a beulaibh 's a cùlaibh;	Your wife is suffering;
'S i bhith caoidh a fir dùcaich,	As she mourns for her worthy husband,
Dh'fhalbh a cuid às gach uair.	Her portion has been lost for all time.

Mo cheist colann na cèille,
'S e do bheul nach robh breugach;
O, 's tu nach labhradh na breugan,
'S tu nach labhradh a' cheilg.

Gu ro bheusach is suairce
Bràthair mo mhàthar a chràidh mi;
Bidh air m' aire gu bràth thu
Gus an càirt' mi san uaigh.

My darling, the embodiment of wisdom,
You, whose word was reliable;
Who would never tell lies
And were never two-faced.

Upright and kindly was he,
My uncle for whom I grieve;
I shall ever remember you
Until I'm laid in my grave.

© James Smith

62. Iorram na Truaighe

In the hope of catching fulmar, a man and his wife went one morning to set snares on the cliffs at the back of *Conachair*. When the snares were in place, they returned to the village. In the forenoon, the man and his brother were among the crew of a boat that set off to catch gannets on *Boreray*. On the return trip, they passed close to the towering cliff at the back of *Conachair* and noticed what they took to be the body of a sheep floating in the sea. They lowered the sail and began to row towards the object, but the current was too strong for them and they were forced to head for the haven of Village Bay.

The man who had been laying snares in the morning with his wife was overcome by a deep sense of melancholy. He began to sing *Iorram na Truaighe*, a lament that he had composed some years earlier in memory of his son who had been killed when his horse bolted.

The boat arrived at the *Dìollaid* without mishap. As usual, there was a crowd of women and children down on the shore ready to drag the boat out of the sea. The boat-crew noticed that one person was missing from the group – the woman who had been setting snares on *Conachair* in the morning. Her husband knew instinctively that the object seen floating at the back of *Conachair* was the body of his wife. Recalling his singing *Iorram na Truaighe* earlier, his brother said to him, 'Not until now have you had reason to sing a lament!'

The widower composed the following *iorram* for his wife.

Nuair a dh'fhalbh uat an tobha	When the rock broke
'S nach robh mo lomhainn gu feum dhut,	And my rope was not of use,
Chaill mi iuchair mo dhorais	I lost the key to my door
Is pàirt de dh'onair mo cheud ghràidh.	And the shared joy of my first love.
Chaill mi 'n stiùir bha air m' fhàrdaich,	I have lost the helm of my household,
Is cuid am bàta an àit' èigheach;	And for a boat-share, I have crying;
Chaill mi cearcall earraich mo thaighe,	I lost the encircling-rope of my home,
Is m' aighear gu lèir leat.	And with you my happiness is gone.
Nuair thilleas mi dhachaigh	When I come home
O thional eunlaith is uighean	From collecting eggs and birds
Gun theine gun lòn air mo choinneimh,	Without a fire or a meal to welcome me,
Nuair a thig mi à eilean,	When I return from an island (expedition),
Cha choinnich (thu) air tràigh mi,	You are not on the shore to greet me.
Is bidh mo chridhe a' bristeadh	My heart breaks
A' faicinn mo phàistean.	When I look upon my children.

63. The First World War on St Kilda

Shortly after the outbreak of the First World War, the Admiralty sent a detachment of fifteen men to garrison Hiort. To house the sailors, wooden barracks were built behind the Village. In January 1915, the island became a War Signal Station and proved to be a thorn in the flesh for the German naval command whose submarines were operating all round the coasts of Britain. The signal station was in regular radio communication with the Naval Centre at Aultbea on the west coast of the Scottish mainland.

Life on Hiort changed dramatically. The islanders were able to buy rations from the garrison, which was regularly supplied with food by HM Depot Ship *Manco*, working out of Stornoway. Throughout the four years of the war, armed trawlers also working out of Stornoway supplied the island with luxuries such as toiletries, cigarettes, magazines and newspapers. Mail was delivered and collected weekly, a service that was of as much benefit to the islanders as to the garrison.

All the able-bodied St Kildans found regular employment helping to unload supplies, labouring on building-sites, digging trenches and, not least, helping to lay the telegraphic cables from the look-out posts on the summits of *Conachair, Mullach Mòr* and *Oiseabhal*. For the first time, the St Kildans were able to earn money throughout the year while working on their native soil.

© The National Trust For Scotland

In addition to the sailors who manned the lookout posts, four St Kildans were employed to keep watch at night. Every ship sighted was reported to the Wireless Signal Station, which then relayed the information to Aultbea, so that, so far as visibility would allow, the Admiralty was kept fully aware of the nature of surface sea traffic within a huge area west of the Outer Hebrides.

After serving for four months on the island, the sailors were withdrawn to make way for a new detachment. No sooner had the St Kildans got to know one group of strangers than they found themselves in the company of others. Thanks to this perpetual turnover, the islanders got to know men from every corner of Britain and from every kind of social background. While some sailors found their isolation on Hiort oppressive, others enjoyed the experience of mixing with the islanders and helping on the crofts whenever they were off duty.

By the spring of 1918, the tide of war was beginning to flow against the enemy. Little by little, the German armies and navies were being subdued. Yet the Kaiser's forces continued to be dangerous and conducted their war of attrition by sea as on land. The islanders were unaware that German submarines had been seen in the vicinity of St Kilda towards the end of April and the beginning of May. At certain hours during the week, they attended lectures at which they were shown what they should do in the event of an emergency.

Since the beginning of the war, German submarines operating in the St Kilda sector had sunk many British cargo ships. However, by May 1918, the war was far from the minds of the islanders. On the morning of 15th May, they awoke to bright sunshine and, after breakfast, prepared to make the best of the good weather. The men working for the Admiralty went to report for duty. The women milked the cows and then drove them out beyond *Gàrradh a' Bhaile* (the Village Dyke) to graze in the *Lag Bho Thuath*. *Bodaich* (old men) attended to the few ewes that had not yet lambed. *Cailleachan* (old women) went to their potato patches to hoe. As the weather was favourable, half a dozen girls went looking for four men who would take them on their annual egg-collecting outing on Boreray and *Stac an Àrmainn*. A sailor hurried from the Factor's House to say that, until further notice, local boats were not allowed to leave Hiort. Before midday, everybody on Hiort knew the reason why.

Shortly after 7a.m. on that day, the lookout on *Conachair* reported seeing a German submarine on the surface close to Boreray. Two hours later, the submarine submerged, but about 10 a.m. it resurfaced at the entrance to Village Bay. A signal to Aultbea was the last received from St Kilda for the rest of that day, and it was correctly assumed that Hiort was under attack.

Walking down his croft, Norman MacQueen spotted two of his ewes which had lambed during the night. He shouted to Neil Ferguson and joyfully lifted twin lambs by their forelegs. But Neil's attention was elsewhere. He was looking out to sea, where he could see two ships on the horizon. But something else on the sea caught his attention – a strange black spot that was no more than a mile away from where he was standing.

Norman shouted, '*Uan fireann agus uan boireann!*' ('A male lamb and a female lamb!')

Neil pointed out to sea and replied, 'We'll have company in the Village before long.'

Norman turned towards the sea and saw the black object on the surface. Just at that moment the siren sounded at the signal station, warning everybody that an enemy was approaching.

The submarine proceeded slowly into the bay until it was about a kilometre from the village, near enough for the German captain's voice to be heard warning everybody by loud-hailer to take cover, as he was about to bombard the wireless station. Soon, young and old were quitting their houses and fields and making for the *Allt Tioram* (Dry Burn), where they believed they would be safe.

Shortly before 11a.m., the bombardment began. Seventy-two shells were fired from a 4-inch gun mounted aft of the conning-tower, one of two such guns on the submarine. The first shells hit the Store House and wrecked two boats lying nearby. The next salvos exploded near the church and badly damaged the manse. The Factor's house received direct hits, as did the huts in which the garrison was billeted. One shell missed its target and destroyed Neil MacKinnon's house. Towards the end of the bombardment, many of the rounds were aimed at the cleits, which the Germans may have mistaken for military emplacements.

As the noise of the bombardment resonated in the hills and cliffs, thousands of seabirds rose off their roosts to seek peace far out to sea. Young dogs ran helter-skelter away from the Village; most of the older dogs lay cowering beside their masters in the *Allt Tioram*. The cattle and sheep were scattered across the island. On the following day, some were discovered grazing in the *Gleann Mòr*. Nobody on the island was hurt. The only casualty was a lamb which was injured and had to be destroyed.

Two armed trawlers and two whalers were dispatched from Stornoway as soon as the first sighting of the German submarine was reported on 15th May. When the German gunners felt sure that the wireless installation had been destroyed, they went below and the submarine began to withdraw. Rounding *Rubha an Uisge*, it travelled west into the open ocean.

The wireless transmitter and aerial were hastily repaired and by 7.30 p.m. were able to transmit an urgent signal reporting that a second enemy submarine had surfaced half an hour earlier and was approaching the island. Shortly afterwards, that vessel altered course so that it arced round the north coast of the island, and it was last seen some miles from Soay travelling south. It is assumed that this vessel intercepted signals from the armed trawlers then approaching Hiort.

In the last week of May, enemy submarines were sighted several times in the vicinity of St Kilda, but there were two Royal Navy auxiliary patrol vessels permanently stationed in Village Bay, and none was prepared to engage them in a duel.

Nevertheless, the enemy continued to strike at shipping in the sector, sometimes within a few miles of Hiort. On 9th July, for example, the lookout on *Mullach Mòr* reported that a submarine was attacking a vessel twelve miles to the south. A signal from the wireless station alerted the armed trawler *Walpole,* which was in the vicinity. It immediately closed with the enemy. After suffering two hits, the submarine was unable to submerge, but with its superior surface speed, it managed to outstrip the trawler and escape. In spite of the efforts of all those holding the remote outpost of St Kilda, the sinking of British ships continued. Within twelve hours of the sinking of the *Atlantic*, eight more ships were torpedoed. Many of the survivors were picked up by the auxiliary patrol vessels stationed at St Kilda.*

In 1918, within three months of the war ending, a 4-inch gun was installed on Hiort in a position overlooking Village Bay. The gun was never fired in anger. Neil Ferguson became its custodian, and for several years after the cessation of hostilities continued to be paid £25 per annum to clean and grease it.

After the war, the authorities refused to pay any compensation to the St Kildans for the damage which their property had sustained during the German bombardment. They claimed that, as the islanders were not included in the government's Insurance Scheme, they were not liable, even though Hiort would never have been targeted had the Navy's signal station not been established there.

In February 1919, the last detachment of sailors was withdrawn. With them went the hearts of some of the local girls. Immediately after the war, a number of St Kildans determined to leave the island and settle on the Scottish mainland. The first to leave were William MacDonald and his wife Mary Ann, who gave up their house and croft at No. 3 and moved away with their young family of seven. Their departure was a nail in the coffin of Hiort. In the months that followed, people wrote sad letters to the MacDonalds telling how they missed seeing a light in their window at night. By 1920 the island's population had fallen by a quarter.

---

* *Soldiering on St Kilda* by James MacKay (Token Press, 2002) gives details of life on St Kilda during the two World Wars.

64. Evacuation

In the 1920s and '30s, tuberculosis (TB) was rife in the Outer Hebrides, particularly in the Isle of Lewis, where the wards of the Stornoway Sanatorium were filled to capacity with patients stricken by the disease. Although inadequate diagnosis may have disguised some cases, it seems that on St Kilda, tuberculosis was rare.

Nurse Williamina Barclay trained at Glasgow Royal Infirmary and studied midwifery at Dundee Royal Infirmary. In 1927, she went to St Kilda under the aegis of the Scottish Health Department and was not long in her new post before discovering a teenage boy who was ill with TB. She advised the rest of the household to leave. Mary Gillies, the boy's mother, refused to abandon her son and nursed him until he died. Shortly afterwards, she herself became ill with appendicitis and Nurse Barclay assumed responsibility for attending to all her needs, including the cooking of her meals.

In February 1930, the skipper of a trawler which had anchored briefly in Village Bay agreed to inform the authorities that the condition of Mary Gillies was critical. Though the weather was atrocious, the fishery-cruiser *Norna* responded to the appeal and, with two doctors on board, fought through heavy seas to reach St Kilda. Once the patient was stretchered aboard, the *Norna* set off for Oban at full speed, but in spite of the effort to save her, Mary Gillies died before reaching Stobhill Hospital in Glasgow. That sad event reduced the St Kildan population to thirty-six, the same number of people as had emigrated to Australia in 1852.

Making the casket for Mary Gillies, who died of tuberculosis three weeks before the day of the evacuation

Since 1927 not one baby had been born, and the morale of the people was deeply affected by the recent death. As an incomer, Nurse Barclay saw signs suggesting that the community was in terminal decline, yet she remained bright and extrovert, always on hand to advise and suggest solutions to the islanders' many problems. She occasionally invited the women to the Factor's House, where she was residing. Over tea and scones, her guests had an opportunity of airing their concerns. One day in April 1930, she extended her invitation to the menfolk. The entire adult population squeezed into the Factor's House to enjoy 'the nurse's wee cèilidh'. The atmosphere was friendly and informal but the conversation soon turned to the weighty subject that was foremost in everybody's mind: the future of Hiort. The consensus was that the community would have to appeal for government help, otherwise it would cease to exist. Nurse Barclay mentioned evacuation as a feasible solution – something that had been discussed a number of times since the crisis of 1852. She said,

> *Transporting you and your valuables to the Scottish mainland would not be a problem, I'm sure, and getting homes for all of you would also be seen to. However, the decision to ask the authorities for assistance to achieve all that must be yours and yours alone.*

After several days of heart-searching deliberation, the islanders unanimously decided that their struggle on St Kilda must come to an end. At a second meeting at the Factor's House, the islanders revealed to Nurse Barclay the extent of their poverty. Six of the children in the largest family had gone barefoot for months and their food barrels were practically empty. The tweed woven by another householder was taken by the Factor as payment for stores delivered to him. As they told of their miserable struggle, some of the old men wept. Dugald Munro, the missionary, was asked to compose a letter expressing their unanimous wish to abandon their homeland. After a few days, he produced it on ruled foolscap paper, written in a meticulous copperplate hand.

> *We, the undersigned, the natives of St. Kilda hereby respectfully pray and petition HM Government to assist us all to leave the island this year and find homes and occupations for us on the mainland. For some years the manpower has been decreasing, now the total population of the island is reduced to thirty-six. Several men out of this number have definitely made up their minds to seek employment on the mainland; this will really cause a crisis as the present number are hardly sufficient to carry on the necessary work of the place. These men are the mainstay of the island at present as they tend the sheep, do the weaving and look after the general welfare of the widows. Should they leave the conditions of the rest of the community would be such that it would be impossible for us to remain on the island another winter.*

> *The reason why assistance is necessary is that for many years St. Kilda has not been self-supporting and with no facilities to better our position, we are therefore without the means to pay for the costs of removing ourselves and furniture elsewhere.*

We do not ask to be settled as a separate community but in the meantime we would collectively be very grateful of assistance and transference elsewhere where there would be a better opportunity of securing our livelihood.

All the adults, twelve men and eight women, having signed the fateful document which was about to bring civilian occupation of St Kilda to a close, it was enclosed in an envelope addressed to William Adamson, Secretary of State for Scotland at Westminster. Within a few hours, the skipper of a homeward-bound trawler which had anchored briefly in Village Bay to deliver a gift of fish to the islanders accepted the letter and promised to post it as soon as he reached his home port.

In response to the petition, Tom Johnstone, then Under-Secretary of State for Scotland, visited Hiort and, after witnessing the extent of the islanders' deprivation, resolved that evacuation should go ahead before the onset of the autumn gales.

Alasdair Alpin MacGregor, a journalist working for a London newspaper who went so far as to petition the Prime Minister to be allowed to witness the evacuation, received a letter from the Scottish office denying him that privilege.

Memories of happier times

The Admiralty are naturally hostile to the idea of publicity and Mr Johnston is strongly of the opinion that the utmost effort should be made to avoid the miseries of the poor people from being turned into a show.

It was estimated that the evacuation would cost £500. The Secretary of the Treasury was none too pleased. He said:

> From the beginning, we have sympathised with the plight of the St Kildans and have made every effort that they get established on the mainland. But this was on the condition that expenses were kept to a reasonable amount. The estimate is more than we expected ... could you please let me know if houses need to be built for those families who have nowhere to go.

The date of the evacuation was set for the 29th of August, 1930. The islanders gathered their cattle and sheep in pens, ready to be sent on the SS *Dunara Castle* to market at Oban. Some of the cattle, tied to the end of a boat, were forced to swim out to the steamer. When she sailed, the ship also had on board a number of government officials, tourists and the last of the journalists who had arrived a few days earlier to cover the story of the evacuation.

The morning of the 28th was fair and HMS *Harebell* from the Fishery Protection Squadron anchored in Village Bay. The evacuees were advised to remove from their houses only items which were likely to be of use to them in their future homes. Sailors from the *Harebell* came ashore to help with the removal of property, but their offer was ignored. The work of assembling their goods and chattels on the pier went on until it was dark, and when it was done, the islanders walked wearily up the crofts to spend their last night in their homes.

The weather was again fair on the morning of the 29th. In the eleven houses, the islanders dressed in their Sunday best and held the family service as usual. On their living-room table, each householder left a small mound of oats and the family Bible open at *Exodus*. Some left fires burning on the hearth. As the keys were turned in their locks, they stood before the doors to their homes and prayed for God's protection. They lingered to take a last walk round the houses and to visit their beloved church to make sure that Bibles were left open at each pew.

As they began to wander down to the pier, the middle-aged and the old felt exhausted by their physical exertions over the previous few days and anxious about their future. By the time the ship weighed anchor and began to transport the islanders to a new life in a very different world, the fires would have burned to an ash, leaving the homes cold, damp and cheerless for the first time in countless centuries.

Most of the St Kildans settled in Morvern, Argyll, working for the Forestry Commission – an ironic turn of events, as the archipelago did not boast one tree. But, as Martin had observed in 1697, the St Kildans were appreciative of the beauty of the forest and would have been delighted if trees had been a feature of their native environment.

One of the things they admired most was the growth of trees; they thought the beauty of the branches admirable, and how they grew to such a height above plants, was far beyond their conception. One of them, much astonished, told me that the trees pulled him back as he traveled through the woods: and they resolved to carry some few of them on their backs to their boats, and take them to St Kilda; but on second thoughts, the length of the journey, being through the greatest part of sky, deterred them from this undertaking; for though they excel others in strength, they are as yet bad travelers on foot, being so much unused to it.

© James Smith

The old classroom

Footnote - I discussed with the St Kildans whom I knew well how the people felt once they had settled on the Scottish mainland. One said that many felt *tàmailt* – a sense of humiliation that they had allowed their way of life to crumble. Lachie Macdonald, who was aged about twenty-four in 1930, believed that although they adapted well in their new environment, they all suffered from *cianalas* – a haunting nostalgia which constantly filled their minds with memories of 'home'. The Rev Dr. Donald John Gillies, on holiday from Canada, believed that the middle-aged and the elderly suffered from *dubhachas* – a moroseness caused by losing control of their destinies to others. He felt that, in the case of the older members, *dubhachas* made them feel like Displaced Persons – refugees who had to flee their homelands during the Second World War.

65. Tuireadh nan Hiortach

The Rev Dr. George Murray composed *Tuireadh nan Hiortach* as a tribute to his friend, the Rev Donald John Gillies of St Kilda. Originally from the village of South Dell in Lewis, Dr Murray was the minister of the United Presbyterian Church in Boston, USA.

Tha sinne brònach 's is beag an t-iongnadh,

Is tha sinn cianail an-diugh
air fògradh;

Tha 'n cuan an iar le chuid thonnan fiadhaich

Gar sgaradh cian bho ar n-àite-còmhnaidh.

No wonder that we are sad;

We feel nostalgic, for today we are
displaced;

The wild billows of the western ocean

Separate us from our homeland.

Tha sinn mar chaoraich an seo gun bhuachaill,

'S sinn sgapt' measg sluaigh air nach eil
sinn eòlach;

Ach 's tric ar smuaintean a' snàmh nan cuantan

Do dh'eilean uaine nan cluaintean bòidheach.

We are as sheep without a shepherd,

Scattered among people whom we do not
know,

But often our thoughts swim across the seas

To the green isle of beautiful meadows.

Tha Hiort nam fuaran 's nan sgeirean gruamach

Am meadhan cuain, 's chan eil duine beò ann;

Na h-eòin mun cuairt air ri gabhail uabhais

On dh'fhalbh an sluagh a bh' ann uair
ri còmhnaidh.

Hiort of the springs and glowering rocks

In mid-ocean, now uninhabited;

The wheeling birds must wonder

Why the people have deserted their native
heath.

Na taighean blàth anns an cluinnte Gàidhlig,

Thèid iad nan càirntean 's bidh tàmh aig
eòin annt';

Cha bhi am buachaill le chù 's
le chuaille

Nas mò gam fuadach le fuaim a
chòmhraidh.

The houses within which Gaelic was spoken

Will become cairns in which birds will
nest;

The shepherd with his dog will not round
his flock,

Nor will they respond to the sound of his
voice.

Tha 'n eaglais fuar 's chan eil clag ga bhualadh,

Cha tionail sluagh ann air
madainn Dòmhnaich;

Cha chluinnear seinn ann no fonn an aoibhneis –

Tha 'n tìr ri caoidh chionn nach till na seòid ud.

No ringing bell in the church now cold,

No congregation gathering there on the
Lord's Day;

Their joyous singing will no more be heard –

The land weeps for those who will not return.

Cha b' e gu h-àraidh a dhol thar sàile

Chuir sinn fo àmhghair 's a dh'fhàg
sinn brònach

Ach mar a sgaoileadh air feadh gach taobh sinn,

'S nach fhaic sinn aon air a bheil sinn eòlach.

It was not so much our being sent overseas

That made us lament and left
us sad

But the way we have been separated

And cannot see anyone we know.

Ged tha an sluagh measg a bheil sinn truasail,

Tha 'n cànan cruaidh 's tha iad fuar
    nan dòighean;

'S ann bha sinn suaimhneach far 'n
    d' thogadh suas sinn,

Le Gàidhlig uasal ga luaidh an-còmhnaidh.

An uair bhiodh àmhghair aig neach san àite,

Gach duine chàich bhiodh le bàidh
    ga chòmhnadh;

Chan fhaighte gamhlas nam measg, no aimhreit –

'S e siud na glinn anns nach cluinnte fòirneart.

Tha sinne cràidhteach on rinn sinn fhàgail;

Chan e gu h-àraidh gun dh'fhàg sinn stòras;

'S e chuir fo phràmh sinn na tha
    dar càirdean

Nan laighe sàmhach 's iad càirt' sna fòid ann.

Soraidh slàn leibh gu 'n teich na sgàilean –

Far bheil sibh tàmh cha bhi càch nur còir ann;

Tha sibhse sìnt' anns an tìr bu mhiann leibh,

Is eòin ri sgreuchail mur n-àite-còmhnaidh.

Mun cuairt don àite sa bheil sibh càirte,

Cha chruinnich càirdean 's cha shilear deòirean;

Bidh ur n-uaighean nan tulaich uaine,

Bidh feur gun bhuain orr' 's an sluagh
    air fògradh.

'S e sguir dem òran as iomchaidh dhòmhsa,

Le briathran beòil meud mo bhròin
    chan innsear;

Ceud soraidh slàn leat, O eilein ghràdhaich

Far 'n deach m' àrach 's bheil tàmh
    mo shinnsre.

Though the folks around us are sympathetic,

Their language is hard and their ways
    cold;

We were truly happy on our familiar
    ground,

Always speaking our noble Gaelic.

When anybody in the place had trouble,

The whole community came with
    tenderness to comfort;

No place for hatred or conflict there,

Nor in the glens were angry voices raised.

We are upset because we had to leave;

It is not so much the leaving of property;

It's sad to think that we've abandoned
    our forebears

Lying silent in the island soil.

Farewell until the trumpet sounds –

Where you lie, no-one will come near you;

You lie in the place that you loved,

With birds calling about your resting-place.

About the place where you are laid

Friends will not gather nor tears be shed;

Your graves will be as green mounds,

Overgrown with grass unreaped and the
    population banished.

It is right that I should end my song,

For words cannot express the depths of
    my sorrow;

A hundred farewells to you, dear isle,

Where I was reared and where rest
    my forebears.

66. Sunderland ML858

During the Second World War, three planes fell on St Kilda: a Beaufighter, a Wellington bomber and a Sunderland Flying-boat.

The Sunderland ML858 which collided with the top of *Mullach Mor* was a relatively new aircraft, delivered to the 302 Ferry Training Unit, Oban, on 14th May 1944. Her crew, consisting of six New Zealanders, three British and one Australian, arrived on the 22nd to complete their training before being sent to North Africa for convoy protection duties. Warrant Officer Cecil Osbourne, a New Zealander, was the Captain – a very experienced pilot, having recorded more than eight hundred flying hours.

The crew boarded the Sunderland at 9 p.m. on the 8th June 1944. There was plenty of daylight and the weather was fair. Although the sea was choppy, her four powerful Bristol Pegasus engines carried the seaplane along the surface effortlessly and lifted her into the sky about 10 p.m.

The Captain's instructions were to follow a course that would take him along the Firth of Lorne to a position south of Colonsay in the Inner Hebrides; then north to a position near Barra in the Outer Hebrides. Finally, he was to take the Sunderland some sixty miles out into the Atlantic to a position south of St Kilda and then retrace his flight-path back to Oban.

Off course, Sunderland ML858 crashed on the Mullach Mòr

By the time she was approaching Barra and turned ninety degrees to port to reach her seaward position, the Sunderland was flying in a blanket of stratus cloud. The further west she flew, the worse the weather became. As she approached the end of her westward run, fog was down to between three and four hundred feet.

Warrant Officer Osbourne had orders to radio back to base every hour. He sent a message at 11 p.m., but not at midnight. By that time, the wreckage of the plane was strewn down a hillside on Hiort in total darkness.

Fully armed, the Sunderland was capable of engaging any enemy she might encounter on the sea or in the air. As she was designed to float, it was hoped that she had come down in the sea and could be towed back to base. On the 9th, a huge expanse of sea west and north of Oban was searched, but nothing was found. The hills of St Kilda were shrouded in mist and rain and prevented close scrutiny, but on Saturday 10th June, three aircraft independently reported seeing the wreckage of an aircraft in the *Gleann Mòr*. That afternoon, a Fairmile motor launch was sent from Stornoway to investigate, and on the following day her radio officer reported that the wreckage of the Sunderland had been found and that none of her air-crew had survived the crash.

The *Walwyns Castle*, one of a flotilla of minesweepers stationed at Stornoway, was sweeping off Tolsta Head when her master received a signal directing him to return to base at once. At Stornoway, the ship berthed for long enough to allow a small group of RAF personnel and a civilian to board her. She then set off at full speed for Village Bay, St Kilda. Her passengers were Wing Commander Campbell, the RAF's Station Commander at Oban, and a group of young airmen who were to be the bearer party and Guard of Honour for the crew of the Sunderland. The civilian was the Rev Lachlan MacLeod, minister of St Columba's Church, Stornoway.

In the wreckage of the Sunderland, the bodies of only seven out of the ten crewmen were found. The RAF team retraced the long path taken by the plane as it plunged downhill. One after another, the remaining crew were discovered, some who had jumped out of the skidding plane or had been thrown clear during her descent.

The reason why the aircraft was in the vicinity of St Kilda and flying at such a low altitude, about 1,000 feet, remains a mystery. Captain Osborne must have been fully aware of the danger of approaching Hiort in poor weather. RAF investigators concluded that the accident resulted from a navigational error or from readings taken from a faulty altimeter.

With the remains of the Sunderland's crew on board, the *Walwyns Castle* steamed slowly north-eastwards until she was in the lee of Boreray. With heads bared, members of her crew watched as the RAF pall-bearers prepared to commit their dead comrades to the deep. The Rev Macleod conducted a religious service which included the singing of the 23rd Psalm. There was not a salute of guns; only a four seconds blast on the ship's horn which caused tens of thousands of gannets to rise off the cliffs of Boreray and the stacks. It was a funeral service that nobody present would ever forget.

As one canvas coffin after another slid silently into the sea, Wing Commander Campbell read the names of the men who perished in the crash:

Warrant Officer C Osborne RNZAF, Captain; Flying Officer R Ferguson RNZAF, 2nd Pilot: Flying Officer W Thompson RNZAF, Navigator; Sergeant R Lewis RAF, Flight Engineer; Warrant Officer J Lloyd, Wireless Officer/Air Gunner; Flight Sergeant B Bowker RAF, Wireless Officer/Air Gunner;   Flight Sergeant O Reed RNZAF (Australia), Wireless Officer/Air Gunner; Sergeant D Roulston RNZAF, Air Gunner; Sergeant F Robertson RNZAF, Air Gunner; Sergeant J.S. Thomson RAF, Air Gunner.

Aircraft flying in the vicinity of Hiort frequently encounter unpredictable air currents caused by the island's unique topography. The prevailing wind is inclined to be deflected into strong swirling eddies which create erratic up-draughts and down-draughts which can cause treacherous flying conditions. In consideration of that, the RAF decided that the wreckage of the Sunderland should be hidden so that other aircraft would not be drawn towards the *Gleann Mòr* to investigate. Having used dynamite to break the wreckage into manageable pieces, a crash-team spent a month burying the debris in twenty-seven deep trenches dug at the foot of *Mullach Mòr*.

At the time of writing, we are trying to trace the family of one of the New Zealanders whose life was lost on that fateful night on 8th June 1944. He was Second Pilot, Flying Officer R. Ferguson. It would be such a strange coincidence if Robert had been a descendant of the St Kildan Fergusons who emigrated to Australia in the nineteenth century.

© James Smith

Dangerous precipices on Dùn

67. Secrets Revealed

With modern technology, it is possible for us to see parts of the archipelago that the St Kildans themselves never saw. The islanders would have found it hard to believe that anyone would willingly go under the surface of the sea to discover what lies hidden in the depths.

Extensive exploration of the 'underworld' of the archipelago began some thirty years ago. As the search for oil has progressed in recent years, more and more has been discovered of the nature of the Continental Shelf far beyond the bounds of St Kilda. This has been achieved, not by divers, but by advanced 3-D seismic imaging technology.

Gordon Ridley of Glasgow, a BSAC First Class Diver and National Instructor, was among the first to visit and explore St Kilda's submarine topography that had lain hidden from humans since the beginning of time. He describes the underwater scenery of the archipelago as spectacular, with huge walls, gullies, boulders and tunnels which, together with the clear water and rich marine life, has the potential to provide the most exciting diving in British waters.

With the permission of the author, the following excerpts are taken from Gordon Ridley's much praised booklet, *St Kilda, a Submarine Guide* (1983).

AN DÙN

The Sawcut   *A sheltered site. The cliffs to the NE of Dun Arch are covered by kelp, then plumose anemones to 24m. Suddenly, at the head of a gully emerges a narrow cut, one to three metres wide, 26m. deep, shooting 60m. straight into Dun. The walls are sheer and coated with technicolour jewel, plumose and sagartia anemones and soft corals. Large boulders, yellow with maxilla sponge, lead up to 10m. at the far end. A beautiful night dive with the moonlit slot above you in 30m. vis.*

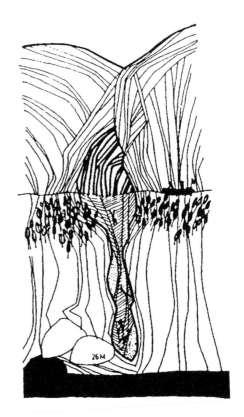

Sgàr Mhòr an Dùine

AM PLASTAIR

The South Face   *This face drops to 24m. and gives a very colourful dive. Further west there are jagged rock teeth rising from 30m. to 10m., with ravines between full of saithe. Crawfish lobster and nudibranchs were everywhere, hiding among their yellow and orange background.*

The Tunnel   *The tunnel is an angled gash that cuts right through the island completely under water. The north entrance is 24m. high and 14m. wide, narrowing to 8m. by 43m. wide just below the surface on the s. face. The whole 40m. tunnel is most impressive and, were it not for the tunnels at Levenish and Sgarbh Stac, it would have to be described in superlative terms.*

The Plastair

STAC LÌ

The East Corner *This dive follows probably the grandest rock wall in British waters. It is difficult to find words to express its scale. In fact, when confronted with the true superb, superlatives are inadequate and seem almost an injustice. Simply stated, the wall is a gentle overhang from the surface to the sea floor 50m. below. Its surface is completed filmed with a riot of browns and yellows, oranges and reds, and blues and greens. Exhaled air slowly trickles to the surface, glistening through this biological barrier. Even in a long diving career, this is a dive to cherish.*

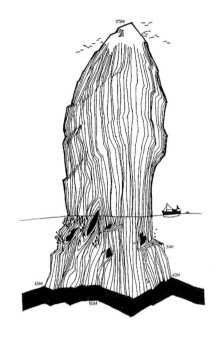

Stac Lì

SGARBH STAC

The South Arch *Discovered in July 1977 by Dave Shuker and Allan Robbie, and first dived by Henry McInnes, Morris Kilmister and Gordon Ridley the next day. This may be the ultimate underwater arch. It certainly provides one of St. Kilda's finest dives ... Seeing nine tiny humans in 40m. visibility gliding through the crystal blue waters of this vast gateway to St. Kilda's underworld is an intense and quite unforgettable experience, in poor visibility and rough conditions this dive would probably be terrifying. The apex of the arch is at a depth of 30m. and it then flares out to meet the seabed at 50m. The arch is about 30m. long and 20m. wide with a broad geological dyke running along the base ... Seals swim through the arch and puffins surround the divers on occasions ... The sides and roof of the arch are solidly lined with sponge, tubularia and anemones, and the life of the arch top traps pockets of glistening exhaled air. Just to the north of the arch there is a 10m. high boulder which one can sit atop while observing the full depth of the water and divers cavorting in the silhouette of the archway.*

Sgarbh-stac

Geologists have known for a long time that the archipelago is the remnant of a large volcano which was active about fifty-seven million years ago. The rocks, mainly of granite, gabbro and dolerite, have been eroded by the continuous action of the ocean and weather, and form the spectacular shapes of the islands and offshore stacks.

Gordon Ridley was one of a team of divers who discovered an area of the seafloor that is believed to represent the core of the extinct volcano.

> ***The Volcano Core*** *A quite sensational site, lying midway between Hirta and Boreray at 57 50 30N and 08 30 00W. This site can be imagined to be at the very core of the old volcano, though this involves some geological licence. The depth is 61m to a flat seafloor consisting of giant smooth slabs of bedrock with some sandy deposits in the cracks. Very little life was observed, but this may have been due to the narcosis. On the descent, the bottom was seen from about 35m. The dive was undertaken for geological samples and cannot be recommended because of the extreme depth.*

68. The Climate

The archipelago creates its own climate. Veils of mist, rising from the cliffs, form clouds so that the hilltops are sometimes entirely hidden. The blanket of cloud can drop to the level of the rooftops of the houses. One of the features of the climate is that the weather can improve or deteriorate very rapidly. While filming on St Kilda in August 1996, our crew experienced *Ceithir Ràithean san Aon* (Four Seasons in One): a brisk spring-like morning with a cold southerly breeze; a warm, sunny afternoon with occasional showers; a cool, glowering evening with sporadic glimpses of the sun; and, during the night, showers of sleet or hail.

St Kilda is said to be the windiest place in the British Isles. In any one year, an average of one day per week has gale-force winds. Gusts of more than 120 mph have been recorded. By contrast, there are also days of perfect stillness, particularly in the late summer and autumn. In her diary, Alice MacLachlan describes a 'simply glorious day' in September followed by an 'exquisite night'. On days and nights like that, it is difficult to imagine that the mood of the weather can change within a few hours with gale-force winds skelping the houses with sudden gusts. During weather like that, the sheep retreat to the shelter of the cliffs, cleits or houses.

While Village Bay is sheltered from northerly gales, Glen Bay, which is open to the full fury of the Atlantic, is pounded by huge breakers. From the shelter of cleits on the south-facing slopes of Boreray, one may watch as the breakers meet the unyielding bastion of *Conachair* and climb several hundred feet up its sheer face. Spume is sometimes blown for a mile to settle inland as far as the Village crofts. During easterly storms, it would be difficult, if not dangerous, for a person to stand near the cliff-top at *Conachair*. Showers of ocean spray, which the up-draught carries over the summit, are often spiced with pebbles from *Mol a' Ghaisgeir*, a small shingle beach at the foot of the cliff.

South-easterly winds blow directly into Village Bay. Gale-force winds from that airt make it highly dangerous for any vessel anchored there. However, modern radio and television weather forecasts give vessels sufficient time to weigh anchor and seek shelter in the calmer waters of Glen Bay.

South-easterly winds of the early spring are generally bitterly cold and pile raging white-caps into the Bay, sending sea-spray over the crofters' field as far as the houses, before rushing up through the *Lag bho Thuath* and escaping by 'the Gap' of *Bearradh na h-Eige*.

In recent years, snow has rarely lain for long, particularly on the lower ground. Two centuries ago, this may not have been so. Calum MacQueen, born in 1828, described the summers as 'very hot' and claimed that, in winter, he had seen 'drifts forty feet deep'. Forty?

During the short days of winter, the weak sun hanging low in the southern sky makes the tall, dark, brooding shapes of *Conachair, Mullach Mòr* and *Ruabhal* look sombre and unwelcoming. The island at that time of the year is surrounded by a restless, slate-coloured sea that looks ice-cold and inimical.

The landscape is transformed during the 'Yellow Months' which come in the late spring and last well into the autumn. As the birds return from the ocean, the windswept, sterile cliffs of winter come to life and the dull ochre and drab brown of the rain-drenched hills change to vibrant colours, ranging from lime to emerald and from oatmeal to amber. The changeable weather continuously alters the mood of the scenery, as it does the intensity of the colours. In a long, breathless sentence, this phenomenon is well described by Macculloch:

> *Fertile as the other islands of the sea in all the accidents of colour and light that arise from these changes, they fall far short of this one, where the variations of the atmosphere are incessant, where they are accompanied by effects, equally various and changeable, of light and shadow, of rain and mist, and storm, and of clouds in a thousand new and romantic forms, and colours such as neither poet not painter ever imagined; the whole producing the most splendid and unexpected combination with the land, and the ever restless and changing sea.*

© Annie MacDonald

69. 'The St Kilda Wedding'

In 1995, Comataidh Telebhisean na Gàidhlig supported my proposal that I produce a Gaelic television drama-documentary depicting the history and lifestyle of the St Kildans. The BBC also supported the proposal and appointed Donalda MacKinnon as my Executive Producer. Paul Murton was hired as film director and Martin Singleton as cameraman – both very experienced in their respective fields. Others were hired to complete our six strong film-crew. We engaged three porters on the understanding that none was to receive payment other than bed and board, and a guaranteed eight days on St Kilda. In return, the porters agreed to support the film-crew by helping them carry heavy equipment to locations all over Hiort. Our first volunteer for that role was Greg MacQueen, who flew from Melbourne, delighted to have an opportunity of visiting his ancestral home – Hiort. Two more porters were recruited: my sons, Iain and Murdo, who readily took leave of absence from their employment in Glasgow and Nova Scotia.

During discussions with officials of the National Trust for Scotland, Scottish Natural Heritage and Col. Stoddart, Commander of the Army in the Outer Hebrides, I gave an assurance that we would work to the strict rules that apply to all visitors to St Kilda.

A yacht was hired to provide us with sleeping-quarters and meals during the scheduled ten days of the shoot. Our production crew, together with two to three hundredweights of equipment and supplies, were loaded on to the yacht at West Loch Tarbert in Harris, and we sailed into the open sea with scarcely a ripple in its surface. Approaching Village Bay, the skipper of the yacht received a radio message from the owner, ordering him to return to West Loch Tarbert as soon as he had disembarked his passengers and their equipment. The skipper appeared to be as nonplussed as the rest of us.

Understandably, the Army's Officer Commanding on Hiort proved unsympathetic to our urgent request for accommodation. Considering the fact that Col. Stoddard had impressed on me the need for our team to live independently of the garrison, the O.C.'s reaction did not come as a surprise.

After discussing our plight with Col. Stoddart by telephone, the O.C. relented and provided us with adequate, if spartan, accommodation. Five members of our crew were allowed to doss down on the floor of the gymnasium, a large aluminium building shaped like a nissen-hut. Our two female personnel were allocated one windowless concrete box-room, and I, nearly twice the age of the eldest of my companions, was allocated another. The three porters slept in lightweight tents which we had brought to the island 'in case of emergency'. Nobody slept well – least of all those committed to the gymnasium. After a night of hail-showers, the assistant cameraman likened his night-time experience to being 'inside a kettle-drum during a drummer's performance!'

Once our work in and around the Village was done, we prepared to venture into the *Gleann Mòr* on the far side of the island. We managed to cadge a lift on an army truck which regularly went to the meteorological station at the summit of *Conachair*. The climb to the pass that leads down into the glen is a very steep one and our porters, particularly, were glad that they were not required to carry heavy loads on that leg of the journey. Some 600 feet above the Village, the truck stopped and, in a thick mist, we began to trek down into the wild and mysterious valley that is the *Gleann Mòr*.

Having descended about 200 feet, we emerged from the mist and became increasingly conscious of strong gusts of wind that, at intervals, came roaring down the glen from the direction of *Mullach Mòr*. Paul Murton, map in hand, finally located the historic *Tobar nam Buadh* (The Well of Virtues). Once the porters arrived with their burdens, the film-crew began to set up their equipment at the well. The gusts were swiping us at thirty-second intervals, each one heralded by a gradually increasing noise, reminiscent of that of an express-train approaching at high speed and then passing in a flurry of swirling detritus. So strong were the gusts that, every time its roar was heard approaching, two porters had to take a firm grip of Martin Singleton to prevent him and his camera and tripod from being toppled. Was the legendary *Bana-ghaisgeach* of the glen warning us not to tarry on her territory? Was the spirit guarding the well upset by our intrusion? With the forces of nature in that moody, overcast glen behaving so aggressively, it was not difficult to understand how the superstitious islanders created imaginary spirits to haunt their minds. Our work at the well 'in the can', we moved to the ruins of *Taigh na Bana-ghaisgich* (The Heroine's House) nearby. What industry to carry all those boulders and build such a structure on a steep slope in such a remote place! But by whose hands and when? Nobody really knows.

On the *Cambair*, about a quarter mile from *Taigh na Bana-ghaisgich*, is 'Bonxie-ville', a half-acre roost occupied by up to 200 pairs of bonxies (great skuas) which nest on St Kilda. The bonxie is a migratory bird which has been known to journey as far afield as Brazil. It is naturally aggressive and will fearlessly attack any human, or other alien creature, that accidentally or otherwise approaches its nest. It is a relative newcomer to St Kilda and preys mainly on the huge population of gannets nesting on Boreray and the stacks.

After seven days, we learned that the yacht was at last approaching St Kilda. With our food supplies running alarmingly low, this was very good news. Unfortunately, a south-easterly gale prevented the yacht from entering Village Bay, so that it had to seek shelter in Glen Bay. Without mentioning to anyone where he was going, the six-foot Greg MacQueen set off across the island and, after helping the yacht's crew to land cargo, headed back to the Village, laden with a heavy hamper of essential provisions. He had lost none of the athleticism of his St Kildan forebears. He climbed from the far shore to the *Blàr*, 800 feet above sea-level, then began the descent of the steep incline that took him down to the Village. Though he was still some way away, somebody drew our attention to the heavy-laden figure of Greg descending the darkening hillside. As I watched him toiling under his load, I was reminded of his island forebears who performed the same journey many times in their lifetime as they carried home their harvest of dead fulmar and peats from the fastness of the *Gleann Mòr*. Jaunty as ever, Greg arrived at our camp to a round of applause from the crew.

From our filming along the coast of Boreray, two incidents remain etched on my memory. The first occurred as we were following the east coast of the island, no more than 200 yards from towering cliffs daubed with white guano and overcrowded with squabbling seabirds. The sky was filled with countless thousands of gannets, some incoming with food for their young and others exiting to hunt in waters which were often scores of miles from St Kilda.

We watched as pairs of bonxies chose incoming gannets to harry. A pair would swoop and continue to chase the chosen victim, tugging at its tail and wings, until it disgorged its hard-won catch of herring or mackerel. As soon as the exhausted gannet complied, the muggers disengaged and swiftly dived to catch the booty before it reached the sea. More than once we saw a gannet, unwilling to submit to the bonxies, plunge beneath the waves. On its reappearing, the two muggers were waiting, ready to resume the chase and, in the end, force it to disgorge.

The second memorable incident relates to the *Uamh Ruadh*, the large cave in the eastern cliff-face of Boreray in which, in 1878, a southerly gale forced Norman Heathcote and his seven companions to spend a night. As our yacht slowly passed the gaping archway at the mouth of the cave, the director decided that a short sequence shot from inside the cave might be included in the film. On the lee side of the yacht, the ubiquitous Martin Singleton lowered himself with his camera into an inflatable and, with a member of the yacht's crew operating the 5 hp outboard engine, set off for the cave.

The tide was ebbing and, though her engine was throbbing gently, the yacht was carried imperceptibly away from the vicinity of the cave. Six or seven minutes after it entered the *Uamh Ruadh*, the inflatable reappeared. Now some 300 yards away from the archway, the yacht immediately raced to intercept it. When it left the shelter of the overhanging cliff and entered the fast-flowing current of the ocean, it rose and fell among the ever-moving green hills and troughs, so that we occasionally lost sight of it. Anxious moments but, in less than five minutes, it drew alongside. The look on Martin's face as he clambered on board clutching his precious camera is unforgettable. He had every right to be unhappy that we had allowed the yacht to drift, forcing the insubstantial inflatable to enter seas in which its occupants felt very vulnerable.

In the evenings, we relaxed in the army's famous *Puff Inn* to enjoy the company of the National Trust volunteers who during the day were kept busy restoring and repairing one of the Village houses. With us also were half a dozen students from Cambridge University who spend time on Hiort every summer studying the island's population of Soay sheep.

The hour-long programme, *Am Pòsadh Hiortach* (St Kilda Wedding), was broadcast on BBC2 in 1996 and again in 1997. Requests for cassette copies were received from all over the world, and particularly from descendants of the St Kildans who emigrated in 1852.

Footnote - Wind and tide were against us, and the former seemed to be freshening every minute. After pulling steadily for an hour and a half, we found ourselves about a mile from the shore [of Boreray]. Three miles of surging ocean lay between us and St Kilda [Hiort] … it had begun to rain and we were beginning to ship a good deal of water … I was for turning back and getting into shelter as soon as possible. By this time the wind looked like developing into a gale … A few minutes of wild excitement and we were flying past the landing-place we had left three hours before … on we sped, the green waves racing behind us, now and again lashing us with spray as if to say it was no time for dawdling, and soon we rounded the south-east point of Boreray and found ourselves in absolute quiet under the sheltering archway of a cave … Presently, Norman MacKinnon, the only English-speaking member of our crew, told us they were going to 'make worship' and then followed one of the most impressive services I ever attended. I could not understand a word, but the earnestness of the men, the intoning of their prayers, the weirdness of the Gaelic tune to which they sang a psalm, and the solemn grandeur of the place, combined to make it a most interesting and impressive ceremony.

(Excerpt from Norman Heathcote's *St Kilda*, 1878)

The film crew looking in vain for a landing place on Stac Lì

70. St Kilda Worldwide

In 1931, St Kilda was purchased by Lord Dumfries, later fifth Marquis of Bute, a keen ornithologist, who wished it to be a bird reserve. Though his main interest was the natural environment of the islands, he was happy for the St Kildans to return to their homes for summer trips. While he was also willing to accommodate tourists and naturalists, he was aware that the houses and church on Hiort were exposed to souvenir-hunters and, worse, to vandals. Anxious to secure the future of the islands, the Marquis offered them in his will to the National Trust for Scotland (NTS).

In March 1957, The Trust accepted responsibility for the future wellbeing of the archipelago and leased it to the Nature Conservancy Council as a national nature reserve. In that year, also, the Ministry of Defence established a base on Hiort to accommodate a small garrison. The War Office had negotiated the establishment of a radar tracking station on the island with the NTS and the Nature Conservancy Council. However, even though the tensions of the Cold War eased from the 1970s, the radar tracking station on Hiort and the missile testing station in South Uist continue to be active. Although the army presence on St Kilda was withdrawn in 1998, the radar and other facilities are now run for the MoD by its agents, QinetiQ Ltd. The army camp remains an intrusion on the landscape, with the buildings still used all year round by QinetiQ Ltd and their sub-contractors.

In 1986, the United Nations Educational, Scientific and Cultural Organisation (UNESCO) inscribed St Kilda as a World Heritage Site in recognition of its natural heritage, for its exceptional natural beauty and for the significant natural habitats that it supports. In February 2003, the UK government presented to UNESCO a revised nomination, seeking further inscription under the natural heritage and cultural landscapes categories, in recognition of the outstanding heritage in the waters surrounding the islands and the unique example of Scottish history and culture that the islands represent.

There are only twenty-three places in the world which enjoy joint natural and cultural heritage inscription as World Heritage Sites. In 2004, the inscription relating to St Kilda was extended to include the surrounding marine environment. In the following year, the archipelago was given dual world heritage site status, placing it on a par with Ayres Rock in Australia, Mount Athos in Greece and the Inca sanctuary at Machu Picchu in Peru.

Also in 2003, following much consultation, a new management regime was put in place for the care of St Kilda. Scottish Natural Heritage (SNH) passed the day-to-day management of this national nature reserve to the NTS, which now works in partnership with SNH, Historic Scotland, Western Isles Council, the MoD and QinetiQ to ensure the long-term future of these unique islands and stacks.

On 29th August 2000, the National Trust for Scotland launched www.hiort.org.uk, a Gaelic version of its highly regarded St Kilda website www.kilda.org.uk. The launch coincided with the anniversary of the evacuation of the archipelago in 1930.

71. Personal Names

The Forty Five Uprising ended in 1746 with the defeat of the Jacobites at the Battle of Culloden. In the years that followed, the Hanoverian government in London passed a series of laws aimed at breaking the clan system and preventing the people of the Highlands and Islands from ever again threatening the stability of the country. The possession of firearms, the wearing of tartan, and the playing of bagpipes were prohibited. The rebels' native language was associated with subversion and although it was not proscribed as a medium of communication, measures were taken to promote English in its stead and to kill off the 'Gaelic nuisance'. In schools, the official campaign against the language continued well into the twentieth century.

By the end of the nineteenth century, many St Kildans were tolerably fluent in English but, in spite of the efforts of school-teachers and others, Gaelic remained the dominant language of the islanders.

As Gaelic christian-names were unacceptable to the authorities, the Registrar of Births was required to record only 'English equivalents'. Inevitably, the translation of Gaelic names gave registrars plenty of scope for invention! For example, Oighrig became Henrietta or Euphemia; Raonailt became Rachel; and Tormod became Norman.

The surnames of Highlanders and Islanders such as the St Kildans, were lumped under clan-names such as MacLeod, MacDonald, Campbell or Ferguson. The practice of doing so was not objectionable to the Gaels who, instinctively, felt a sense of allegiance to their respective clans. However, within Gaelic-speaking communities, individuals continued to be identified, not by an official surname, but by the age-old custom of coupling the person's christian-name to those of his immediate forebears. For example, John whose father was Finlay and whose grandfather was Donald would be known as 'Iain Dhòmhnaill Fhionnlaigh' (John of Donald of Finlay). In addition to that patronymic, some individuals were given bye-names such as 'Am Pìobaire' (The Piper) or 'Am Bàrd'(The Poet); or by applying to the christian-name an epithet (often ironic) such as 'Bàn' (Fair-haired), 'Beag' (Little) or 'Stuama'(Sober).

The following are the English 'equivalents' of St Kildan personal names:

Aonghas - Angus

Anna – Ann, Anne, Annie

Barabal - Annabel

Calum - Malcolm

Cairstiona, Ciorstaidh – Christian, Christina, Kirsty

Catrìona – Catherine, Kate

Dòmhnall – Donald

Eachann – Hector

Eòghann – Ewen

Fionnlagh – Finlay

Isbeal – Bella, Bessy, Betsy, Isobel, Elizabeth,

Iain – John

Lachlan – Lachlan, Lachie

Màiread – Margaret

Màiri – Mary

Mòr– Marion

Niall – Neil

Oighrig – Euphemia, Effie, Henrietta, Henny

Raonailt – Rachel

Ruairidh – Roderick, Rory

Tormod – Norman

Uilleam – William

Left to right: Mrs Gillies, Mrs MacDonald, Mary MacDonald, Mary MacQueen, Mrs MacKinnon (widow), Mrs Ferguson

Their work done, fowlers on Boreray wait for the boat to arrive

Neil Ferguson, junior, carrying the last sack of St Kildan wool to the jetty

Ewen MacDonald (right)

© Alasdair Alpin MacGregor Collection (N.M.S.)

Donald Ewen MacKinnon on his way to
the pier on the day of the evacuation

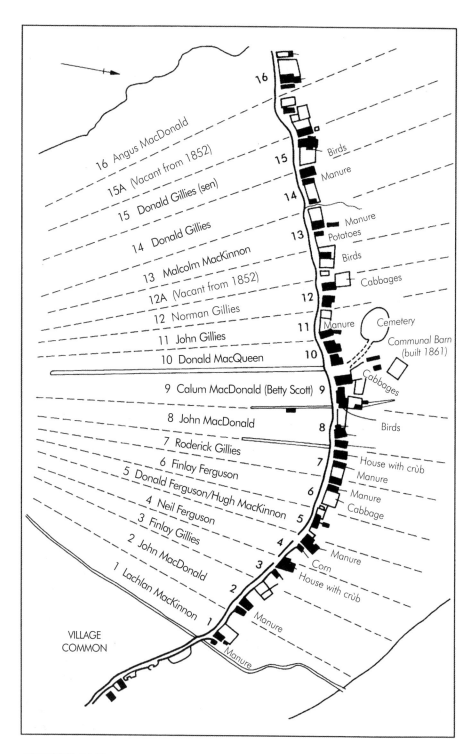

CROFTS 1860

16 Angus MacDonald
15A (Vacant from 1852)
15 Donald Gillies (sen)
14 Donald Gillies
13 Malcolm MacKinnon
12A (Vacant from 1852)
12 Norman Gillies
11 John Gillies
10 Donald MacQueen
9 Calum MacDonald (Betty Scott)
8 John MacDonald
7 Roderick Gillies
6 Finlay Ferguson
5 Donald Ferguson/Hugh MacKinnon
4 Neil Ferguson
3 Finlay Gillies
2 John MacDonald
1 Lachlan MacKinnon

VILLAGE COMMON

Birds
Manure
Manure
Potatoes
Birds
Cabbages
Manure
Cemetery
Communal Barn (built 1861)
Cabbages
Birds
House with crùb
Manure
Manure
Cabbage
Manure
Corn
House with crùb
Manure
Manure

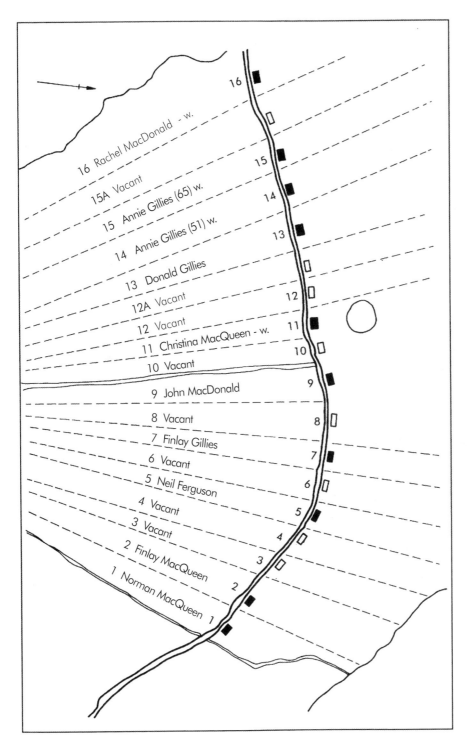

16 Rachel MacDonald - w.

15A Vacant

15 Annie Gillies (65) w.

14 Annie Gillies (51) w.

13 Donald Gillies

12A Vacant

12 Vacant

11 Christina MacQueen - w.

10 Vacant

9 John MacDonald

8 Vacant

7 Finlay Gillies

6 Vacant

5 Neil Ferguson

4 Vacant

3 Vacant

2 Finlay MacQueen

1 Norman MacQueen

CROFTS 1930
Based on Lawson, 1993

72. A Population in Decline

According to James Wilson's 'Voyage Round the Coasts of Scotland and the Isles' (pub. A. & C. Black, Edinburgh, 1842), there were 105 people resident on St Kilda in 1841. The minister's household accounted for nine. By the time of the Evacuation in 1930, the population was reduced to 36.

	No. in Family		No. in Family
Finlay Gillies	6	Catherine Ferguson (unmarried) (83)	1
Neil MacKinnon	3	Mary MacDonald & natural dau'r	2
Angus MacDonald	3	Roderick Gillies	4
Finlay MacQueen	5	John Ferguson	4
John Gillies	6	Donald MacCrimmon	2
Malcolm MacDonald	5	Neil Ferguson	4
Finlay MacQueen	6	Finlay Gillies	5
Donald MacQueen	3	John MacDonald	4
John Gillies	4	Margaret MacLeod w.	2
Anne MacQueen w	2	Lachlan MacKinnon	5
Malcolm MacDonald	3	Euphemia (unmarried & niece)	2
John MacDonald	3	Mary MacKinnon w.	1
Mary Morrison w.	2	Roderick MacDonald	6
		Finlay Ferguson	2
		Finlay MacLeod (83)	1
		Rev. Neil MacKenzie	9

Total - 105

1861 (Census)

1. MacKinnon, Lachlan (54) = Rachel (37)

    Ewen (26), Donald (23), Norman (16), Neil (13), Catherine (2)

2. MacDonald, John (55) = Betsy (51)

    Donald (25), Annie (18)

3. Gillies, Finlay (56), = Mary (46)

    Ewen (19), Angus (14), John (23), Marion (21), Mary (17), Christian (9)

4. Ferguson, Neil (55) = Catherine (46)

    Donald (27), Mary (21), Margaret (18), John (11)

5. Ferguson, Finlay (46) = Betsy (51)

    Mary (18)

6. MacDonald, John (50) = Christian (42)

    Margaret (22), Catherine (19), Mary Ann (17), Marion (4), Christian (8)

7. Gillies, Roderick (47) = Catherine (60)

    Anne (23)

8. MacDonald, Malcolm (52) = Betsy (47)

    Neil (22), Anne (19)

9. MacQueen, Donald (56) = Christian (53)

    Donald (21), Rachel (9)

10. Gillies, John (51) = Flora (50)

    Alexander (25), Rachel (22), Marion (19), Catherine (13),   Christian (9) #

11. Gillies, Norman (37) = Anne (31)

    Christian (6), Finlay (5), Mary J. Otter (1)

12. MacKinnon, Malcolm (31) = Marion (32)

    Christian (70, w)

13. Gillies, Donald (41) = Margaret (38)

    Neil (16), Mary (13)

    Gillies, Donald (22)

    Betsy (32) - sister

    Rachel (27) - sister, Anne (20) - sister, Anne (57, w.)

15. Kennedy, Duncan (67) Catechist, from Ardchattan

16. MacDonald, Angus (45, w.)

17. MacDonald, Catherine (40, w.)

      Donald (17)

18. MacCrimmon, Annie (60, w.)

      Rachel (30)

19. MacCrimmon, Effie (82)

20. Gillies, Roderick (47)

      VACANT

Total 78

1891   (Census)

1. Fiddes, Angus (48) - minister

      MacLennan, Catherine (43) - servant

      Chisnell, Jessie (45) - nurse

2. MacCrimmon, Rachel (59)

3. MacKinnon, Lachlan (83) = Rachel (66)

      Neil (42) = Christina (35) – dau'r-in-law

      Christine (20)

      Norman (11)

4. MacDonald, John (83) = Jessie (80)

      MacQueen, Finlay (29) = Mary (30)

      Donald (6), Annie (2)

5. Gillies, Maria (46)

      MacQueen, Mary Ann (19), niece

6. Ferguson., Neil (84) = Catherine (76)

      Margaret (47)

      Rachel (56, w.), daughter-in-law

7. Ferguson, Donald (57) = Rachel (50)

     Alexander (18), Neil (15), Donald (12)

8. Gillies, Angus (44) = Annie (50)

     Finlay (13)

9. Gillies, Rory (76, w.)

     Annie (52) - daughter

     Finlay (35) = Catherine (40)

     Donald (6), Neil (5), Annie (2)

10. MacDonald, Malcolm (29) = Christina (38)

     Margaret (50, w.); Catherine (48) - aunt, Catherine (24) - aunt

11. MacDonald, Neil (50) = Maria (48)

     William (16), Bella (8), John (6)

12. MacQueen, Donald (49) = Maria (35)

     Ann (14), Norman (11), Christina (7) , Donald (5)

13. Gillies, Christina (38)

14. Gillies, Norman (65) = Mary (50)

     Annie (19), Mary (12), Ewen ((9)

15. MacKinnon, Malcolm (60) = Maria (61)

16. Gillies, Bessie (62, w.) = Ann (88, w.)

17. Gillies, John (29)   = Annie (24)

     Margaret – mother (68, w.)

18. MacDonald, Donald (46) = Rachel (26)

     Donald (15), Ewen (3), Catherine (1)

Total - 71

1901   (Census)

1.   Fiddes, Angus (58) - minister

      MacDonald, Kate   (34) - servant

      MacKenzie, James   (19) - Assist. Teacher

      MacCrimmon, Rachel   (69)

1.   Main Street   MacKinnon, Neil (52) = Christina (47)

      Norman (21), Lachlan (3)

2.   MacQueen, Finlay (38) = Mary Otter (41)

      Donald (15), Annie (12), Mary Ann (8), Christina (6), John (3), Elizabeth (8m)

3.   MacDonald, William (27) = Mary Ann (29)

      John (4), Finlay (3), Annabella (10m.)

      Gillies, Marion (60) – aunt-in-law

4.   Ferguson, Margaret (52)

      Rachel (65) – sister-in-law

5.   Ferguson, Donald (66) – Ground Officer

      Neil (24) = Annie (23)

      Neil (18mths)

6.   Gillies, Angus (53) = Ann ((58)

7.   Gillies, Finlay (44) = Catherine (52)

      Donald (16), Neil 14, Annie (12), Catherine (9), Norman (7),

      Ann (65) – aunt-in-law

8.   MacDonald, Malcolm (38)   = Christina (46)

      Donald (8), Mary (5),

      Margaret (59, w.), Catherine (57)

9.   MacDonald, Neil (59) = Marion (58)

      Isobella (18), John (15)

10. MacQueen, Donald (60) = Marion (43)

    Christina (17) , Donald (14), John (9), Mary (6),

    Norman (21) = Christina (29)

11. VACANT

12. Gillies, Norman (76) = Mary (60)

    Ann (29), Mary (22) , Ewen (19)

13. MacKinnon, Malcolm (67) = Christina (48)

    Christina (5)

14. Gillies, Elizabeth (71, w.)

15. Gillies, John (38) = Ann (35)

    Donald (9), John (7), Neil (4)

16. MacDonald, Donald (58) = Rachel (37)

    Ewen (12), Catherine (11), Angus (7), Donald (5) , Rachel (18 m.)

Total 77

1930 (Lawson)

1. MacKinnon, Norman (50) = Annie (42)

    Norman (20), Donald Ewen (19), Finlay (16), Rachel (13), John (10),

    Christina (9), Mary (5), Neil (4)

2. MacQueen, Finlay (68, w.)

    Kirsty Ann (36, w.)

3. VACANT

4. VACANT

5. Ferguson, Neil (54) = Annie (53)

    Neil (31) = Mary Ann (29)

6. VACANT

7. Gillies, Finlay (74 w.)

    Catherine (41). w.

    Donald (12), Ewen (9)

8. VACANT

9. MacDonald, John (59)

    Gillies Anne (36) w..

    Mary Ann (16)

10. VACANT

11. MacQueen, Christina (59 w.)

12. VACANT

13. Gillies, Donald (39) = Christina (35)

    Catherine (12), Rachel (8)

14. Gillies, Annie (51 w.)

    Rachel Annie (20), Flora (11)

15. Gillies, Annie (65, w.)

    Norman (6)

    MacDonald, Rachel (67, w.)

    Ewen (42), Lachlan (24)

Total 36

Bibliography

Buchan, Alexander (1704-29) *A Description of St Kilda,* Lumsden & Robertson, reprinted with alterations by Jean Buchan, John Wylie & Co., 1773

Buchanan, Meg (ed.) *St Kilda (The Continuing Story of the Islands),* Glasgow Museums, 1995

Atkinson George Clayton, ed. D. A. Quine *Expeditions to the Hebrides,* Maclean Press, 2001

Fleming, Andrew *St Kilda and the Wider World,* Windgather Press, 2005

Harman, Mary *An Isle Called Hirte,* Maclean Press, 1997

Heathcote, John Norman (1898-99) *St Kilda,* Longmans, Green & Co., 1900

Hebridean Naturalist No. 14 The Western Isles Natural History Society; Curracag

Lawson Bill, '*St Kilda and its Church*' and *Croft History of St Kilda:* Pub. Bill Lawson Publications 1993

Love, John *St Kilda: A World Apart,* Scottish Natural Heritage,

MacAulay, Kenneth (1764) The *History of St Kilda;* James Thin, 1974

MacGregor, Alasdair A *A Last Voyage to St Kilda,* Cassell & Co. Ltd, 1931

Mackay, James A *Soldiering on St Kilda,* Token Publishing Ltd, 2002

MacKenzie, Neil (1829-43) *Antiquities and Old Customs of St Kilda,* compiled from notes by the Rev Neil MacKenzie ed. J.B. MacKenzie: Proceedings of the Society of Antiquaries of Scotland 38, pp 397-402

MacLachlan, Alice (1906-9) Diaries typescript in NTS Archive
Maclean, Charles *Island on the Edge of the World,* Canongate Ltd, 1977

MacLean, Lachlan *Sketches on the Island of St Kilda,* McPhun, Glasgow, 1938

MacQueen, Callum *St Kilda Heritage,* ed. Kelman and Ewen G. MacQueen, Edinburgh, Scottish Genealogical Society, 1995

Martin Martin, *A Voyage to St Kilda* (1697), 1818

Mitchell, W. R. *Finlay MacQueen of St Kilda,* House of Lochar, 1992

Ridley, Gordon *St Kilda: A Submarine Guide,* Gordon Ridley, 1983

Sands, John *Out of the World: Life on St Kilda,* MacLachlan & Stewart, London

Seton, George *St Kilda: Past and Present,* William Blackwood & Sons, 1878

Small, Alan (ed.) *A St Kildan Handbook,* National Trust For Scotland, 1979

Steel, Tom *The Life and Death of St Kilda,* Harper Collins, 1994

Quine, David A. 1982 *St Kilda Revisited,* Dowland Press, 1982

Quine, David A. *St Kilda Portraits* Quine, 1988

Quine, David A. *St Kilda,* Colin Baxter Photography Ltd., 1995

Ordnance Survey 1970 Maps, Scale 1:25,000 (Pathfinder), Sheet 1373, *St Kilda NA00/10* and *NF 09/19*

Lorne Gillies, Anne *An Long Hiortach* (CD of songs from St Kilda), Brìgh, 2004

Index

'Jackal' - 176, 177

James McRaild - 174

James Wilson - 26, 244

Jean Buchan - 63, 251

John MacDiarmid - 17, 31

John MacPherson MacLeod - 129

John McCallum - 194

John Sands - 46, 105, 108, 176, 177, 187, 189, 190, 191, 193

John Stuart Blackie - 196

Ketil - 179

labaid - 177

Lachie MacDonald - 82, 152, 204, 207, 219

Lachlan MacKinnon - 244-246

Lachlan MacLean - 71

lament - 69, 89, 92, 95, 105, 180, 193, 208, 210, 222

Laird - 104

Leif Erickson - 37

lisp - 152

Liturgy - 152

Loch a' Bhaile - 60

Loch Portain - 20, 21

lockjaw - 146

lullaby - 55, 154

'*Lysander*' - 168

MacDonald of Sleat - 15, 70

'MacIntosh's Lament' - 193

MacLeod of MacLeod - 127

maor - 63, 64

Marquis of Breadalbane - 163

Marquis of Bute - 236

Marion Gillies - 104

Marion Morrison - 102-105

Martin Martin - 15, 38, 50, 51, 150, 252

Mary Gillies - 215

Mary MacSwain - 171

'Mary's nut' - 176

Mealasta - 174

Melbourne - 16, 163, 168-170, 172, 232

merriment - 57

mogais/*mogais* - 27, 28, 100

Moluccan beans - 176

mongrel - 30

Morvern - 216

Muldonich - 52

music - 10, 35, 57, 64, 156, 180, 183, 185, 193

Neil Ferguson - 151, 177, 206, 212, 214, 244

Neil Gillies -10, 198, 202, 204, 206

Norman Heathcote - 79, 195, 234, 251

Nurse Williamina Barclay - 215

Ob/Obbe - 105

Oiseabhal - 14, 31, 34, 42, 61, 121, 174, 200, 204, 205, 211

oystercatcher - 25, 85

Peter MacLachlan - 196, 204, 205

'Peti Dubrovacki' - 176

pirates/*pirates* - 42, 43, 202

pony races - 58

Port Phillip Bay - 167

'*Priscilla*' - 165-169, 187

puffin - 35, 46, 55, 60, 78, 80, 82, 87, 181, 184, 193

Quarantine - 167-172

quern - 119, 190

Rachel Chiesley - 70

razorbill - 35, 60, 80, 82, 83, 87, 152

Red Ruairi - 50-54

Rev. Alexander Buchan - 63, 64, 251

Rev Angus Fiddes - 147, 177

Rev Donald John Gillies - 204, 220